MW00772774

VERSE BY VERSE

THE BOOK OF MORMON

VOLUME TWO

Other volumes in the Verse by Verse series
by D. Kelly Ogden and Andrew C. Skinner

The Four Gospels

Acts through Revelation

The Book of Mormon, volume 1:
1 Nephi through Alma 29

VERSE BY VERSE
THE BOOK OF
MORMON

VOLUME TWO
ALMA 30 THROUGH MORONI 10

D. KELLY OGDEN
ANDREW C. SKINNER

DESERET
BOOK

SALT LAKE CITY, UTAH

Library of Congress Cataloging-in-Publication Data
Ogden, D. Kelly (Daniel Kelly), 1947– author.
    Verse by verse : The book of Mormon. Volume 2, Alma 30 through Moroni 10 / D. Kelly Ogden and Andrew C. Skinner.
        pages cm
    Includes bibliographical references and index.
    ISBN 978-1-60641-477-4 (hardbound : alk. paper)
    1. Book of Mormon—Commentaries. I. Skinner, Andrew C., 1951– author. II. Title.
    BX8627 .O33 vol. 2 2011
    289.3'22—dc23   2011019598

Printed in the United States of America
Publishers Printing, Salt Lake City, UT

10   9   8   7   6   5   4   3   2   1

CONTENTS

PREFACE

The series Verse by Verse, which began with *The Four Gospels* and *Acts through Revelation,* continues with *The Book of Mormon,* a verse-by-verse commentary that is one book in two volumes.

This is the second of the two volumes. The division between the volumes reflects the way in which courses on the Book of Mormon are structured in seminary, in the institutes of religion, and on the various campuses of Brigham Young University: 1 Nephi 1 through Alma 29, and Alma 30 through Moroni 10.

The introduction appears in the first volume, and the index to both volumes is found at the end of the second. Each volume contains its own table of contents, notes, and sources. Occasionally, cross-references between the two volumes appear in the text.

We acknowledge the assistance of many colleagues and students at Brigham Young University for their helpful suggestions during the years of preparation of these books. We extend particular appreciation to the production team at Deseret Book Company: Cory Maxwell, director of publishing; Suzanne Brady, senior editor; Shauna Gibby, designer; and Rachael Ward, typographer.

We dedicate these writings to Marcia Hammond Ogden and Janet Corbridge Skinner, our dear wives, who are also ardent students and teachers of the Book of Mormon, and to our children and grandchildren.

Most of all, we thank our Heavenly Father and his Son,

Jesus Christ, and all the prophets and other faithful record keepers for their dedicated attention to preserving eternal truths that they knew would be crucial for us in these last days.

THE BOOK OF ALMA
(CONTINUED)

Alma 30

Korihor is our third example of an anti-Christ in the Book of Mormon. Before him we met Sherem (Jacob 7) and Nehor (Alma 1). Once again we remind ourselves that the contents of this great book are meant for our day, the last days, as President Ezra Taft Benson taught:

"The Book of Mormon was written for us today. God is the author of the book. It is a record of a fallen people, compiled by inspired men for our blessing today. Those people never had the book—it was meant for us. Mormon, the ancient prophet after whom the book is named, abridged centuries of records. God, who knows the end from the beginning, told him what to include in his abridgment that we would need for our day. . . . The Book of Mormon exposes the enemies of Christ. It confounds false doctrines and lays down contention. (See 2 Ne. 3:12.) It fortifies the humble followers of Christ against the evil designs, strategies, and doctrines of the devil in our day. The type of apostates in the Book of Mormon are similar to the type we have today. God, with his infinite foreknowledge, so molded the Book of Mormon that we might see the error and know how to combat false educational, political, religious, and philosophical concepts of our time."[1]

Read 2 Nephi 28:4–5, 14 and notice how, as Korihor's arguments unfold, his reasoning perfectly fits the descriptions and warnings of Book of Mormon prophets and modern-day prophets, including President Benson.

1. No one can know of anything in the future (v. 13).

Sherem said exactly the same thing (Jacob 7:7), denying the foreknowledge of God and his power to reveal his secrets to his servants, the prophets.

2. Your religious beliefs are merely handed-down foolish traditions (v. 14). They are superstition, folklore, legend, myth, and other such convenient labels.

3. You cannot know anything that you cannot experience with one or more of the five physical senses (vv. 15, 28). That is the scientists' traditional method. Only those things known through the five physical senses are "real."

4. Your traditions and beliefs are no more than the effect of a frenzied mind; your minds have become deranged (v. 16).

5. God doesn't save anyone in this world; everyone fares in this life "according to the management of the creature," prospers "according to his genius," and conquers according to his strength (v. 17). That is the old "every man for himself" philosophy, the "survival of the fittest."

6. Go ahead and lift up your heads in your wickedness (v. 18); that is, feel good about your sins. And if you feel guilty, just lower your standards. When you are dead, you are dead. Better take in all the pleasure you can while there is time, especially satisfying the desires of your body. If you do not believe you will become immortal, then here you will likely become immoral.

In other words, Korihor denied the existence of prophecy (v. 13), faith (v. 15), the Atonement (v. 17), and the resurrection from the dead (v. 18). Someone has observed that Korihor was the headmaster in the school of Satan's curriculum. He represented religion as Karl Marx would some nineteen hundred years later: "the opiate of the masses," unworthy of sophisticated thinkers.

Korihor criticized and fought against the Lord's anointed ones, His chosen leaders. Joseph Smith said, "That man who rises up to condemn others, finding fault with the Church, saying that they are out of the way, while he himself is righteous, then know assuredly, that that man is in the high road to apostasy; and if he does not repent, will apostatize, as God lives."[2]

Korihor espoused the false educational, philosophical, and social concepts of those who live without God in the world, and he did it with eloquence and finesse: "he did rise up in great swelling words before Alma, and did revile against the priests and teachers, accusing them of leading away the people after the silly traditions of their fathers, for the sake of glutting on the labors of the people" (v. 31). The most common result of canceling God out of one's life is to become immoral.

The following paraphrased conversation between the Christlike prophet (Alma) and the anti-Christ (Korihor) is revealing (vv. 35–45):

"Do you think we're deceiving this people with something that causes such joy in their hearts?"

"Yes."

"Do you believe there is a God?"

"No."

"Will you again deny God and Christ? I know there is a God and that Christ will come. Now, Korihor, how do you know there is no God? Did he reveal it to you? I have all the evidence in the world—all things testify of God. But you have cast the Spirit of God out of you and allowed the devil to take over your mind." The burden of proof that there is no God rests with those who claim there is no God. No one in earth's history has proven there is no God, whereas millions have gained a witness that he lives—some with direct personal contact with him.

"Well, okay, I will be convinced if you show me a sign."

Joseph Smith taught that demanding a sign in order to believe is sure evidence of an adulterous or immoral person (see commentary at Jacob 7:13–17).[3] In every priesthood dispensation the righteous have been given the promise that "signs shall follow them that believe" (Mormon 9:24). Signs flow from faith and are a product of it. Signs strengthen the faithful but only if they have responded to the invitation to have faith. A chief purpose of signs and miracles is to reward faith—not to create it out of nothing (D&C 63:7–11).

Alma proceeded to list the evidences and the witnesses, among others the prophets, the scriptures, the earth itself, the regularity and stability of the planetary system—all things created are evidences of a creator.

Korihor persisted in requesting a sign, so he got one. He was struck dumb, nevermore to open his mouth and deceive people (v. 47). Face-to-face with the power of God, he could deny no longer and admitted that he always knew of God's existence, but the devil deceived him—even appearing as an angel—inciting him to do things that were pleasing to the carnal mind. Korihor was so successful in the deceptions he taught others that he became convinced of them himself (vv. 52–53). Korihor, like all others who fight against God, came to an ignominious end. His eventual death illustrates the scriptural maxim, "It is by the wicked that the wicked are punished" (Mormon 4:5).

"And thus we see" (Mormon's lesson-defining introductory phrase) "the end of him who perverteth the ways of the Lord" (v. 60). He alienated his God; and his master, the devil, who cared nothing for him, abandoned him. Brigham Young's famous parallel to Mormon's teaching was, "All that want to draw a party from the church after them, let them do it if they can, but they will not prosper."[4] Only God will uphold his promises (D&C 82:10), for God cannot lie (Enos 1:6).

Alma 31:1–4

After the ignominious death of Korihor, Alma had to face yet another problem—the news that the Zoramites, another splinter group from the Nephites, were in the throes of apostasy and idolatry. Under the law of Moses, idolatry was one of the worst sins—described in graphic terms as spiritual adultery (Leviticus 17:7; Jeremiah 3:6, 8, 9). Such reports evoke in us an appreciation for the faithfulness of the Lord's servants, who do not face lives of ease and do not flinch from doing hard things.

Alma 31:5

The preaching of the word of God had a more powerful effect on the minds of the people than using methods of force to reach them. That is why—in order to resolve the social, philosophical, moral, and political ills and tensions of peoples all over the world—the missionaries are sent out to "try the virtue of the word of God." The word *virtue* derives from a Latin word and means "power" or "strength." A superb example of success in turning a people around by the preaching of the word is found in Helaman 5, especially verses 50–51.

The power of the word is infinite and limitless, as opposed to finite, worldly means. For the "word" means not only the scriptures but also the Being to whom the scriptures point—Jesus Christ (John 1:1–4). His is the power to change lives, as described by President Ezra Taft Benson: "The Lord works from the inside out. The world works from the outside in. The world would take people out of the slums. Christ takes the slums out of people, and then they take themselves out of the slums. The world would mold men by changing their environment. Christ changes men, who then change their environment. The world would shape human behavior, but Christ can change human nature."[5]

Alma 31:6–7, 32

Armed with the word and not with worldly weapons, Alma went forth with his companions to change their part of the world. The zone of missionaries working among the Zoramites included Alma, Ammon, Aaron, Omner, Amulek, Zeezrom, Shiblon, and Corianton—a power group with seventeen years of missionary experience.

Alma 31:8–10

To *dissent* means to disagree, or to differ in opinion with contentious quarrelling. In terms of the Church, dissenters are apostates, those who have a degree of knowledge and even testimony of the truth and take a stand against the heads of the Church—the Lord Jesus Christ and his chosen, authorized leaders—and openly publish their contrary views (Alma 24:30). Not only did the dissenters fail to keep the commandments, but they had failed to stay worthy to perform ordinances and had stopped praying—a sure formula for disaster.

Alma 31:12–14

The adversary seldom promotes principles and practices that are diametrically opposite those of the Lord; he sponsors cheap imitations of the true order of things: Build a place of worship, have a day of the week for worship, offer vocal prayer, go through all the motions of religiosity—outer motions without pure inner motives.

Alma 31:15–18

The Zoramites' self-righteous prayer was spoken only on their holy stand. It was a set, memorized prayer that included the false doctrine that God is a spirit and a denial of the veracity and divinity of Christ. Are there parallels today, where worship is done only in a church, with memorized prayers, teaching that God is a spirit? Are there those who teach that Christ was a great moral teacher but not the Son of God?

Why does Satan want people to believe that God is a spirit-nothing too mysterious to comprehend? Because life eternal is to know God and Jesus Christ (John 17:3), and we can't know and become like a spirit-nothing. All false religions teach that God is an incomprehensible mystery.

And the Zoramites' brazen presumptuousness in regarding themselves as the exclusive holy children, the elect who would be saved while others were destined for hell! They prayed, "O God, I thank thee that we are better than our brethren" (Alma 38:14). That sanctimonious approach to "worship" is more pharisaic than the Pharisee in Jesus' later parable who stood and prayed "with himself" and thanked God that he was not as other men (Luke 18:11), with a "holier than thou" attitude (Isaiah 65:5).

The Zoramite concept of election anticipates the later false Christian idea of predestination, which Augustine and Luther worried about, and the idea of double predestination that John Calvin taught. Such doctrine not only negates agency but also, worse still, tries to destroy faith in Christ, as the Zoramites' attitude demonstrates. Having been automatically elected by God to be his holy children, the Zoramites did not need Christ, and all others around them could not have Christ because they were destined to hell anyway.

Alma 31:21

Their place of worship was a "holy stand" called Rameumptom. The Semitic root word *ram* means "high place," as in the alternate name for the Hill Cumorah: Ramah (Ether 15:11; compare LDS Bible Dictionary, "Ramah," "Ramoth-gilead").

Alma 31:22–25

Zoramite troubles were rooted in pride, which led to elitism and worldliness. Literally as well as symbolically the Zoramites were a people high and lifted up. They engaged in vain, empty repetitions (Matthew 6:7); they worshipped once a week—truly a religion of convenience; and their hearts were set so much upon the things of the world that they claimed riches to be the mark of favor with God.

Alma 31:26–35

Alma, deeply agitated for the perversity and hypocrisy that he saw among the Zoramites, poured out his soul in mighty prayer. Contrast the Zoramites' set prayer with the humble, heartfelt prayer of Alma. He admitted his own weakness in dealing with such blatant sacrilege. He pled for patience, comfort, and success for himself and also for his brethren while suffering afflictions because of the gross behavior around them. He importuned the Lord for success in bringing the apostates and less-actives back to the fold.

Alma 31:36–38

After Alma's prayer of faith and priesthood blessings, the Spirit came. That kind of praying also caused the missionaries' afflictions to be swallowed in the joy of Christ. It is good to know that whatever we are afflicted with while we are serving the Savior, it can be consumed by the joy we have in him (see also commentary at Alma 27:28).

Alma 32:1–8

After a lot of hard work, the missionaries began to have success among the poor class of people, those who were poor in worldly things and also poor in heart—that is, lowly or meek in heart (compare the opposite, "stubbornness of heart," in v. 16). As is often the case in missionary work today, their afflictions had humbled the people, and they were prepared to listen.

Alma 32:12–16

President Ezra Taft Benson taught that "God will have a humble people. Either we can choose to be humble or we can be compelled to be humble."[6] Of course, it is far better to humble ourselves. The progress toward perfection is faster, and we bypass the "hard lessons" that pride and worldliness thrust upon us. Humility is a prerequisite to faith and wisdom.

President Dieter F. Uchtdorf gave us this assessment of the perils of pride: "My beloved fellow disciples of the gentle Christ, should we not hold ourselves to a higher standard?

. . . We must realize that all of God's children wear the same jersey. Our team is the brotherhood of man.

"When we become obsessed with our status; when we focus on our own importance, power, or reputation; when we dwell upon our public image and believe our own press clippings—that's when the trouble begins; that's when pride begins to corrupt. . . .

"We are not given the priesthood so that we can take our bows and bask in praise. We are here to roll up our sleeves and go to work. . . . We seek not our own honor but give praise and glory to God. . . .

"We seek to do the will of the Father, just as the Savior did. . . . We give all glory to the Father, just as the Savior did. . . .

"Some suppose that humility is about beating ourselves up. Humility does not mean convincing ourselves that we are worthless, meaningless, or of little value. Nor does it mean denying or withholding the talents God has given us. We don't discover humility by thinking less *of* ourselves; we discover humility by thinking less *about* ourselves. . . .

"The moment we stop obsessing with ourselves and lose ourselves in service, our pride diminishes and begins to die. . . .

"There are so many ways we could be serving. We have no time to become absorbed in ourselves."[7]

Alma 32:17–27

Some think that spiritual witness comes from physical evidence and by seeing signs from heaven (see commentary at Jacob 7:13–17). Genuine faith, however, involves fervent hope and desire to know things that are not physically apparent, that are not visible but are nevertheless real and true. Korihor and many others have pursued the philosophy that seeing is believing, but in the realm of godly things and pure religion the opposite is true: *believing is seeing.* Revelation of truth comes to the faithful (those full of faith), not only to men—the priesthood holders—but also to women as well as little children, and signs do follow as a reward for faithfulness.

Men, women, and children of the covenant do not start from positions of knowledge. Rather, they begin with a desire to believe and hope that their *efforts* and works will yield fruit. In this regard, Elder Bruce R. McConkie stated: "We grow in faith; we go step by step from a lower degree to a higher degree. We add grace to grace until eventually we get to a state where we have perfected our faith, as far as at least the generality of righteous, mortal men can. . . . Don't go out now and try to cast sycamine trees into the sea. Don't go out and try to move mountains, but go out and start in a small degree to do the thing that you need to do in your life to get what you ought to have temporally and spiritually. 'Faith without works is dead.' (James 2:20). Work on the projects ahead, and when you have taken one step in the acquiring of faith, it will give you the assurance in your soul that you can go forward and take the next step, and by degrees your power or influence will increase until eventually, in this world or in the next, you will say to the Mt. Zerins in your life, 'Be thou removed.' You will say to whatever encumbers your course of eternal progress, 'Depart,' and it will be so."[8]

In verse 27 Alma explained how to obtain faith. We must be willing to test and try the truth of spiritual things, to experiment, to begin with earnest desire—then we are in a position to learn and live the truth.

Elder John A. Widtsoe, a noted scientist and university administrator who later became a member of the Quorum of the Twelve, stated: "The gospel of the Lord Jesus Christ advises men to test its truths in human life. It approves distinctly of the experimental method. The Savior laid down the principle in a luminous statement: 'My doctrine is not mine, but his that sent me. If any man will do his will, he shall know of the doctrine, whether it be of God, or whether I speak of myself.' (John 7:16, 17) On another occasion He repeated the thought: 'If I do not the works of my Father, believe me not. But if I do, though ye believe not me, believe the works.' (John 10:37, 38) The words of the Apostle Paul, 'Prove all things; hold fast that which is good' (1 Thessalonians 5:21), are of the same import. There is constant advice in the scriptures to let the effects of gospel living be evidence of its truth, as for example: 'Let your light so shine before men, that they may see your good works, and glorify your Father which is in heaven' (Matthew 5:16); or 'Having your conversation honest among the Gentiles: that, whereas they speak against you as evil-doers, they may by your good works, which they shall behold, glorify God in the day of visitation.' (1 Peter 2:12)

"Joseph Smith, the Prophet, recognized this method of testing truth. He read the words of James, 'If any of you lack wisdom, let him ask of God, that giveth to all men liberally, and upbraideth not; and it shall be given him' (James 1:5); and, believing in God, he went into the grove to test the reality of the promise there made. Thus came the great First Vision."⁹

Alma 32:28–43

Alma described the process of growth from desire, to belief, to faith, to knowledge. One of the favorite teaching techniques of ancient scripture writers was to compare something in nature to something in the human experience. The prophets and the Savior, the Master Teacher, did that often.

Alma compared the word of God to a seed that is planted in our hearts. The good seed (the good word, or the good Word—the Savior) begins to enlarge our soul and enlighten our understanding and begins to be delicious. The good seed can swell and sprout and eventually develop into a full-grown tree, which bears fruit. There is no end to the tree's capacity; it continues to produce seeds, which in turn produce more fruit, and so on. There is a clear hint in all of this of our own eternal potential: everlasting life consists of producing seed forever, that is, continually regenerating. Each of us is like a tree of life, with the capacity and potential to bear seed and

THE BOOK OF MORMON

produce fruit forever (the "continuation of the seeds forever and ever"; D&C 132:19). "There is no end to matter; there is no end to space; there is no end to spirit; there is no end to race."[10]

Young missionaries are called to serve, and many of them begin with barely a seed of faith and knowledge. They arrive at a missionary training center, where the Spirit is abundant and seeds become plentiful, and "Miracle Growth" is poured on those seeds which sprout. Throughout their missions their trees will grow, becoming more and more productive, and the missionaries partake of the fruit of their labors. If they nourish their trees with great care—with prayer, scripture study, and service—the trees will sink deep roots and become stable and solid. If they neglect their trees and will not nourish them—that is, they are not obedient and faithful in mighty prayer, scripture study, and dedicated service—the trees will not develop deep roots and will wither away. Some Church members, even returned missionaries, get a good tree growing, even an impressive tree, and then for various reasons stop nourishing it; the tree becomes dormant, or inactive, and unproductive. That makes it good for nothing but to be cut down and cast out. All this can happen, not because the seed itself was not good but because *the ground is barren* (compare the parable of the four kinds of soil in Matthew 13:3–8, especially v. 5). If they will not continue to nourish the tree, fruit is impossible. If we refuse to pray, study, obey, work hard, and love our companion (mission or marriage) and other people, too, we will bear no fruit here or in eternity. If we refuse to nourish the word, we can never taste of the fruit of the tree of life.

So Alma encouraged us to experiment with the word, and the Savior *is* the Word. Isaiah 11:1 speaks of new shoots out of the root; we are new shoots out of the Root. He is our nourishment. With him we can also sink deep roots and become firm and steadfast. The secret is *constant nourishment.*

Alma 33:1–11

Alma continued the subject of his great discourse. The people wanted to know how they might obtain the fruit of which he spoke, or how they could know the truth and receive faith. This recalls the inquiry of King Lamoni's father, "What shall I do?" (Alma 22:15). The key questions are once again asked and answered. (Repetition is God's way of teaching his children.) How do we plant the seed? How do we have faith? Answer: By prayer and by study of the word. Prayer or worship may be done anytime, anywhere. Then, as other scriptures add, we must go out and do something about it—serve!

Alma 33:14

Alma is a master of asking thought-provoking questions. Two of his most decisive questions are these: Have ye "read the scriptures?" And "If ye have, how can ye disbelieve on the Son of God?"

JESUS IS THE SON OF GOD

Many in the modern, scholarly world question whether Jesus ever really claimed to be the Son of God. Book of Mormon prophets leave no doubt concerning the matter, plainly and constantly testifying that Jesus announced himself as the Son of God. In addition, Joseph Smith's translation of the Gospels—called "Testimonies" in that inspired revision of the Bible—contains at least forty declarations beyond those in the King James Version that Jesus is the Son of God. In his mortal ministry Jesus consistently testified that he was sent by his Father and that he spoke the words and did the works of the Father. Some of the Jews believed and accepted his witness; others did not. Those who rejected his claims to divinity labeled as blasphemy Jesus' claim to have been sent from God or to actually be God, and thus making himself "equal with God" (John 5:18). Some might also have had a problem with Jesus' claim because they believed in one God only, so his claim of being God's Son would be blasphemous. For that capital offense against Jewish law, they sought to kill him.

Yet there are *numerous* testimonies of Jesus as the Son of God. The greatest of all testimonies is the Father's own testimony, "This is my beloved Son," at Jesus' baptism (Matthew 3:17; D&C 93:15); at the Transfiguration (Matthew 17:5); at the appearance of the resurrected Christ to the Nephites (3 Nephi 11:7); and at Joseph Smith's First Vision (Joseph Smith–History 1:17). Additional testimonies by the Father include the vision of Moses (Moses 1:33; 2:1, 26); the vision of glories (D&C 76:20–23); and others (1 John 5:9–11; D&C 29:42; 49:5).

To all of the following, Jesus bore his own testimony that he is the Son of God: Adam (Moses 5:9); Moses (Moses 4:2); the Jews (Matthew 27:43; Luke 10:21–22; John 5:18–27; 10:36; 19:7); a blind man (John 9:35–37); the apostles (John 20:21); Caiaphas (Matthew 26:63–64); Nephites and Lamanites (3 Nephi 9:15; 20:31); Latter-day Saints in general (D&C 6:21; 10:57; 45:52; 50:27); Hyrum Smith (D&C 11:28); David Whitmer (D&C 14:9); Joseph Smith and Sidney Rigdon (D&C 35:2); Edward Partridge (D&C 36:8); elders of the Church (D&C 42:1); William W. Phelps (D&C 55:2); and four men who would later be called as apostles: Orson Hyde, Luke Johnson, Lyman Johnson, and William E. McLellin (D&C 68:6, 25).

Others testified that Jesus is the Son of God and the Only Begotten of the Father: Moses (Alma 33:18–19; Helaman 8:13–15); Isaiah and Jeremiah (Helaman 8:20); Zenos and Zenock (Alma 33:13–17; Helaman 8:19–20); the angel Gabriel (Luke 1:32, 35); John the Baptist (John 1:34; D&C 93:14); apostles (Matthew 14:33); Nathanael (John 1:49); Mark (Mark 1:1); Peter (Matthew 16:16; John 6:69; Acts 3:13, 26); Martha (John 11:27); John (John 1:14; 3:16, 35; 20:31; 1 John 3:8, 23; 4:10, 14–15; 5:5, 10–13); a Roman soldier (Matthew 27:54); an Ethiopian officer (Acts 8:37); Paul (Acts 9:20; Romans 1:4; 8:3, 32; 15:6; 2 Corinthians 1:19; Galatians 2:20; 4:4; Ephesians 4:13; Colossians 1:13; 1 Thessalonians 1:10; Hebrews 1:2; 4:14); Silas and Timothy (2 Corinthians 1:19); Nephi (1 Nephi 10:17; 11:7,

18, 21, 24; 13:40; 2 Nephi 25:12, 16, 19); Jacob (Jacob 4:5, 11); King Benjamin (Mosiah 3:8); Benjamin's people (Mosiah 4:2); Abinadi (Mosiah 15:2); Amulek (Alma 11:32–35; 34:2, 5); Alma the Elder and Alma the Younger (Alma 36:17–18); Alma the Younger (Alma 5:48; 6:8; 12:33–34; 13:5, 16; 33:14, 22); Samuel the Lamanite (Helaman 14:2, 8, 12); Mormon (Helaman 3:28; 3 Nephi 5:13, 26; Mormon 5:14; 7:5–7); Moroni (Ether 12:18); Joseph Smith (D&C 20:21); and Joseph Smith and Sidney Rigdon (D&C 76:20–25).

So, to conclude this listing of witnesses that Jesus is the Son of God, we ask again the same questions Alma asked: "Now behold, my brethren, I would ask if ye have read the scriptures? If ye have, how can ye disbelieve on the Son of God?" (Alma 33:14).

Alma 33:17

When true prophets of earlier times have testified of the Messiah in profound ways, they have often faced harm or death. Zenock and Zenos are two of them. Compare 1 Nephi 1:20; Mosiah 7:26–28; 17:7–8, 20; Helaman 8:12–23; and many other passages, including Doctrine and Covenants 135.

Alma 33:19–20

When the Lord sent poisonous serpents among the impatient and rebellious Israelites in the Sinai wilderness, Moses prayed for the people to be spared.

"The Lord said unto Moses, Make thee a fiery serpent, and set it upon a pole: and it shall come to pass, that every one that is bitten, when he looketh upon it, shall live.

"And Moses made a serpent of brass, and put it upon a pole, and it came to pass, that if a serpent had bitten any man, when he beheld the serpent of brass, he lived" (Numbers 21:8–9).

New Testament writers saw in that event a type or similitude in anticipation of the Messiah:

"As Moses lifted up the serpent in the wilderness, even so must the Son of man be lifted up:

"That whosoever believeth in him should not perish, but have eternal life" (John 3:14–15; see also Helaman 8:13–15).

As Israel had looked to the serpent on a pole to live, so they were now encouraged to look to their Redeemer, who would be lifted up and live. The serpent was apparently a symbol of God.

From the very beginning, however, there was a perversion of the true symbol. Lucifer, or Satan, usurped the image to represent himself. "The great dragon was cast out, that old serpent, called the Devil, and Satan, which deceiveth the whole world" (Revelation 12:9; see also 20:2). "The serpent beguiled [deceived or tricked] Eve through his subtilty" (2 Corinthians 11:3).

Moses' serpent on a pole was able to heal; and the Savior who was lifted up on the cross is able to heal. The serpent's healing powers persisted in the mythologies of Near Eastern religions, even down to the Greco-Roman Asclepius, the god of healing and medicine. Healing or medical centers were established throughout the Roman Empire, for example the Asclepieum at Pergamum and the Asklepeion on the island of Cos, where Hippocrates practiced for many years. The symbol of Asclepius was a serpent wrapped around a pole. Serpent images used as symbols of deities are found in most ancient Near Eastern and Mediterranean cultures.[11] Today the serpent wrapped around a pole is the symbol of the American Medical Association and other medical associations.

The parallel of the serpent with God penetrated other ancient cultures as well. For example, the Aztec god Quetzalcoatl, "Precious Serpent," reputedly lived in Coatzacoalcos, which means "sanctuary of the serpent." To ancient Mesoamericans, the serpent was associated with fertility, wisdom, and power.

So Moses is one of the greatest testators of the Messiah. He is famous for that unique type he raised up in the wilderness. To rescue his people he crafted the bronze serpent and lifted it up so the people could look upon it and avoid the deadly plague. It was easy to look (1 Nephi 17:41), so "many did look and live."

"But," Alma sadly commented, "few understood the meaning of those things, and this because of the hardness of their hearts. . . . There were many who were so hardened that they would not look, therefore they perished." Imagine! A simple matter of glancing up to the symbol of the Savior, and they refused. Why? "Now the reason they would not look is because they did not believe that it would heal them." There it is! It is exactly the same reason why many people stubbornly refuse to look to the Master Healer: they don't really believe that he will heal them. They don't believe that he is real, or that he lived and suffered for every one of us, or that he *can* heal them. If people will look to him, they can be healed and live (3 Nephi 9:13–14). He not only suffered for our sins but for our sicknesses. Through our faith in him, he can make us whole. Some of us refuse to look to him because we adopt the unbelieving attitude of Laman and Lemuel: "The Lord maketh no such thing known unto us" (1 Nephi 15:9)—or, in other words, he may heal others, but he wouldn't heal us.

See also commentary at 1 Nephi 17:41–42.

Alma 33:21, 23

If we could be healed of all our maladies just by casting our eyes toward him, wouldn't we do it? "All this can ye do if ye will."

Alma 33:22–23

The message of these verses and all of chapter 34 is that the seed is the Savior and his word and work. He was, in Alma's day, about to come into the world to suffer and die to atone for people's sins, to provide immortality through resurrection, and to provide a fair judgment. He would redeem people, not just in the abstract "save all mankind" concept but in a literal, personal redeeming of every one of us who will look to him. If the Father has helped you to know and feel that great truth, then "your burdens may be light, through the joy of his Son."

Alma 34:6–8

Alma and Amulek were a dynamic and unified missionary team, testifying of the Atonement and affirming each other's witness. Alma prepared his listeners to hear the crowning teachings of Amulek: the deep meaning of Christ's atoning sacrifice. Those men, plus all the other prophets since the world began, testified "that the word is in Christ unto salvation." They dedicated their lives to proving Christ (Helaman 8:13–24).

Alma 34:9–12

Nothing short of the shedding of the blood of both an infinite and perfect Being could meet the demands of justice (pay for broken laws) and redeem (exalt) individuals whose progress has been stopped by transgression. No sacrifice of animals or of humans could pay for sins; only an infinite and eternal sacrifice of God himself could do that. Joseph Smith taught: "It must be shedding the blood of the Only Begotten to atone for man, for this was the plan of redemption, and without the shedding of blood was no remission. And as the sacrifice was instituted for a type by which man was to discern the great Sacrifice which God had prepared, to offer a sacrifice contrary to that, no faith could be exercised, because redemption was not purchased in that way. . . . Certainly, the shedding of the blood of a beast could be beneficial to no man, except it was done in imitation, or as a type, or explanation of what was to be offered through the gift of God Himself—and this performance done with an eye looking forward in faith on the power of that great Sacrifice for a remission of sins."[12]

Jesus Christ is an infinite being and can provide immortality and possible redemption for all. There is a vast difference between mere payment and complete redemption (D&C

19:16–19). Ultimately, justice will demand payment for every single sin, whether by the individual or by a proxy, but redemption moves the penitent forward on the path to perfection. The infinite atonement extends to all of the Savior's worlds (see commentary at 2 Nephi 9:7).

Alma 34:13–14

Sacrifice began with Adam as an ordinance of the gospel and continued under the preparatory gospel (the law of Moses). All the hundreds of thousands of sacrifices on temple altars over the centuries pointed to the great and last sacrifice of the Son of God himself. The twenty-four-hour period that included Gethsemane and Golgotha was *the* Day of Atonement.

Alma 34:15–17

In order for the bowels of mercy to overpower the demands of justice, we must exercise our faith unto repentance. The phrase "faith unto repentance" appears four times in these three verses. The single most important act we do to set in motion the personal benefit of Jesus' great atoning sacrifice is to repent of our sins.

Alma 34:17–27

This is the third chapter in a row in which we read of mighty prayer—one of the keys to appreciating and personalizing the Atonement in our lives. These verses detail where and when and how to pray. "Closets," "secret places," and "your wilderness" all suggest places to which we may go for private, quiet introspection (contrast that personal setting with the vain, public praying of the Zoramites on their Rameumptom). Verse 27 encourages us always to have a prayer in our hearts; to be "drawn out in prayer" means praying for an extended period of time or repeatedly praying over an indefinite period of time. We pray for ourselves, and we pray for others, specifically, by name. And always we express gratitude.

Alma 34:28–29

If we don't get up off our knees and go to work to meet the needs of others, our prayers are in vain, and Amulek said we are as hypocrites (Greek *hypokritēs,* meaning "actor," one who just *pretends* to believe). If we do not show the love of Christ, Amulek said we are as "dross," which is worthless scum or waste matter.

Alma 34:30, 33

We have indeed "received so many witnesses"; see commentary at Helaman 8:13–24.

Alma 34:31–32

Amulek emphasized the urgency of his message: "Now is the time and the day of your salvation." Scriptures teach that a thousand years in our time is as a day in God's time (Psalm 90:4; 2 Peter 3:8; Abraham 3:4). Someone has calculated that 12,000 months, or 365,000 days, in earth's time is equal to one day in the Lord's time, or 1,000 years in our time is 24 hours in God's time. Five hundred years in our time is 12 hours in God's time; 250 years, 6 hours. One hour of celestial time is equal to 41 years and 8 months in our time. One minute in God's time is over 8 months in our time. On that scale, if we live to be 70 years old, we will have been out of the presence of God for 1 hour and 40 minutes. Amulek said that "this life is the time for men to prepare to meet God." We have on average about an hour and 40 minutes to work out our salvation. We have no time to waste.

Time flies on wings of lightning;
We cannot call it back.
It comes, then passes forward
Along its onward track.

And if we are not mindful,
The chance will fade away,
For life is quick in passing.
'Tis as a single day.[13]

Actually, according to the above calculations, life is not even "a single day"; it is a small fraction of a day by heavenly reckoning.

Alma 34:33

Procrastination is the thief of exaltation. The rabbis used to say that you can't repent the day before you die because you don't know what day you'll die. So repent every day![14]

Alma 34:34

"I will repent. . . . I will return to my God." The Hebrew verb *lashuv*, translated "to repent," means "to return." The two words are appropriately used together here. They are used together in other passages also: Helaman 13:11; 3 Nephi 9:13; 10:6; 18:32; Doctrine and Covenants 109:21.

When we depart this mortal sphere, we will be taking with us into the spirit world our same attitudes, our same cravings, our same prejudices toward people, and our same inclinations toward sins. We will remain the same basic person. Taking bad habits and dispositions into the spirit world to work on them is like trying to learn to play the violin without a violin. Professor Rodney Turner wrote: "'That same spirit' is one's distilled, fundamental self, stripped of all the transitory, superficial baggage acquired in mortality. It is what the soul really is in its fixed, resurrected state, rather than what it appeared to be at any given moment in its fluid, probationary state. What it really is determines what it really desires. These desires, free of all mitigating entanglements, constitute the soul's own self-judgment."[15]

THE BOOK OF MORMON

Alma 34:35

We are choosing, by our daily behavior, whether our sins will be blotted out (Isaiah 43:25; Acts 3:19) or our names will be blotted out (Mosiah 26:36; Moroni 6:7; D&C 20:83). We will either remain an enemy to God, a natural man (Mosiah 3:19), or we will become a friend of God, as Abraham did (Isaiah 41:8; James 2:23). In the end, either God will "seal [us] his" (Mosiah 5:15), or the devil will "seal [us] his" (Alma 34:35) and have all power over us. It is our choice.

Alma 34:36

"The Lord hath said he dwelleth not in unholy temples." That is, "the *Spirit* of the Lord doth not dwell in unholy temples" (Helaman 4:24; emphasis added) "but in the hearts of the righteous doth he dwell." The *Spirit* of the Lord can dwell in our hearts. As Doctrine and Covenants 130:3 teaches us, that is a *symbolic* dwelling in one's heart, not a literal one (see also D&C 130:22).

On garments being made white through the blood of the Lamb, see commentary at 1 Nephi 12:10–11.

Alma 34:37–41

Amulek, the new convert-turned-prophet, teaches great wisdom to live by: "Work out your salvation with fear [reverence] before God"; "contend no more against the Holy Ghost"; "take upon you the name of Christ"; "humble yourselves even to the dust"; "live in thanksgiving daily"; "be watchful unto prayer continually"; "bear with [patience] all manner of afflictions." Then, a happy promise is assured: "Ye shall one day rest from all your afflictions."

Patience in the face of affliction is a hallmark of faith, meekness, and true discipleship. On one occasion the Lord said to Joseph Smith, "Be patient in afflictions, for thou shalt have many; but endure them, for, lo, I am with thee, even unto the end of thy days" (D&C 24:8). On another occasion he said, "Be patient in afflictions, revile not against those that revile. Govern your house in meekness, and be steadfast" (D&C 31:9). Such instructions are important keys to a life well lived.

Alma 35:1–14

The truth of Alma 31:5 is confirmed—"the word" had a greater power to effect righteous change than anything else. Some Zoramites converted to the gospel and were expelled by the wicked, taken in by the people of Ammon, and ministered to "according to their wants." True charity extended by sincere disciples comprehends both needs and wants. Nevertheless, the work of the adversary also increased, and war was initiated again, as reported in a latter part of the record (see Alma 43:3).

Alma 35:15

The Lord expects exact obedience. In fact, he *requires* that we be strictly obedient. And he warns us not "to be offended because of the strictness of the word."[16]

Alma 36–42

These seven chapters record the final counsel and blessing upon each of Alma's sons: Helaman, Shiblon, and Corianton. In the next twenty chapters (Alma 43–62), Mormon continued the account of the wars between the Nephites and the Lamanites that he began in Alma 35.

Alma 36:1–2

It seems significant that the very first thing Alma chose to teach was one of the major themes of the whole Book of Mormon: "Inasmuch as ye shall keep the commandments of God ye shall prosper in the land" (see also v. 30; 37:13). "Remembering" is a righteous focus with Alma, and it becomes so with Helaman (Helaman 5:5–14).

Alma 36:3, 27

Every one of us is going to experience serious trials, troubles, and afflictions in this life, but Alma reassured us that "whosoever shall put their trust in God shall be supported in their trials, and their troubles, and their afflictions, and shall be lifted up at the last day" (see vv. 27–28 for Alma as an example of that truth). In fact, Alma went on to teach that there is a direct and proportional relationship: The extent to which we trust the Lord indicates the extent to which we will be delivered (Alma 38:5). It is comforting to know that if we trust God—put our confidence in him—in the end we will be not cast down but lifted up, and we will have heaven's help to make it through the inevitable hard times and to find purpose in them.

One student related that he started his mission in the land of Armenia and was enjoying becoming acquainted with the people and helping them learn of the gospel and come unto Christ. But all of that changed on a cold night when he slipped on ice and damaged his back; a few months later he had to be sent home to the United States to receive treatment for a herniated disc. It was a serious trial for the elder, but he took note of scriptures that teach "God . . . shall consecrate thine afflictions for thy gain" (2 Nephi 2:2) and "all things wherewith you have been afflicted shall work together for your good" (D&C 98:3).

The elder felt lost, and he wondered why God had allowed him to fall into such trials. He questioned why he had to be home with nothing to do.

Eventually he was reassigned to the California Arcadia Mission with a special call. He was to help revive an Armenian group that had been dissolved fifteen years earlier. Soon after he began the daunting task, his best companion from Armenia became sick and later joined him in California. With great effort and the Lord's blessings, they reestablished that unit of the Church, and when the injured elder finished his

Alma, Arise, *by Walter Rane.*

mission, there were thirty active members and a continuous flow of new investigators. The Lord really did consecrate this elder's afflictions for his good and for the good of the many thousands of Armenians in California who could now hear the gospel in their own language.

Alma 36:5–23

Alma's conversion story is repeated. Refer to the detailed commentary, combining both accounts of this experience, at Mosiah 27:24–29, and especially Mosiah 27:28–29.

Alma 36:24–26

When we are truly converted we want to help others experience the joy of spiritual rebirth also (see Mosiah 28:3).

Alma 36:28

"I know that he will raise me up at the last day." Alma knew that he was sealed up to eternal life, having his calling and election made sure, and guaranteed exaltation, as were his father (Mosiah 26:20); Abraham, Isaac, and Jacob (D&C 132:37); the brother of Jared (Ether 3:13); Lehi (2 Nephi 1:15); Jacob (2 Nephi 2:3); Enos (Enos 1:27); the sons of Mosiah—Ammon, Aaron, Omner, and Himni (Mosiah 28:7); the Nephite Twelve (3 Nephi 28:1–3); Mormon (Mormon 2:19); Moroni (Ether 12:37); Peter, James, and John (2 Peter 1:19); Paul (2 Timothy 4:8); and Joseph Smith (D&C 132:49). President Marion G. Romney declared, "In this dispensation many have received like assurances."[17]

Alma 37

This chapter teaches the importance of written records, with encouragement for us to keep a book of remembrance and a personal journal.

THE IMPORTANCE OF RECORD-KEEPING

1 Nephi 1:1–3

[First thing, first page!] "I make a record of my proceedings in my days. . . . I make a record in the language of my father. . . . And I know that the record which I make is true; and I make it with mine own hand; and I make it according to my knowledge."

Alma 37:2–14

"I also command you that ye keep a record of this people, . . . and keep all these things sacred . . . ; for it is for a wise purpose that they are kept. . . . Now ye may suppose that this is foolishness in me; but behold I say unto you, that by small and simple things are great things brought to pass; and small means in many instances doth confound the wise. . . . By very small means the Lord . . . bringeth about the salvation of many souls. And now, it has hitherto been wisdom in God that these things should be preserved; for behold, they have enlarged the memory of this people, yea, and convinced many of the error of their ways, and brought them to the knowledge of their God unto the salvation of their souls . . . [and] brought them to . . . rejoice in Jesus Christ their Redeemer. . . . And now remember . . . God has entrusted you with these things, which are sacred, . . . for a wise purpose . . . that he may show forth his power unto future generations."

3 Nephi 27:23–25

[To the Twelve] "Write the things which ye have seen and heard. . . . Write the works of this people, which shall be . . . [and] that which hath been. For behold, out of the books which have been written, and which shall be written, shall this people be judged."

Doctrine and Covenants 21:1

"There shall be a record kept among you."

Doctrine and Covenants 85:1–2

"It is the duty of the Lord's clerk, whom he has appointed, to keep a history, and a general church record of all things that transpire in Zion, and of . . . their manner of life, their faith, and works."

Abraham 1:31

"The records of the fathers . . . the Lord my God preserved in mine own hands; therefore a knowledge of the beginning of the creation, . . . as they were made known unto the fathers, have I kept even unto this day, and I shall endeavor to write some of these things upon this record, *for the benefit of my posterity that shall come after me*" (emphasis added).

Pages of Personal Journals Have Become Scripture

What if Joseph had not recorded his experiences in Egypt, including his sensitive feelings during the estrangement from his brothers, during injustices perpetrated against him, and in the poignant scenes of reconciliation in Egypt? What if he had failed to write down his revelations? "And the prophecies which he wrote, there are not many greater. And he prophesied concerning us, and our future generations; and they are written upon the plates of brass" (2 Nephi 4:2).

What if Nephi had felt reluctant to record those very personal glimpses inside his heart when, after numerous chapters of scripture we have him up on a pedestal of perfection, he exclaims: "O wretched man that I am! . . . My soul grieveth because of mine iniquities . . . , because of the temptations and the sins which do so easily beset me. . . . My heart groaneth because of my sins" (2 Nephi 4:17–19). He admitted, "I write the things of my soul" and all "for the learning and the profit of my children" (2 Nephi 4:15).

What if Enos had been embarrassed or ashamed to tell us of the wrestle he had when he needed to be cleansed of his sins? Doesn't it help to know that there are others who have struggled with their own success and happiness? And he didn't just tell us it happened, he gave us details of how it happened:

"I cried. . . . I was thus struggling in the spirit. . . . I did pour out my whole soul. . . . [I] prayed and labored with all diligence" (Enos 1:4–12).

And Alma. He could have hidden his rebellious past and started his life story after the turning point; he could have avoided recounting the spiritual labor pains leading to his own new birth; but he was willing to go back and briefly reconstruct his experience for our benefit, describing the ugliness of his rebellion. Alma is the personification of hope. If one so vile, so antagonistic, so rebellious can become president of the Church, then what of us? Thank goodness he wrote the story!

What if the New Testament apostles had not kept journals? We would not even have the meager accounts we now have of the one perfect life we are supposed to emulate.

What if Joseph Smith had not kept a journal? We would have no six-volume *History of the Church*.

What if Wilford Woodruff had not kept a journal? We would have fewer details of important Church history.

What if we kept no journal? Jacob 4:3 says that "we labor diligently to engraven these words . . . , hoping that our beloved brethren and our children will receive them with thankful hearts, and look upon them that they may learn with joy and not with sorrow . . . concerning their . . . parents."

Alma 37:6–7

From small and simple things great things can come. President Boyd K. Packer said: "You can put it down in your little black book that if you will not be loyal in the small things, you will not be loyal in the large things. If you will not respond to the so-called insignificant or menial tasks which need to be performed in the Church and kingdom, there will be no opportunity for service in the so-called greater challenges."[18] See commentary at 1 Nephi 16:28–29; Doctrine and Covenants 64:33.

Alma 37:11–14

On mysteries that are not yet fully known and so it is un-wise to talk about them, see commentary at 1 Nephi 10:15–22; 2 Nephi 28:30; and especially Alma 12:9.

On things being preserved for "a wise purpose" known by God, see commentary at Words of Mormon 1:7.

On God's course being "one eternal round," see commentary at 1 Nephi 19:22–24, under "Why Study Isaiah," 3 Nephi 23:1–3; and commentary at Alma 7:20–21.

On the strictness of the commandments of God, see commentary at Alma 57.

Alma 37:21–26

These verses refer to the record of the Jaredites inscribed on the twenty-four gold plates found during the time of kings Limhi and Mosiah. Verse 23 tells of the Lord saying that "my servant Gazelem" would use a stone specially prepared to translate the record and publish it to the world. That record is the Book of Mormon, including the book of Ether (an abridgment of the Jaredite record), and it was translated and published by the Prophet Joseph Smith. In editions of the Doctrine and Covenants before 1981, some code names were used in several sections. There the Prophet was called "Gazelam," a likely variant of the Book of Mormon name (see a pre-1981 edition, D&C 78:9; 82:11; 104:26).

Alma 37:27–32

Some things need to be recorded but should not be circu lated. Revealing secret oaths, covenants, signs, and abomina-tions could possibly corrupt more societies (see commentary at Helaman 6:21–25).

Alma 37:33–37

These verses offer inspiring counsel to youth and adults: Be aware and informed of the secret works of darkness, but when teaching others, focus on the open works of light. "Never be weary of good works"; "learn in thy youth to keep the commandments"; "let all thy thoughts be directed unto the Lord; yea, let the affections of thy heart be placed upon the Lord"; and "counsel with the Lord in all thy doings, and he will direct thee."

Alma 37:38–40

To assist Lehi's colony in journeying through the great Arabian Desert and across the great seas, the Lord prepared a ball or director—what they called the *Liahona,* which means "compass"—the equivalent of an early twenty-first-century global positioning system. But instead of functioning through electrical power, it operated on faith and obedience.

In addition to its literal function, it had—like most gospel concepts—a symbolic function. It was a real object that typified an underlying reality. The Liahona was a type and shadow of Christ, who points the way all of us should go in life (see commentary for Alma 37:43–47). This is the first mention of the proper name of this device. We do not know the specific derivation or origin of the word.

Alma 37:41

Another lesson for today: Even though miracles could be worked by daily diligence in the regular rhythm of their schedule, and marvelous works and success could follow, regrettably some "were slothful, and forgot to exercise their faith and diligence and then those marvelous works ceased, and they did not progress."

Alma 37:43–47

It was easy for the members of the Lehite colony, if they would so choose, to look to the Liahona to keep them on a straight course to the promised land. It is likewise easy for us, if we will so choose, to follow our Liahona—the Holy Ghost and the words of Christ and his prophets—to keep us

31

on a straight course to our eternal home. The scriptures are full of such meaningful types, shadows, and similitudes. Other examples are the following:

1. The Flood, like baptism	1 Peter 3:20–21
2. Abraham offering Isaac	Jacob 4:5
3. Joseph's coat	Alma 46:23–24
4. The serpent on a pole	Alma 33:19–21; Helaman 8:14–15
5. The law of Moses	Mosiah 13:30–31; 16:14; Alma 25:15; 34:14
6. All things!	2 Nephi 11:4; Moses 6:63

Alma 38

Alma gave nine admonitions to his missionary son that are recorded in chapter 38:

1. Keep the commandments and endure to the end;
2. Remember that you will receive help in your troubles and afflictions in the same degree as you trust God;
3. Learn that there is no other way to obtain salvation except through Christ;
4. Continue to teach with diligence and temperance;
5. See that you are not lifted up in pride;
6. Use boldness but not overbearance;
7. Bridle all your passions;
8. Refrain from idleness; and
9. Pray for forgiveness and for mercy on behalf of your fellow human beings.

Alma 38:2, 5

All righteous fathers hope to find great joy in their sons because of the sons' steadiness and faithfulness to God. And even though life is hard—and it has to be so, for our sake—as long as we will put our trust in God, the promise is that we will be "delivered out of [our] trials, and [our] troubles, and [our] afflictions" and at the last be exalted.

Alma 38:11, 14

"Do not boast in your own wisdom, nor of your much strength," but "acknowledge your unworthiness before God at all times." "Boasting," Elder Marvin J. Ashton taught, "is to glorify oneself, to talk in a vain or bragging manner, or to talk especially about one's deeds."[19] King Benjamin advises us to remember the greatness of God and our own nothingness; or, in other words, "humble [our]selves even in the depths of humility" (Mosiah 4:11).

Alma 38:12

Here is one of the most important single-line teachings in all of scripture: "Bridle all your passions, that ye may be filled with love." Note that passion and pure love are not the same thing. In fact, the word *passions* here is referring to feelings much broader than simply romantic love or immoral ideas. It refers to any strong emotions in a variety of contexts that, left unchecked, will drive away the Spirit of the Lord—whether those emotions are social, political, sexual, and so on. If we want to feel real love toward God and toward other persons, we must bridle our passions or emotions. A bridle does not *suppress* the spirited creature (whether horse or human) but is used to *control* or *direct*.

"[Alma] did not say eliminate or even suppress your passions, but *bridle* them—harness, channel, and focus them. Why? Because discipline makes possible a richer, deeper love."[20]

One of our Book of Mormon students inadvertently misspelled the word on an exam, but the mistake was rather instructive: he spelled it "*bridal* all your passions." All right, *get married;* that is a positive way of properly directing our passions!

Sexual restraint or control is particularly imperative for

young people. Will and Ariel Durant insightfully wrote: "No one man, however brilliant or well-informed, can come in one lifetime to such fullness of understanding as to safely judge and dismiss the customs or institutions of his society, for these are the wisdom of generations after centuries of experiment in the laboratory of history. A youth boiling with hormones will wonder why he should not give full freedom to his sexual desires; and if he is unchecked by custom, morals, or laws, he may ruin his life before he matures sufficiently to understand that sex is a river of fire that must be banked and cooled by a hundred restraints if it is not to consume in chaos the individual and the group."[21]

Other excellent counsel in verse 12 is for all youth: Be bold, but don't be overbearing, and refrain from being idle. An old Spanish saying reminds us, "The devil is the king of idleness, but he is not idle!"

Alma 39

Corianton had moral problems because he didn't possess the sure doctrinal foundation and understanding that keep individuals from sinning and which are at the heart of behavior. In other words, lack of doctrinal understanding is really at the heart of misbehavior. That is one reason why President Boyd K. Packer said: "True doctrine, understood, changes attitudes and behavior. The study of the doctrines of the gospel will improve behavior quicker than a study of behavior will improve behavior. Preoccupation with unworthy behavior can lead to unworthy behavior. That is why we stress so forcefully the study of the doctrines of the gospel."[22] And Elder Neal A. Maxwell said: "Doctrines believed and practiced do change and improve us, while ensuring our vital access to the Spirit. Both outcomes are crucial."[23]

Alma 39:2–4

Alma commanded his missionary son Corianton to repent. He had disobeyed mission rules by leaving his proselyting area to go after a woman. One of his first problems leading up to his immoral behavior was *pride*. He was boasting in his own strength and wisdom. "It's my life; I can handle this!" and then the tragedy ensued. In a way, pride is a denial of the Fall and the need for the Atonement—in short, it is a rejection of our dependency on Christ.

Alma 39:5–14

Alma did as a good father should do: He chastised and corrected his son and commanded him to repent, *for his good* (compare the Old Testament priest Eli, whose "sons made themselves vile, and he restrained them not"; 1 Samuel 3:13). He told him to "cross" himself in the lusts of his eyes, that is, to refrain or abstain from the lusts of the flesh. Joseph Smith's translation of Matthew 16:26 says, "For a man to take up his cross, is to deny himself of all ungodliness, and every worldly lust, and keep my commandments."

The basic issue is control. We came into this life not just to obtain a physical body but to learn to control it. And "life" is really at the heart of the matter. The three "greatest" sins mentioned by Alma all have something to do with life: murder—the unauthorized taking of life; immorality—the unauthorized use of the sacred force of life; and denying the Holy Ghost—the purposeful rejection of the spiritual component of life. The secret is to love the things of the Spirit, to be constantly filling ourselves with spiritual things, so that the spiritual stimulation will be more appealing and satisfying than giving in to the passions of the body. As another great missionary, Paul, taught, "Walk in the Spirit, and ye shall not fulfil the lust of the flesh" (Galatians 5:16).

The Church's *For the Strength of Youth* booklet gives frank, direct counsel to all youth regarding the sacred law of chastity:

"Do not have any sexual relations before marriage, and be completely faithful to your spouse after marriage. Satan may tempt you to rationalize that sexual intimacy before marriage is acceptable when two people are in love. That is not true. In God's sight, sexual sins are extremely serious because they defile the power God has given us to create life. . . .

"Before marriage, do not do anything to arouse the powerful emotions that must be expressed only in marriage. Do not participate in passionate kissing, lie on top of another person, or touch the private, sacred parts of another person's body, with or without clothing. Do not allow anyone to do that with you. Do not arouse those emotions in your own body.

"In cultures where dating or courting is acceptable, always treat your date with respect, never as an object to be used for your lustful desires. Stay in areas of safety where you can easily control your physical feelings. Do not participate in talk or activities that arouse sexual feelings."[24]

Self-control and self-mastery must continue after marriage. President Thomas S. Monson explains: "Choose a companion carefully and prayerfully; and when you are married, be fiercely loyal one to another. Priceless advice comes from a small framed plaque I once saw in the home of an uncle and aunt. It read, 'Choose your love; love your choice.' There is great wisdom in those few words. Commitment in marriage is absolutely essential."[25]

"THE LUSTS OF YOUR EYES" (ALMA 39:9)—THE DESTRUCTIVE NATURE OF PORNOGRAPHY

While serving as president of Brigham Young University, Elder Dallin H. Oaks warned about the damage caused by pornography: "We are surrounded by the promotional literature of illicit sexual relations, on the printed page and on the screen. For your own good, avoid it. Pornographic or erotic stories and pictures are worse than filthy or polluted food. The body has defenses to rid itself of unwholesome food. With a few fatal exceptions bad food will only make you sick but do no permanent harm. In contrast, a person who feasts upon filthy stories or pornographic or erotic pictures and literature records them in this marvelous retrieval system we call a brain. The brain won't vomit back filth. Once recorded, it will always remain subject to recall, flashing its perverted images across your mind and drawing you away from the wholesome things in life."[26]

President George Albert Smith taught:

"My grandfather [George A. Smith, a counselor in the First Presidency to Brigham Young] used to say to his family, 'There is a line of demarkation, well defined, between the Lord's territory and the devil's. If you will stay on the Lord's side of the line you will be under his influence and will have no desire to do wrong; but if you cross to the devil's side of the line one inch, you are in the tempter's power, and if he is successful, you will not be able to think or even reason properly, because you will have lost the spirit of the Lord.'

"When I have been tempted sometimes to do a certain thing, I have asked myself, 'Which side of the line am I on?' If I determined to be on the safe side, the Lord's side, I would do the right thing every time. So when temptation comes, think prayerfully about your problem, and the influence of the spirit of the Lord will enable you to decide wisely. There is safety for us only on the Lord's side of the line."[27]

President Thomas S. Monson taught: "Constantly before us is the [temptation] of immorality. Almost everywhere we turn, there are those who would have us believe that what was once considered immoral is now acceptable. . . .

"The evil one . . . would have us believe that the viewing of pornography really hurts no one. . . .

"Some publishers and printers prostitute their presses by printing millions of pieces of pornography each day. No expense is spared to produce a product certain to be viewed, then viewed again. One of the most accessible sources of pornography today is the Internet, where one can turn on a computer and instantly have at his fingertips countless sites featuring pornography. President Gordon B. Hinckley has said: . . . 'It is vicious. It is lewd and filthy. It is enticing and habit-forming. It will take [you] down to destruction as surely as anything in this world. It is foul sleaze that makes its exploiters wealthy, its victims impoverished' [Ensign, Nov. 2000, 51].

"Tainted as well is the movie producer, the television programmer, or the entertainer who promotes pornography. Long gone are the restraints of yesteryear. So-called realism is the quest, with the result that today we are surrounded by this filth.

"Avoid any semblance of pornography. It will desensitize the spirit and erode the conscience."[28]

Referring to the Internet, President Monson warned: "On one hand, it provides nearly limitless opportunities for acquiring useful and important information. Through it we can communicate with others around the world. The Church itself has a wonderful Web site, filled with valuable and uplifting information and priceless resources.

"On the other hand, however—and extremely alarming— are the reports of the number of individuals who are utilizing the Internet for evil and degrading purposes, the viewing of pornography being the most prevalent of these purposes. My brothers and sisters, involvement in such will literally destroy the spirit. Be strong. Be clean. Avoid such degrading and destructive types of content at all costs—wherever they may be! I sound this warning to everyone, everywhere. I add—particularly to the young people—that this includes pornographic images transmitted via cell phones.

"My beloved friends, under no circumstances allow yourselves to become trapped in the viewing of pornography, one of the most effective of Satan's enticements. And if you have allowed yourself to become involved in this behavior, cease now. Seek the help you need to overcome and to change the direction of your life. Take the steps necessary to get back on the strait and narrow, and then stay there."[29]

Alma 39:10–13

Alma is in effect saying, Corianton, listen to your older brothers. Pay attention to their counsel. You've been a bad example! "When [the Zoramites] saw your conduct they would not believe in my words." The Lord could say the same thing to any openly disobedient missionary. "I command you, my son, in the fear of God, . . . [to] refrain from your iniquities." "Return unto [the people], and acknowledge your faults and that wrong which ye have done." Confession—acknowledging and admitting our sins—is an indispensable part of true repentance; going through all the other steps but avoiding confession is not complete repentance and will not bring complete forgiveness.

Alma 39:14

Corianton had another problem. His father, Alma, taught him, "Seek not after riches nor the vain things of this world; . . . you cannot carry them with you." Paul made the same point: "We brought nothing into this world, and it is certain we can carry nothing out" (1 Timothy 6:7). As Brother Skinner tells his students, "You never see a hearse pulling a U-Haul."

Getting things seems to be a serious problem for humans. How foolish to spend so much time and effort to get things, only to leave them all behind when we die and return to our God. "Beware of covetousness," Jesus warned, "for a man's life consisteth not in the abundance of the things which he possesseth. . . . So is he that layeth up treasure for himself, and is not rich toward God" (Luke 12:15, 21). The psalmist tersely described why this is so foolish: "When he dieth he shall carry nothing away: [his riches] shall not descend after him" (Psalm 49:17). Think about the implications of the word *descend* in that verse!

Alma 39:15–16

Look to Christ. He is our only hope for getting our sins taken away. Alma says, in effect, Corianton, you had better apply the saving power of Christ to yourself. Once you have resolved your own situation, then your mission is to teach others about the glad tidings of their Savior.

Alma 40

Alma was a model of a perceptive father who is trying to counsel with and bless his son, and, through the inspiration available to all parents, he began to zero in on Corianton's real issue—a profound doctrinal question. Why was Corianton "worried concerning the resurrection of the dead"? Because if a person claimed that there is no life after this one and no resurrection to live forever, that reasoning could be used to further justify sinning: Live it up here in mortality; go after whatever your body wants here in this life because there's nothing afterwards. It was important for Alma to resolve his son's doubt.

At that time, about 73 B.C., there was understandably some curiosity about the nature of resurrection. There was still no such thing as resurrection; for nearly four thousand years people had been dying and their bodies remained dead. The Savior had not yet lived and died to overcome the effects of physical death and provide immortality for all of Heavenly Father's children. There was still relatively little revealed on the subject, except for what the prophets had specifically asked about. Alma had inquired diligently to know about resurrection, and this chapter is full of what he learned from heavenly sources:

1. There is no resurrection until after the coming of Christ, who would be, as the scriptures attest, "the firstfruits of them that slept" (1 Corinthians 15:20), the first to be resurrected from the dead to immortality (Acts 26:23; Colossians 1:18; Revelation 1:5; 2 Nephi 2:8–9).
2. There is a time appointed for everyone to rise from the dead (v. 4).
3. There is a time period between death and resurrection (v. 6).
4. Between death and resurrection our spirits in some way report back "home" to God (v. 11).

5. There is a partial judgment at death to determine one of two general destinations in the world of spirits (vv. 12–13).
6. The righteous enter a state of happiness called paradise, and the wicked are cast out into outer darkness, or spirit prison, or hell (vv. 12–13).
7. The first resurrection begins at the resurrection of Christ and includes the righteous who lived and died before his mortal ministry (vv. 16–21).
8. Resurrection means the reuniting of the soul (that is, the spirit) and the body (vv. 21–23).

Alma 40:3

"There are many mysteries which are kept, that no one knoweth them save God himself" (compare D&C 25:4). There are many things that, in our present mortal state of weakness and nothingness and with our limited scope of understanding, we are not yet prepared to receive. Articles of Faith 1:9 clearly teaches that God will "yet reveal many great and important things pertaining to the Kingdom of God" (see also D&C 101:32–34; 121:26–32). We should never lose faith in the things we already know because of the things we do not yet know. We are, however, at liberty to inquire of the Lord about things we sincerely want to know, as Alma did.

Here is one example: "To the world and to the worldly the resurrection is a mystery. In fact, even to those of the household of faith it is incomprehensible and inexplicable. How is it that a dead body can return to life, join with the immortal spirit, and acquire godlike glory and power in the process? It is beyond mortal mind to fathom such a thing. But the Spirit whispers and experience teaches that such is true and real."[30]

Alma 40:8

"As one day with God"; see commentary at Alma 34:31–32.

Alma 40:11

"The spirits of all men . . . are taken home to that God who gave them life." Of that teaching of Alma, President George Q. Cannon wrote: "He does not intend to convey the idea that they are immediately ushered into the personal presence of God. He evidently uses that phrase in a qualified sense."[31]

President Joseph Fielding Smith explained: "'Taken home to God' [compare Ecclesiastes 12:7] simply means that their mortal existence has come to an end, and they have returned to the world of spirits, where they are assigned to a place according to their works with the just or with the unjust, there to await the resurrection."[32] On this point, the Savior is our best, most important witness. We know that not even he was taken immediately into the presence of his Father after his death. He went to the world of spirits (D&C 138), and even after his own resurrection, being "the firstfruits of them that slept" (1 Corinthians 15:20), he said to the first mortal to see his resurrected body, "Touch me not; for I am not yet ascended to my Father" (John 20:17).

In Latter-day Saint theology there are actually two heavens where God resides and where his jurisdiction extends to his children on this earth. Brother Ogden realized after his father died that he now had two fathers in heaven—his immortal Father and his mortal father—although their two places of residence are the two different definitions we have of heaven. One heaven is where the Father, Son, and Holy Ghost reside, far out in space near Kolob. The other heaven is the immediate surroundings, the atmosphere around this earth—that is, the earth's spirit, or the spirit world. That's where Brother Ogden's father is now.

President Brigham Young helped us understand the difference between these two heavens: "When you lay down this tabernacle, where are you going? Into the spiritual world. . . . Where is the spirit world? It is right here. Do the good and evil spirits go together? Yes, they do. Do they both inhabit one kingdom? Yes, they do [that is, the righteous and the wicked occupy together one world of spirits, although there are separate venues in that world for each, and a chasm, gulf, or some kind of barrier separates them there; see D&C 138:12, 20–22, 29]. . . . Do they go beyond the boundaries of the organized earth? No, they do not. They are brought forth upon this earth."[33]

Alma's increasing understanding of the doctrine of "heavenly home" is another example of revelation that comes line upon line, precept upon precept.

Alma 40:12

Troubles, care, and sorrow are an intentional and essential part of mortality. We were not sent down here to be comfortable. Earth life is a testing ground of faith and obedience, and it purposefully includes adversity. However, there will come a deserved rest from the troubles, care, and sorrow—but only for the righteous.

Alma 40:13–19

Implied in these verses are the several partial or intermittent judgments that occur during the postmortal phase of our eternal existence. The righteous are those who have been baptized and remained faithful in mortality. At death they are judged worthy to be gathered to one part of the spirit world—paradise. All others go to other parts of the spirit world.[34] Verses 13–14 speak of that part of the spirit world reserved for those who once *knew* the ways of righteousness but ultimately rejected the things of God. It does not refer to those who died in ignorance.

"Outer darkness, or hell, is made up of those who in

mortality spurned the ways of righteousness, those who de-
fied the word of truth, those who chose to walk in their own
paths or in paths of disobedience. Joseph Smith pointed out,
'The great misery of departed spirits in the world of spirits,
where they go after death, is to know that they come short
of the glory that others enjoy and that they might have enjoyed themselves, and they are their own accusers' (*Teachings*,
pp. 310–311; compare p. 358). Thus hell or outer darkness
is both a *place*—a part of the world of spirits where suffering and sorrow and appropriate preparation go on—and a
state—a condition of the mind associated with remorseful
realization."[35]

The "first resurrection" in verse 16 is the same one discussed by Abinadi (see Mosiah 15:21–26).

Alma 40:20

Sometimes a prophet's or an apostle's opinion becomes
scripture. Paul also gave his opinion (1 Corinthians 7:10, 12,
25). See commentary at Alma 7:8.

Alma 40:23

Resurrection is a miraculous blessing to everyone. There
is no fulness of joy possible without a reunion of body and
spirit. Three prophets—Joseph Smith, Joseph F. Smith, and
Joseph Fielding Smith—taught us more about how resurrection works.

The Prophet Joseph Smith taught: "All your losses will be
made up to you in the resurrection, provided you continue
faithful."[36] "As concerning the resurrection, I will merely
say that all men will come from the grave as they lie down,
whether old or young; there will not be 'added unto their
stature one cubit,' neither taken from it; all will be raised
by the power of God, having spirit in their bodies, and not
blood."[37]

President Joseph F. Smith declared: "The body will
come forth as it is laid to rest, for there is no growth nor

development in the grave. As it is laid down, so will it arise."[38] "From the day of the resurrection, the body will develop until it reaches the full measure of the stature of its spirit, whether it be male or female."[39]

President Joseph Fielding Smith elaborated on the meaning of his father's words: "President [Joseph F.] Smith was in full accord with Amulek and Alma. He taught that the body will be restored as stated in Alma 11:42–45 and 40:22–23. While he expresses the thought that the body will come forth as it was laid down, he also expresses the thought that it will take time to adjust the body from the condition of imperfections. This, of course, is reasonable, but at the same time the length of time to make these adjustments will *not* cover any appreciable extent of time.

"President Smith never intended to convey the thought that it would require weeks or months of time in order for the defects to be removed. These changes will come naturally, of course, but *almost instantly.*"[40]

President Joseph Fielding Smith also observed: "*Bodies will come up . . . as they were laid down, but will be restored to their proper, perfect frame immediately. Old people will not look old when they come forth from the grave. Scars will be removed. No one will be bent or wrinkled.* How foolish it would be for a man to come forth in the resurrection who had lost a leg and have to wait for it to grow again. Each body will come forth with its *perfect frame.*"[41]

Elder Dallin H. Oaks explained that all defects and deficiencies will be corrected and resolved in the resurrection: "What a comfort to know that all who have been disadvantaged in life from birth defects, from mortal injuries, from disease, or from the natural deterioration of old age will be resurrected in 'proper and perfect frame.' . . .

"The assurance of resurrection gives us the strength and perspective to endure the mortal challenges faced by each of us and by those we love, such things as the physical, mental, or emotional deficiencies we bring with us at birth or acquire during mortal life. Because of the resurrection, we know that these mortal deficiencies are only temporary!"[42]

One student wrote about a sacred experience that formed part of her "family scripture." She said: "In about 1967 my uncle lost his right arm (at the shoulder) in a farming accident. I have no memory of him with his arm. My earliest memory of him was the first time I saw him after the accident. Years later, one of my aunts died. I was going to school at BYU. My mother flew here for the funeral. We were seated during the funeral with me in front of my mother, who was seated on my uncle's right side. During the meeting I turned to check on my mother. I could not believe what I saw. At first I wondered what was wrong with what I saw. When I figured it out, I turned again to double-check what I was experiencing. I saw my uncle's right arm around my mother, his hand wrapped around her right shoulder. This 'vision' continued through the entire funeral service. When I told my mother about this experience, she replied that if he did have his arm, that is exactly where it would have been. . . . Because of this experience I *know* that the body parts will be restored and that deformities will be fixed. I know that our spirits are in perfect form and that is what our bodies will be perfected to when that transition is made."[43]

Alma 40:26

The wicked figuratively receive the just deserts of their evil deeds: the dregs of a bitter cup. The cup in ancient scripture was sometimes symbolic of experiences of suffering. Elder James E. Talmage wrote: "Our Lord's frequent mention of His foreseen sufferings as the cup of which the Father would have Him drink (Matt. 26:39, 42; Mark 14:36; Luke 22:42; John 18:11; compare Matt. 20:22; Mark 10:38; 1 Cor. 10:21) is in line with Old Testament usage of the term 'cup' as a symbolic expression for a bitter or poisonous potion typifying experiences of suffering. See Ps. 11:6; 75:8; Isa. 51:17, 22; Jer. 25:15, 17; 49:12."[44] Compare also 3 Nephi 11:11.

"Dregs" are sediment, the bits of matter that settle to the bottom of a container of liquid; they are the worthless, least desirable part.

Alma 41

This whole chapter describes the law of restoration or the law of the harvest: We get what we worked for. Restoration is a foundational principle of the Father's plan of happiness. The meaning of the word *restoration* is to bring back again evil for evil and good for good. "For that which ye do send out shall return unto you again." It is most unwise, even dangerous, to assume that God will overlook our disregard of his laws, maybe beat us with a few stripes (2 Nephi 28:8), punish us a bit, and then let us into his glory; we would feel quite out of place there. "Do not suppose . . . that ye shall be restored from sin to happiness. . . . Wickedness never was happiness."

Alma 41:1–6

The justice of God is at the core of the principle of restoration, and the resurrection of the physical body through the atonement of Christ is a powerful example of both restoration and the justice of God. All individuals who have lived on this earth will be resurrected (1 Corinthians 15:22). Nonetheless, a telestial spirit cannot be resurrected with a celestial body. Good is restored to good, and bad to bad. Amulek taught earlier that "that same spirit which doth possess your bodies at the time that ye go out of this life, that same spirit will have power to possess your body in that eternal world" (Alma 34:34). We will be resurrected with the type of body we will possess for eternity, based on the purity and condition of our spirits (1 Corinthians 15:40–42).

Alma 41:7

"They are their own judges"; see commentary at Mosiah 3:25–26; 2 Nephi 9:13–16; 9:46–49.

Alma 41:10–11

Wickedness never was happiness, but righteousness always brings happiness—if not immediately, ultimately. Jesus was a righteous person and, therefore, a happy person—and we want to be like Jesus.

Those who live "without God in the world" are certainly not living "after the manner of happiness" (2 Nephi 5:27) but are walking in darkness—living a life without light. Walking with God, there is happiness and light.

Alma 41:15

The Old Testament "preacher" taught this principle in different language: "Cast thy bread upon the waters: for thou shalt find it after many days" (Ecclesiastes 11:1).

Alma 42:1

Alma's son Corianton needed help understanding some basic doctrine of the kingdom "concerning the justice of God in the punishment of the sinner." He questioned, by way of justification of his sinning: Is it right that God would punish his own children if he loved them?

Alma would certainly have already taught this principle to his son, but he had to teach it again because sin without repentance causes one to lose knowledge.

Alma 42:2

Alma was a loving and patient parent and teacher. "Now behold, my son, I will explain this thing unto thee." To show the justice of God and our own accountability for our actions in mortality, he launched into a full-scale doctrinal exposition—once again—of two of the three pillars of the plan of salvation: the Fall and the Atonement. These teachings are all basic to understanding the purposes of our earth life, and they are the theological rationale behind missionary work, why we go out to try to rescue or save all of our Father's children.

Alma 42:2–6

On "cherubim," a "flaming sword," becoming "as God, knowing good and evil," and our need for this "probationary time," see commentary at Alma 12:21–26, 30 and 12:31–37.

Alma 42:7–31

The purposeful transgression of Adam and Eve helped all of us become as God, learning by our own experience the difference between good and evil. So here we are, in a fallen condition and on probation. We are cut off physically and spiritually from God's presence (though we can enjoy his presence here as we spiritually obey). It was not a good idea to merely rescue us from physical death—"that would destroy the great plan of happiness." We need to experience physical death, too. But in our helpless condition we did need to be reclaimed or redeemed from the spiritual death. God himself would provide the needed redemption. Were it not for that redemption we would have remained in the grasp of justice, cut off from our eternal home, and we would be miserable forever.

Justice is a law of consequences. For every act of obedience there is a blessing; for every violation of divine law a punishment. Mercy is a law of redemption and restoration. Through the Atonement, individuals are redeemed or rescued from the demands of broken laws and restored to the path leading to perfection. Individuals are first declared not guilty and then they begin to be cleansed internally. Every broken law is still paid for: it is not dismissed but paid for by Christ's suffering. Without Christ's redemption, all of humankind would have been "lost forever" (Alma 42:6). Each of us would have become subject to the devil forever (2 Nephi 9:7), which is the same fate the sons of perdition suffer.[45] Thus, all of us would have become like sons of perdition.

Justice cannot be robbed, but it can be appeased. The eternal plan provided for payment of the demands of justice by the Atonement, or sacrifice, of God himself. The Savior redeems us by his suffering in place of our suffering! Laws and punishments are fixed, all infractions must be paid for, but repentance is provided, and mercy claims the penitent.

The Atonement provides resurrection, and therefore *all are brought back into the presence of God* (see commentary and "Two Inseparable Parts of the Plan" at 2 Nephi 2:8–10), thus undoing all the consequences of the Fall: all of humankind being physically and spiritually separated from his presence. Thus—and here is the key to the whole plan—"justice exerciseth all his demands, and also mercy claimeth all which is her own"; in other words, justice and mercy are both satisfied, and "none but the truly penitent are saved." All sin has been paid for, and all suffering has been accomplished—if we will only repent. That is our indispensable part.

Alma 42:27–30

Alma's concluding words to his son contain some of the most beautiful and powerful language in the Book of Mormon. These words reflect an ancient Near Eastern mindset, affirm the fundamental doctrine of agency, and come full circle to the principle of restoration—which centers in the Atonement because only the atonement of Jesus Christ makes restoration possible. "Therefore, O my son, whosoever will come may come and partake of the waters of life freely; and whosoever will not come the same is not compelled to come; but in the last day it shall be restored unto him according to his deeds." "Waters of life" is a significant phrase. In the land from which Lehi's family originated, water *is* life. Jesus Christ is the embodiment of the waters of life. The waters of baptism are the waters of life; the gospel contains the waters of life (John 3:5; 4:10–14; Revelation 21:6; 22:1, 17; 1 Nephi 11:25; Alma 5:34). The Lord offered the same invitation to all individuals in our day that Alma offered to his son: "Yea, if they will come, they may, and partake of the waters of life freely" (D&C 10:66).

THE BOOK OF ALMA

Alma asked his son to not deny the justice of God: "Do not endeavor to excuse yourself in the least point because of your sins, by denying the justice of God." That is merely a doctrinal facade for a covered-up problem with sin. "Let your sins trouble you, with that trouble which shall bring you down unto *repentance*" (emphasis added).

Alma 42:31

Finally, Alma reminded his son of his calling and encouraged him to go forth and declare the word that "the great plan of mercy may have claim upon them." Given the gross sin of which Corianton was guilty—a missionary, a personal representative of the Lord Jesus Christ, who had gone lusting and sinning with a harlot (Alma 39:3–5)—it might be supposed that he was unworthy to continue his mission. Judging from the words of his father, Alma, in this final verse, the mission call was still in effect, the misguided missionary could fully repent out in the mission field, and he had a solemn duty to go out and bring others to understand and live these saving principles that he now understood and had personal experience applying for his own rescue and redemption.

How did Corianton turn out? He repented, preached the word, and would have become the custodian of the sacred records had he not been away on a missionary welfare assignment (Alma 49:30; 63:10).

Alma 43:1

When we are "desirous that salvation should be declared to every creature" and we cannot "bear that any human soul should perish" (Mosiah 28:3), the same will be written of us: we had to go forth and share the gospel. We "could not rest" (Alma 43:1).

Alma 43–62

Account of wars. It sounds like a lot of wars, but there were not as many wars in Book of Mormon lands, during any one time period, as in the last one hundred years of United States history. It is a spiritual account, too. The Book of Mormon was written for us. Not counting the book of Ether, 50 percent of the Book of Mormon is devoted to 12 percent of the time period involved—just before the coming of Christ. The books of Alma, Helaman, and the first part of 3 Nephi are the closest parallel to our time and situation in the last days.

President Ezra Taft Benson defined the purpose of these war chapters: "In the Book of Mormon we find a pattern for preparing for the Second Coming. A major portion of the book centers on the few decades just prior to Christ's coming to America. By careful study of that time period, we can determine why some were destroyed in the terrible judgments that preceded His coming and what brought others to stand at the temple in the land of Bountiful and thrust their hands into the wounds of His hands and feet. *From the Book of Mormon we learn how disciples of Christ live in times of war.*"[46]

The opposing sides had various reasons for the continual warring: the Lamanites' reasons were anger, hatred, and the desire to usurp power (Alma 43:29); the Nephites' reasons were to preserve homes, wives, children, rights, religion, and freedom of worship (Alma 43:30, 45–47; 46:12, 20; 48:10, 13; 53:17; 54:10; 58:12).

THE BOOK OF MORMON ON WAR

1. Is war always evil?

3 Nephi 11:29	Contention is of the devil.
Alma 50:21	Some causes of war: quarrelings, contentions, murderings, idolatry, immorality, and general wickedness.
Alma 62:41	Some effects of war: some become hardened; others, softened or humbled.

Mormon 2:12–15	Sorrowing of the damned, open rebellion.
Moroni 9:18–19	Without order and mercy; brutal, perverse, unfeeling.

2. When does the Lord justify war?

D&C 98:32–38	When the Lord commands, after lifting the standard of peace *several* times.
Alma 48:14–16	In a *defensive war;* as the Lord warns his people when to fight.
Alma 43:45–47	Reasons for going to battle: to defend homes, families, lands, freedoms, God, and religion.
Alma 61:11–14	To resist evil, such as rebellions and dissensions.

President David O. McKay: "War is incompatible with Christ's teachings. The gospel of Jesus Christ is the gospel of peace. War is its antithesis, and produces hate. It is vain to attempt to reconcile war with true Christianity. . . .

"Notwithstanding all this, I still say that there are conditions when entrance into war is justifiable, and when a Christian nation may, without violation of principles, take up arms against an opposing force.

"Such a condition, however, is not a real or fancied insult given by one nation to another. When this occurs proper reparation may be made by mutual understanding, apology, or by arbitration.

"Neither is there justifiable cause found in a desire or even a need for territorial expansion. The taking of territory implies the subjugation of the weak by the strong—the application of the jungle law.

"Nor is war justified in an attempt to enforce a new order of government, or even to impel others to a particular form of worship, however better the government or eternally true the principles of the enforced religion may be.

"There are, however, two conditions which may justify a truly Christian man to enter—mind you, I say *enter, not begin*— a war: (1) An attempt to dominate and to deprive another of his free agency, and, (2) Loyalty to his country. Possibly there is a third, viz., Defense of a weak nation that is being unjustly crushed by a strong, ruthless one. . . .

"So fundamental in man's eternal progress is his inherent right to choose, that the Lord would defend it even at the price of war. Without freedom of thought, freedom of choice, freedom of action within lawful bounds, man cannot progress. The Lord recognized this. . . . Throughout the ages advanced souls have yearned for a society in which liberty and justice prevail. Men have sought for it, fought for it, have died for it. Ancient freemen prized it, slaves longed for it, the Magna Charta demanded it, the Constitution of the United Stated declared it.

"'This love of liberty which God has planted in us,' said Abraham Lincoln, 'constitutes the bulwark of our liberty and independence. It is not our frowning battlements, our bristling seacoasts, our army, and our navy. Our defense is in the spirit which prizes liberty as the heritage of all men, in all lands, everywhere. Destroy this spirit, and we have planted the seeds of despotism at our very doors.'

"A second obligation that impels us to become participants in this world war is loyalty to government. . . .

"As a Church:

"'We believe that all men are justified in defending themselves, their friends, and property, and the government from the unlawful assaults and encroachments of all persons in times of exigency, where immediate appeal cannot be made to laws, and relief afforded. (D. & C. 134:11.)'

"Even though we sense the hellish origin of war, even though we feel confident that war will never end war, yet under existing conditions we find ourselves as a body committed to combat this evil thing. With other loyal citizens we serve our country as bearers of arms, rather than to stand aloof to enjoy a freedom for which others have fought and died.

"One purpose of emphasizing this theme is to give encouragement to young men now engaged in armed conflict and to reassure them that they are fighting for an eternal principle fundamental to the peace and progress of mankind."[47]

3. If war is inevitable, should a nation strike first?

3 Nephi 3:20–21	No.
Mormon 3:9–16	Offensive war signaled the beginning of the end for the Nephites.
Alma 43:53–54	Stop fighting when the enemy is overwhelmed.

4. What about disarmament or preparation for war?

Alma 24 and 27	Anti-Nephi-Lehis experimented with disarmament because they were addicted to bloodlust; otherwise disarmament is self-annihilation.
2 Nephi 5:14	Nephi armed his people.
Jarom 1:8–9	Nephites armed themselves.
Alma 43:19–20	Superior preparations of the Nephites.
Alma 48:7–10	*Spiritual* preparation as well as military.

5. What is the duty of civilians in time of war?

Alma 60 and 61 (note especially 60:11, 15–17; 61:14)	Moroni-Pahoran correspondence.
Alma 53:10–22	The people of Ammon supported the war effort.
Doctrine and Covenants 134:5	People must sustain their governments; sedition and rebellion should be punished.

6. Will the righteous be protected in time of war?

1 Nephi 22:16	The righteous need not fear; with some exceptions (see below), the Lord will not allow the wicked to destroy them.
Alma 56:55–56	2,000 young warriors of Helaman protected and preserved.
Alma 46:18	Followers of Christ are destroyed when they bring it on themselves.
Alma 14:8–11	Why the righteous are allowed to be slain.
Alma 60:12–13 (also 40:12)	For a testimony and judgment against the wicked. They go to find rest and the fulness of God's glory (D&C 84:24).

7. What should one's attitude be toward the enemy? Can a man retain the Spirit of the Lord on the battlefield?

Alma 44:1–2	"We do not desire to be men of blood" (that is why Ammon's converts buried their weapons).
Alma 48:23	They did not delight in the shedding of blood.
Alma 48:11–16	Moroni's reliance on the Lord and noble attitudes during wartime.
Jarom 1:7	Leaders were mighty men in the faith of the Lord.
3 Nephi 3:19	It is good to have spiritual men as leaders.

8. What is a nation's best defense? What is the formula for success in fighting a war?

2 Nephi 4:34	Do not trust in the arm of flesh.
1 Nephi 13:15–19; Jarom 1:7–9; Alma 44:3–4; 3 Nephi 4:8–10	What happens when people are righteous and fight with the strength and power of God.

Alma 43:23–24	Seek guidance from the Lord through his prophets.
3 Nephi 3:19	Leaders have the spirit of revelation and prophecy.
Alma 48:14–16	The Lord will reveal what should be done.

Elder John A. Widtsoe: "Preparedness is today on every tongue. There is danger ahead, and defenses must be set up. Preparedness is not a new word to Latter-day Saints. For one hundred and ten years our voice has been one of warning to prepare against the commotion and calamities of the last days. We have taught and continue to teach that full preparedness and complete defense against the devastation by evil is the acceptance of the Gospel of Jesus Christ. When every knee shall bow and every tongue confess that Jesus is the Christ we may look for the peace of Eden, but not before.

"Our land is setting up defenses of powder and steel. That is well enough. But there are intangible defenses more powerful which direct the use of material defenses. These must be fostered, if our preparedness shall be adequate."[48]

President Ezra Taft Benson: "The gospel is the only answer to the problems of the world. . . . We may cry peace. We may hold peace conferences. And I have nothing but commendation for those who work for peace. But it is my conviction that peace must come from within. . . . It can come only by following the teachings and the example of the Prince of Peace."[49]

President Gordon B. Hinckley: "Those of us who are American citizens stand solidly with the president of our nation. The terrible forces of evil must be confronted and held accountable for their actions. . . .

" . . . as a Church, we must get on our knees and invoke the powers of the Almighty in behalf of those who will carry the burdens of this campaign [the war in Iraq]. . . .

"Now, brothers and sisters, we must do our duty, whatever that duty might be. Peace may be denied for a season. Some of our liberties may be curtailed. We may be inconvenienced. We may even be called on to suffer in one way or another. But God our Eternal Father will watch over this nation and all of the civilized world who look to Him. He has declared, 'Blessed is the nation whose God is the Lord' (Ps. 33:12). . . . Let us pray for the forces of good. Let us reach out to help men and women of goodwill, whatever their religious persuasion and wherever they live. Let us stand firm against evil, both at home and abroad."[50]

President Gordon B. Hinckley: "In a democracy we can renounce war and proclaim peace. There is opportunity for dissent. Many have been speaking out and doing so emphatically. That is their privilege. That is their right, so long as they do so legally. However, we all must also be mindful of another overriding responsibility, which I may add, governs my personal feelings and dictates my personal loyalties in the present situation.

"When war raged between the Nephites and the Lamanites, the record states that 'the Nephites were inspired by a better cause, for they were not fighting for . . . power but they were fighting for their homes and their liberties, their wives and their children, and their all, yea, for their rites of worship and their church.

"'And they were doing that which they felt was the duty which they owed to their God' (Alma 43:45–46). The Lord counseled them, 'Defend your families even unto bloodshed' (Alma 43:47).

"I believe that God will not hold men and women in uniform responsible as agents of their government in carrying forward that which they are legally obligated to do. It may even be that He will hold us responsible if we try to impede or hedge up the way of those who are involved in a contest with forces of evil and repression."[51]

Perhaps we may struggle to understand why nearly a fourth of the Book of Mormon is about war, why Mormon would include so much about warfare—what he wanted us to learn from it. We believe Nephi when he said we should liken the scriptures unto us. But maybe we have come away unsatisfied. We may well ask if there is not some motif in these chapters much deeper than the surface reporting of specific battles. What is the underlying meaning of these chapters? What is the deep message?

We believe that Captain Moroni and the later editor, General Mormon, wanted to emphasize the military preparations, the armaments and fortifications, but *first* they usually mentioned the spiritual preparations, "preparing the minds of the people to be faithful unto the Lord their God" (Alma 48:7).

There was a war fought in heaven to preserve our right to freedom. Lucifer was cast down because he sought to destroy the agency of man; then should it surprise us to find there are many on earth now who want to do the same? The battlefield has changed, but the battle is the same.

President Boyd K. Packer said: "In the Church we are not neutral. We are one-sided. There is a war going on, and we are engaged in it. It is the war between good and evil, and we are belligerents defending the good. We are therefore obliged to give preference to and protect all that is represented in the gospel of Jesus Christ, and we have made covenants to do it."[52]

President Henry B. Eyring declared: "This is not a time of peace. . . . Since the creation of Adam and Eve, the conflict has continued. We have seen it intensify. And the scriptures suggest that the war will become more violent and the spiritual casualties on the Lord's side will mount."[53]

So the war rages on in our lives. We sometimes have little skirmishes and sometimes major battles, but we should keep our eye on our glorious objective: to bring the message of salvation to all of God's children.

In times of war, however, we can get sidetracked. We lose perspective. President Spencer W. Kimball said:

"We are a warlike people, easily distracted from our assignment of preparing for the coming of the Lord. When enemies rise up, we commit vast resources to the fabrication of gods of stone and steel—ships, planes, missiles, fortifications—and depend on them for protection and deliverance. When threatened, we become antienemy instead of pro–kingdom of God; we train a man in the art of war and call him a patriot, thus, in the manner of Satan's counterfeit of true patriotism, perverting the Savior's teaching:

"'Love your enemies, bless them that curse you, do good to them that hate you, and pray for them which despitefully use you, and persecute you;

"'That ye may be the children of your Father which is in heaven.' (Matt. 5:44–45.)

"We forget that if we are righteous the Lord will either not suffer our enemies to come upon us—and this is the special promise to the inhabitants of the land of the Americas (see 2 Ne. 1:7)—or he will fight our battles for us."[54]

LATTER-DAY SAINT HYMNS ON WAR

Our hymns teach us proper focus in our mortal warfare:

Let Us All Press On

Let us all press on in the work of the Lord,
That when life is o'er we may gain a reward;
In the fight for right let us wield a sword,
The mighty sword of truth.

We will not retreat, though our numbers may be few
When compared with the opposite host in view;
But an unseen pow'r will aid me and you
In the glorious cause of truth.[55]

Onward, Christian Soldiers

Onward, Christian soldiers!
Marching as to war. . . .

Like a mighty army
Moves the Church of God. . . .[56]

We Are All Enlisted

We are all enlisted till the conflict is o'er; happy are we!

Happy are we! Soldiers in the army, there's a bright
   crown in store;
We shall win and wear it by and by.
Haste to the battle, quick to the field;
Truth is our helmet, buckler, and shield.
Stand by our colors; proudly they wave!
We're joyfully, joyfully marching to our home.

Hark! the sound of battle sounding loudly and clear;
   come join the ranks!
Come join the ranks! We are waiting now for soldiers;
   who'll volunteer?
Rally round the standard of the cross.
Hark! 'tis our Captain calls you today;
Lose not a moment, make no delay!
Fight for our Savior; come, come away!

Fighting for a kingdom, and the world is our foe; . . .
Glad to join the army, we will sing as we go;
We shall gain the vict'ry by and by.
Dangers may gather—why should we fear?
Jesus, our Leader, ever is near.
He will protect us, comfort, and cheer.[57]

Behold! A Royal Army

Behold! A royal army,
With banner, sword, and shield,
Is marching forth to conquer
On life's great battlefield.
Its ranks are filled with soldiers,
United, bold, and strong,
Who follow their Commander
And sing their joyful song:

Chorus:
Victory, victory,
Thru him that redeemed us!
Victory, victory,

Thru Jesus Christ, our Lord!
Victory, victory, victory,
Thru Jesus Christ, our Lord!

And now the foe advancing,
That valiant host assails,
And yet they never falter;
Their courage never fails.
Their leader calls, "Be faithful!"
They pass the word along;
They see his signal flashing
And shout their joyful song: [Chorus]

Oh, when the war is ended,
When strife and conflicts cease,
When all are safely gathered
Within the vale of peace,
Before the King eternal,
That vast and mighty throng
Shall praise his name forever.
And this shall be their song: [Chorus][58]

Hope of Israel

Hope of Israel, Zion's army,
Children of the promised day,
See, the Chieftain signals onward,
And the battle's in array!

See the foe in countless numbers,
Marshaled in the ranks of sin.
Hope of Israel, on to battle;
Now the vict'ry we must win!

Strike for Zion, down with error;
Flash the sword above the foe!
Ev'ry stroke disarms a foe-man;
Ev'ry step we conq'ring go.

Soon the battle will be over;
Ev'ry foe of truth be down.

Onward, onward, youth of Zion;
Thy reward the victor's crown.

Hope of Israel, rise in might
With the sword of truth and right;
Sound the war-cry, "Watch and pray!"
Vanquish ev'ry foe today.[59]

We sing about war, battles, conflicts, soldiers, armies, the foe, the battlefield, banners, swords, helmets, bucklers, shields, signals, war cries, and victory—and we put it all in an eternal context. The battle we are fighting is much wider and much more important than a Vietnam war or a Persian Gulf war, a war in Iraq, or Afghanistan, or any other place of our world in these last days.

It is a battle not to save physical bodies, for all physical bodies will eventually be resurrected to a perfect condition, but to save the souls of humankind. With all our emotions telling us to support this or that military thrust or tactic, we should remember that our ultimate goal is to get the gospel into all countries and to help save, as much as possible, the souls of all of Heavenly Father's children.

Alma 43:3

Alma 43:3 through Alma 49:29 covers two Nephite wars, thus indicating the intense interest of Mormon (the compiler and abridger of the records until about A.D. 385) in the subject of warfare. Why? Because his own period was one of war; he was a military man and a prophet like Captain Moroni; and Alma prophesied of Mormon's own day, as had Nephi (Alma 45:10–14; 1 Nephi 12:19). The Book of Mormon was written for our day, and we must learn how to live righteously and optimistically even in times of war.

President Dieter F. Uchtdorf declared: "I have seen enough ups and downs throughout my life to know that winter will surely give way to the warmth and hope of a new spring. I am optimistic about the future."[60]

Alma 43:4

The Lamanites began to grow in numbers and strength, intimating that only righteousness and the power of God could account for any kind of victory by the Nephites over the Lamanites.

Alma 43:9–11

The Nephites were motivated by more noble causes than the Lamanites. Verse 9 anticipates Moroni's title of liberty (see Alma 46:12–13).

Alma 43:16–54

Moroni's leadership qualities as a commander began to shine forth. He prepared his people for conflict in meaningful ways using technological innovations. He used two kinds of advanced intelligence: he asked Alma to inquire of the Lord, and he sent out spies—he was a superb strategist. He inspired his people when their courage waned. He was merciful, and he was a spiritual giant, which translated into supernatural help for his people.

Thus, the advantages of the Nephites may be summarized as follows: superior technology—better clothing and armor (vv. 19, 20, 37); better intelligence (vv. 23, 30); better strategy (vv. 30, 35); inspiration by a better cause (vv. 45–47); better leadership (v. 48); and better connections with heaven (v. 50).

Alma 44:2–5

During times of war or peace, the most important thing for us to do is remain faithful to God. As long as we do that, our future is secure. Nephites were fighting a religious war, for religious reasons. God will support and preserve those who are faithful to him. If we fail in war, it is because we fall into transgression and deny our faith.

Alma 44:15

Mercy in the conduct of war has a healing effect on those who must fight it, lessens the brutality of conflict, and brings the blessings of the Lord (compare 43:54). As the Lord said, "For intelligence cleaveth unto intelligence; wisdom receiveth wisdom; truth embraceth truth; virtue loveth virtue; light cleaveth unto light; *mercy hath compassion on mercy and claimeth her own*" (D&C 88:40; emphasis added). Those who are merciful may lay hold on the power of the Merciful One to make things right and whole.

Alma 45:1

Do we sometimes fast solely to give thanks, or are we always asking for something? Note what the Lord has said in our dispensation: "And in nothing doth man offend God, or against none is his wrath kindled, save those who *confess not his hand in all things,* and obey not his commandments" (D&C 59:21; emphasis added).

Alma 45:2–9, 15

Here, between Alma and Helaman, is a good scriptural example of a father's interview. Notice the pattern: inquire, instruct, and bless. Children need to know and feel that they are loved, wanted, and appreciated. They need to be assured of that frequently.

Alma 45:18–19

For unstated reasons, Alma departed out of the land and apparently was "taken up" or translated, as were Enoch (Genesis 5:24; Hebrews 11:5; D&C 107:49), Melchizedek (JST, Genesis 14:32–34, in Bible appendix), Moses (Deuteronomy 34:5–6), and Elijah (2 Kings 2:11; D&C 110:13) before him, and Nephi (3 Nephi 1:2–3), John (John 21:22; D&C 7:3), and three Nephite apostles (3 Nephi 28:6–8) after him.

The Prophet Joseph Smith said: "Translated bodies

cannot enter into rest until they have undergone a change equivalent to death. Translated bodies are designed for future missions."[61] Thus, the purpose of translated beings is to bless future generations of our Heavenly Father's children. Alma must have fulfilled such a role.

Alma 46:1–11

Here (and in Alma 47:4–19) we are told of a traitor to the Nephites and his opposition to the things of righteousness. Amalickiah was "a Nephite by birth" (Alma 49:25), dissented from the Church of God, and eventually became king of the Lamanites (Alma 47:19). His lust for power motivated him to use his talents to bring about evil and misery. He was cunning and believed in flattery. Flattery appeals to vanity. It is cynical and a tool used to manipulate people for selfish purposes. It advances ulterior motives and is adversarial. It is different from a sincere praise or compliment, which validates the honest work of others. See the effects of flattery in Alma 50:35.

Alma 46:8

President Spencer W. Kimball used to say that the most important word in the English language may be *remember* (see commentary at Helaman 5:5–12). The Book of Mormon constantly iterates and reiterates: "Oh, remember, remember . . ." The Baal Shem Tov, leader of Hassidic Jewry in Eastern Europe over two and a half centuries ago, made a famous remark that for many years was emblazoned in giant letters at the exit of the Yad Vashem Holocaust Memorial in Jerusalem: "Forgetfulness leads to exile, but remembrance is the secret of redemption."

Alma 46:9

How great the wickedness one evil man can cause! Twentieth-century examples include Joseph Stalin, 1930s–1940s; Adolf Hitler, 1940s; Mao Zedong, 1950s–1970s; and Saddam Hussein, 1980s–1990s.

Alma 46:11–17

Moroni, righteously indignant, prayed mightily and poured out his soul to God. His display of patriotism and the message of his title of liberty have modern parallel in the words of Francis Scott Key:

Oh, thus be it ever, when free men shall stand
Between their loved homes and the war's desolation!
Blest with vict'ry and peace, may the heav'n-rescued
*   land*
Praise the Pow'r that hath made and preserved us a
*   nation!*
Then conquer we must, when our cause it is just,
And this be our motto: 'In God is our trust!'
And the star-spangled banner [as Moroni's title of lib-
*   erty] in triumph shall wave*
O'er the land of the free and the home of the brave!"[62]

"Moroni prayed that the cause of the Christians, and the freedom of the land might be favored." He labeled the land—north and south—"a chosen land, and the land of liberty."

The first recorded use of the term *Christian* in the Old World occurred in the postresurrection period of the apostolic Church in Antioch (Acts 11:26), but the term was used in the New World a century earlier—and we might add that the first Christians, or believers in the Christ who should come, were actually our first parents, Adam and Eve.

Alma 46:13, 21–24

These verses attest to the use of garments, or even fragments of garments, as symbols of covenant-making or witnessing and affirming certain actions. Treading upon one's garments is an ancient ritual practice attested in early Christian Coptic texts where individuals became members of the early church by trampling their clothes as a token of trampling old sins or the old life. It is traced back to the Jewish interpretation of Genesis 3:21.[63]

Verse 24 attests that a remnant of Joseph's coat was preserved beyond his being sold into slavery into Egypt. Jacob prophesied regarding the seed of Joseph by using his son's coat as an object lesson. We have only a remnant of this prophecy preserved in our current Old Testament (Genesis 44:28). Joseph's coat or garment was an emblem of his primacy in the priesthood, and evidently it had special markings on it.

Alma 46:31

This verse reminds all freedom-loving nations in our modern day that sometimes we have to maintain armaments to keep the peace. It is ironic but true; righteous nations have to *fight* for *peace*. The Mormon Miracle Pageant presented annually for decades on Temple Hill in Manti, Utah, includes this memorable idea: "Through all the years of peace Moroni never disarmed. *You cannot compromise with evil; if you do, evil always wins.*"

Alma 46:35

In times of war those who refused to submit to the cause of freedom, who willfully and knowingly continued to seek to subvert the cause of freedom and agency, or who remained defiantly rebellious were justifiably put to death. One is reminded of General George Washington executing subverters and traitors to the American cause during the Revolutionary War, even though they were members of the Continental Army.

Alma 46:40

An interesting medicinal note for the naturalists (and everyone else) among us: God prepared excellent-quality plants and roots to remove the cause of diseases. Also of interest to Book of Mormon geographers is this revealing comment regarding the climate of the Book of Mormon lands, which caused seasonal fevers.

Alma 47:1–35

We are given an account of Amalickiah's murderous treachery to claim the throne of the Lamanites. He is further described here as "a very subtle man to do evil." Through his cunning servants and his own great fraud he obtained the kingdom.

Alma 47:36

Dissenters are apostates, those who break away or desert the cause of truth—the "spiritually challenged" of the Church. Once they come to know the inner workings of the kingdom and then intentionally rebel, they do become more hardened and impenitent and entirely forget the Lord their God. Elder Neal A. Maxwell described them:

"There are the dissenters who leave the Church, either formally or informally, but who cannot leave it alone. Usually anxious to please worldly galleries, they are critical or at least condescending towards the Brethren. They not only seek to steady the ark but also on occasion give it a hard shove! Often having been taught the same true doctrines as the faithful, they have nevertheless moved in the direction of dissent. . . . They have minds hardened by pride."[64]

Alma 48

Moroni didn't just prepare his people with armaments, he prepared their minds to be faithful to God. "The Nephites' most dangerous enemy was not outside the city walls but inside the people's hearts. . . . Nephite pride was more dangerous than Lamanite aggression."[65]

Still, Moroni strengthened their defensive fortifications.

President Gordon B. Hinckley declared: "We are people of peace. We are followers of the Christ who was and is the Prince of Peace. But there are times when we must stand up

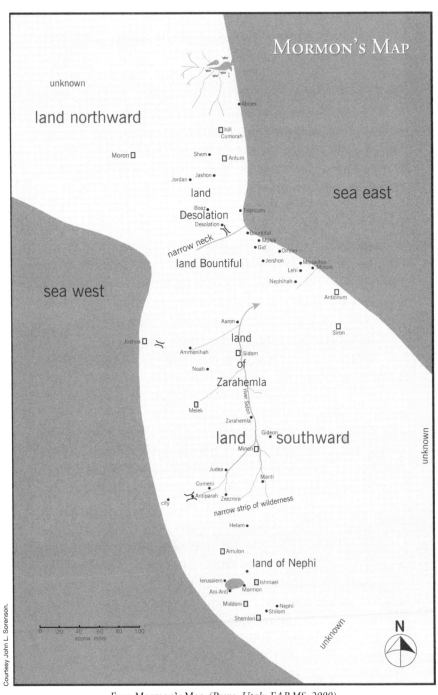

From Mormon's Map *(Provo, Utah: FARMS, 2000).*

for right and decency, for freedom and civilization, just as Moroni rallied his people in his day to the defense of their wives, their children, and the cause of liberty (see Alma 48:10)."[66]

Nephites were taught to defend themselves even if it meant some died because a defensive war was justifiable. They were also never to give offense; if they lived righteously, God would be their chief strategist and would prosper them.

An impressive group of leaders arose during this preparatory period before the coming of the Savior. The mighty men of God preparing the way were Ammon and the other sons of Mosiah, Alma and his sons, Helaman and his brethren, and Moroni. Of all these great leaders, the superlative exclamation was recorded that if all men were like Moroni, "the very powers of hell would have been shaken forever" and the evil one would be powerless to influence the children of men.

Alma 48:16–17

The towering greatness of Moroni is described. His attributes and spiritual power are those that will bind Satan during the Millennium (compare verse 17 here with 1 Nephi 22:26). In speaking to the missionaries at the Missionary Training Center in Provo, Utah, Elder Charles Didier of the Seventy said that if we were all like Moroni, truly baptized by the Holy Ghost, we wouldn't need all the rules to dictate behavior.[67]

Alma 49

The complete portrait of Amalickiah and his stark contrast to Moroni is fleshed out. He was a bloodthirsty man, who murdered to get gain, exhibiting the Mahanic principle or cornerstone of Satan's kingdom (Moses 5:31). In addition, in verse 30 Corianton's rehabilitation is noted.

Alma 50

Moroni's righteous leadership strengthened the Nephites, who built new cities, prospered exceedingly, and were blessed by the Lord. However, the specter of civil war was then raised at a time when they could have had security and peace.

What causes wars? "It has been their quarrelings and their contentions, yea, their murderings, and their plunderings, their idolatry, their whoredoms, and their abominations, which were among themselves, which brought upon them their wars and their destructions." In times of war, focus on keeping the commandments. Is it possible to be happy during times of war? "Behold there never was a happier time among the people of Nephi, since the days of Nephi, than in the days of Moroni."

Peace was finally restored to the people of Nephi, and Pahoran ascended to the offices of chief judge and governor over the people. What would happen in our modern world if our leaders took office with "an oath and sacred ordinance" to judge righteously, keep the peace and freedom of the people sacrosanct, grant to all people their sacred privileges to worship, maintain the cause of God all their days, and bring the wicked to justice?

Alma 51

The epic struggle between the kingmen and freemen is recounted. This contention came at a particularly critical time because Amalickiah of the Lamanites began to stir up old antagonisms and hatred against the Nephites. Eventually and ironically Amalickiah was murdered, as had been his predecessor. Thus, we see that those who live by the sword die by the sword (Matthew 26:52).

Alma 51:15–17

Moroni demanded fellow-citizens' loyalty in fighting to defend their country or be executed. Dissenters were considered traitors. Rebels or insurrectionists who would not fight in defense of their country, or who promoted civil disobedience, were speedily executed (62:9–10). However, this reality of war must be measured against Moroni's reluctance to take up the sword in the first place and his willingness to lay it down quickly when opportunity presented itself (52:37).

Alma 52

Another war and another victory over the Lamanites is described. Truly, Moroni did not delight in bloodshed. He slew only those who would not lay down their weapons and make peace (compare vv. 25, 32 with Alma 48:16 and 55:19). Again we are reminded that war is contrary to the gospel of the Prince of Peace (see "The Book of Mormon on War" in commentary at Alma 43–62).

Alma 53

Chapters 53 through 57 are a testimony to the power and influence on young people of righteous family life. The two thousand stripling warriors (*stripling* means "young") had decided to fight for liberty for the sake of their families inasmuch as their fathers had made a covenant not to take up arms. Thus, the sons covenanted to fight in order to protect the covenant of their fathers not to fight, which had God's approval (56:6–8). Helaman was their commander and later explained the source of their courage, strength, and commitment:

"Now they never had fought, yet they did not fear death; and they did think more upon the liberty of their fathers than they did upon their lives; yea, they had been taught by their mothers, that if they did not doubt, God would deliver them.

"And they rehearsed unto me the words of their mothers, saying: We do not doubt our mothers knew it" (56:47–48).

Thus we see that there is hardly a force for good in society comparable to a righteous home. It is the foundation of a strong, courageous, moral, just, and *free* society.

Alma 54

This chapter offers an account of the negotiations and counter-negotiations that always seem to accompany attempts to resolve conflicts among antagonists.

Alma 54:13

Moroni determined to preserve his people's freedom in their current lands and also to retake their ancestral homeland.

Alma 54:20

Eternal war is Satan's objective, not the Lord's. The Lord is the Prince of Peace! It is sad to realize that these kinds of sentiments are very real and exist in the world today. On 1 February 1991, during the first Gulf War, Brother Ogden wrote in his journal: "How the Israelis are hated. Iran, who has insisted on its neutrality in this Gulf War but who has received over 100 Iraqi jet aircraft that have sought refuge there, today announced that it would fight alongside Iraq if Israel joined the war. It is incredible to hear that after nine years of bitter war between Iran and Iraq, with over one million dead, that Iran would stand united with Iraq if Israelis were to join the war. Maybe that is an example of what the Book of Mormon describes as eternal hatred between Lamanites and Nephites."

Alma 56

In a letter written by Helaman to Moroni, the former recounted battles begun four years previously. Truly, Helaman loved Moroni. He described his love for the stripling warriors and why their sacrifice was so important. They fought to protect the covenant their fathers made with God not to fight. According to the law of Moses the minimum age for Israelite soldiers was twenty years old (Numbers 1:3). We do not know exactly how old the stripling warriors were, but clearly their youth continued to impress the prophets.

Alma 56:11

This is a valuable and comforting commentary on those righteous ones who die in combat: "They have died in the cause of their country and of their God, yea, and they are happy." Indeed, the righteous are not lost to us just because they are slain in war. They receive the Lord's reward—his "rest," which is the fulness of his glory, according to Doctrine and Covenants 84:24 (also Alma 60:13).

Alma 56:27, 47–48

The young men of Ammon received care packages from home—"many provisions from the fathers"—just as many missionaries and servicemen and -women do today. They also received spiritual support from the teachings of their parents. They had no fear of death, they valued the liberty of their people more highly than their own lives, and they had learned, especially from their mothers, to get rid of doubt and have faith and trust in their God. The fervent testimony of their mothers had burned deeply into their own hearts: "We do not doubt our mothers knew it."

Alma 57

Helaman continued his account of battles involving the stripling warriors. Verses 27 and 21 present an important theme for today's stripling warriors, the missionaries: "They are young, and their minds are firm." "They [do] obey and observe to perform every word of command with exactness." And Alma 58:40 adds, "They are strict to remember the Lord their God from day to day." That is the instruction or the command taught in all missionary training centers and by all mission presidents: exact obedience, or strict obedience, is the only way to lasting success in the work of God.

One missionary wrote to her father:

"There's a missionary rumor floating around that I hate. It's *so* false. Everyone says, 'Don't try to keep all the rules in

THE BOOK OF MORMON

the mission; you'll just be unhappy and stressed and won't accomplish anything.' That has to be the biggest misconception. . . . I've discovered I'm *only* happy when I'm trying to obey all the rules I know! God gives you [laws] to follow on one level, and then when you're obedient to those things, He moves you up to the next level. So if I'm obviously not complying with a rule that I know about, why should he give me higher rules and more important things to follow? . . . Our district leader is really good at following all the rules and getting baptisms and strictly following what he knows. Like it says in Alma 57:21: 'they did obey and observe to perform every word of command with exactness . . . according to their faith.'"

Exact obedience and quiet dignity are the Lord's standards. These verses teach an additional lesson in personal honesty: *almost* is a terrible word—"almost honest," "almost clean," "almost obedient," and so on. Our generous and merciful God will certainly bless our sincere efforts, kindly acknowledging and rewarding us as we struggle to overcome our weaknesses, but as he says, if we want any blessing from him, we must obey the law upon which that blessing is predicated (D&C 130:20–21; see also D&C 46:9).

Alma 57:25

The two thousand stripling warriors exhibited the mark of true greatness. They kept going when circumstances became extremely difficult, even when they were wounded, even when a great toll had been exacted—physically, emotionally, and spiritually. No wonder Helaman loved them.

Alma 58–61

There were problems with the government sending adequate numbers of soldiers, equipment, and supplies. Military leaders were angry with government leaders for neglecting the needs on the war front. Moroni wrote a strongly worded epistle of condemnation to a seemingly indifferent government. He wondered if government leaders were traitors to their country (60:18) and accused them of being sinners against God (60:28, 33). Moroni threatened heads of government with death if they did not immediately do something to assist the war effort (60:30).

His letter, as it turned out, was unjustified but understandable. It is the old misunderstanding between the "office" and the "field," resentment against the easy-living VIPs in the capital. Internal divisiveness, dissension, and insurrection in the capital had caused the devastating neglect. Those defending the cause of freedom, true patriots, were willing to "resist wickedness even unto bloodshed" (61:10) to fight against traitors.

Alma 60:23

"God has said that the inward vessel shall be cleansed first, and then shall the outer vessel be cleansed also." There seems to be a fixed order for retributions to be meted out. "And upon my house shall it begin, . . . saith the Lord; first among those . . . who have professed to know my name and have not known me" (D&C 112:25–26).

Alma 61

Book of Mormon–period insurrection, rebellion, and intrigue have their Old Testament counterparts in the conspiracies of Abimelech at Shechem (Judges 9:1–6), Absalom at Hebron (2 Samuel 15:10–17), and Adonijah at Jerusalem (1 Kings 1:5–30).

Alma 61:11–14

When does God approve of war? Whatever evil cannot be resisted with words (negotiations) must be resisted with weapons, in order to maintain freedom, religious privileges, and the cause of our Redeemer and God—that kind of war is justifiable. See further at "The Book of Mormon on War," question 2, at Alma 43–62.

Alma 62:9

Those who refused to take up arms to defend their country and their liberty were considered guilty of treason. Those who fought against or even taught against the cause of freedom were put to death as traitors.

Alma 62:41

A protracted war can cause cynicism or build faith. Boiling water hardens eggs but softens carrots; so a long, drawn-out war causes some to be hardened, while others are softened in their afflictions. Each of us must decide how anything outside us will affect us, negatively or positively.

Alma 63:1–7

Three righteous record keepers had continued to inscribe the history of the Nephites: Alma, Helaman, and now Shiblon. Shiblon noted that 5,400 families migrated northward out of the land of Zarahemla, and later many more followed.

Alma 63:5

Hagoth, the shipbuilder, was an exceedingly "curious" man. We might think that means he was inquisitive or strange or adventurous, but *curious* or *curiousness* in Joseph Smith's day when the Book of Mormon was translated into English meant "made with care," "wrought with care and art," "elegant," "exactness of workmanship,"[68] so Hagoth himself, and the ships he built, were apparently careful, elegant, exact, and precise. Compare "curious workmen" mentioned in Helaman 6:11 and the "ball of curious workmanship" mentioned in 1 Nephi 16:10.

THE BOOK OF HELAMAN

The Book of Helaman is an example of annalistic, or annual, writing: almost every year is mentioned. Mormon, the prophet-historian, was very selective, though; only the best lessons are noted ("and thus we see that . . ."). This half-century record, just before the Savior's coming into the world, is full of political intrigue and social destruction by highly professional, organized, and sophisticated "secret combinations." The motives and objectives of the Gadianton robbers, and other such secret societies, were power, wealth, and popularity—the glory of men (Helaman 2:8; 7:21). The methods they used were murder, political assassination, robbery, extortion, and so forth. It is revealing to note how often "contentions" and "dissensions" are mentioned (see, for example, Helaman 1:2; 3:1–3, 17). Notice also that pride and riches are often at the top of the list of spiritual and social ills (for example, in Helaman 4:12). The secret societies used covenants, oaths, signs, and tokens (all perversions of true principles and sacred precepts).

As in that day, so in ours: secret combinations are best fought with our open combinations—the righteousness of the Saints, especially the missionary force. In the face of increasing societal maladies, the Church of God flourished, and tens of thousands of people came to a knowledge of their Redeemer (Helaman 3:26). Despite the cunning, snares, and wiles of the devil ("wiles" are tricks or lures), many were able to fast and pray, humble themselves, show faith, and become purified or sanctified by yielding their hearts unto God and becoming children of Christ (Helaman 3:29–30, 35).

Helaman 1

When men of consuming pride and self importance, such as Paanchi and his supporters, refuse to follow the voice of the people in an established democracy, contention, then murder, then the rise of secret combinations occur.

Helaman 2

Upon the foundation laid by Kishkumen, a new secret combination, the Gadianton band, emerged. Note that Satan, who was behind the perpetuation of these secret combinations and conspiracies (Helaman 6:24–30; 3 Nephi 6:28), inspires leaders who use the same tactics over and over again: expertise in many words, secret murder, robbery, and flattery. These are virtually the same challenges Moroni faced with Amalickiah (Alma 46:5; Helaman 1:7). The secret combination of Gadianton would prove the downfall of the Nephite nation. It is hard to overstate the importance of this comment for our day and time.

President Ezra Taft Benson sounded the warning voice to us: "From the Book of Mormon we see the evils of secret combinations portrayed in graphic and chilling reality. . . .

"Secret combinations flourished because, as Helaman tells us, the Gadianton robbers 'had seduced the more part of the righteous until they had come down to believe in their works and partake of their spoils.' (Helaman 6:38.)" In the Book of Mormon, however, we find "the power to avoid deception."[1]

Helaman 2:8–9

Perhaps invoking a bit of a rhetorical flourish, Mormon wrote that when Helaman's servant came to know "all the heart of Kishkumen," the servant stabbed Kishkumen "even to the heart."

The heart made a big difference to him as it does for all of us. The importance of the disposition and orientation of a person's heart in ancient Near Eastern cultures is monumental. For instance, the final judgment scene in ancient Egyptian religious imagery (remember the Book of Mormon's strong connection to Egypt) is the "weighing of the heart" ceremony—where an individual's heart is weighed against the feather of Ma'at (goddess of truth, justice, righteousness). The more evil a person's deeds in life, the heavier his heart would weigh, until it weighed more than Ma'at, and then horrible consequences awaited the candidate. The lighter the heart, the more righteous the person was. The Egyptian concept akin to repentance was called "swallowing the heart." In at least two passages in the book of Exodus, the original Hebrew text says that Jehovah will cause or allow Pharaoh's heart to be heavy (Exodus 7:3; 10:1), meaning that Jehovah would weigh his evil deeds and his intractable attitude toward the Israelite slaves.

Helaman 3

In a period of calm before the storm, the people of Nephi enjoyed a two-year period largely free of contention. But then society began to unravel. Some Nephites migrated to locations northward and embarked on a major building program as well as commerce by merchant marine.

Helaman 3:15

Many records were kept of every kind. This seems to be confirmed by Brigham Young, who in 1877 quoted Oliver Cowdery as saying that at the time Joseph Smith received the gold plates, he witnessed "more plates than probably many wagon loads."[2]

Helaman 3:20–21

Helaman filled the judgment-seat with honor. He and his two sons, Nephi and Lehi, are examples of men of Christ (on their names see commentary at Helaman 5:6).

Helaman 3:29–30

In the scriptures, the term *man* or *mankind* is a generic word for a human—male or female. For example, Doctrine and Covenants 20:18 notes that God "created man, male and female, after his own image."

"The man of Christ," therefore, refers to any person, male or female, who has the desire and determination to follow Christ. These verses provide us with a pattern by which we may know how the man or woman of Christ can operate in a world filled with secret combinations and corrupt government.

On the meaning of "strait and narrow" see commentary at 2 Nephi 9:39–41. On the meaning of "right hand" see commentary at 1 Nephi 20:13.

Helaman 3:35

Fasting and prayer naturally go together to increase humility and faith. Humility is not weak but strong; faith is not flimsy but firm. Sanctification, the process of becoming true Saints or "holy ones," comes by sacrificing our pleasure for God's pleasure, giving up our desire to do his will—submitting or yielding our hearts to God (see also commentary at Mosiah 3:19).

Helaman 4

Contentions and dissensions in Nephite society, especially in the Church, where unity should have prevailed, caused much bloodshed—a high crime rate. The Nephite dissenters sought to destroy the Nephites by joining with the Lamanites, who conquered all Nephite possessions in the land southward. And it was the Nephites' own fault—their wickedness.

Helaman 4:12–13, 21–24

Ills of society, then and now. How many of these evil characteristics can we identify in our present-day society of Saints?

Indulging in pride, accumulating excessive riches, oppress-
ing the poor, withholding food from the hungry, withholding clothing from the naked, smiting the humble, mocking
sacred things, denying prophecy and revelation, murdering,
plundering, lying, stealing, committing adultery, being contentious, boasting in one's own strength, depreciating God's
commandments, and altering, corrupting, and trampling on
civil laws.

No wonder the Nephites began to "dwindle," and "the
judgments of God did stare them in the face." The Spirit of
the Lord withdrew from them collectively, because he cannot
"dwell in unholy temples."

Brigham Young University professor Douglas Brinley
compared our time to that of the Nephites: "Could it be that
we have so many more material possessions than the Nephites
did that our level of pride, selfishness, and arrogance dwarfs
theirs? Without BMWs, TVs, VCRs, radial tires, wristwatches,
dishwashers, central air and heat, wrinkle-free clothing, and
medical cures, they still managed to become prideful. We have
been inundated with many more conveniences and luxuries
conducive to prideful feelings than they were. Yet, pride destroyed the Nephites. And our prophets are describing us as
having similar tendencies. Are we so money conscious, materi-
ally oriented, and insecure that we are headed down the same
Nephite path?"[3]

Helaman 4:24

Elder M. Russell Ballard warned: "Do not fall into the
trap of thinking you can sin a little and it will not matter.
Remember, 'the Lord cannot look upon sin with the least degree of allowance.' (D&C 1:31.) . . . Some youth foolishly
rationalize that it is 'no big deal' to sin now because they can
always repent later when they want to go to the temple or on
a mission. Anyone who does that is breaking promises made
to God both in the premortal life and in the waters of baptism. The idea of sinning a little is self-deception. Sin is sin!

Sin weakens you spiritually, and it always places the sinner at eternal risk. Choosing to sin, even with the intent to repent, is simply turning away from God and violating covenants."[4]

Helaman 4:26

Elder Neal A. Maxwell "had once wondered how the society described in the Book of Mormon could change as rapidly as it did ('thus had they become weak, because of their transgression, in the space of not many years'; Helaman 4:26), but now he understood: 'Anybody who watched the sixties [the 1960s, with its hippies and its sexual revolution, etc.] understands how our society changed quickly.'"[5]

Helaman 5:1

Cezoram turned out to be wicked. He was murdered, and so was his son who succeeded him (Helaman 6:15–19). And from that point on, Gadianton robbers started filling or usurping the judgment seats (7:4).

Helaman 5:2

It is a frightening prospect that those who choose evil will be more numerous than they who choose good. Are we there yet? Elder Joseph B. Wirthlin offered the following example of how the deterioration of a society's standards can be measured:

"Mr. Frank Stanton, CBS president emeritus, told a Brigham Young University audience that network television standards will continue to decline because they are based on society's standards. He said, 'Standards come from the audience . . . ; the audience determines the programming and program content.' Further, he said, 'I believe there will be more infractions with respect to [immorality] and violence and it will get a lot worse before it gets better because of the changing standards of our society.' (*The Daily Universe*, 2 Feb. 1989, p. 1.)

"What a sad commentary on our society! Again we can

learn a great principle from the Book of Mormon. When King Mosiah proposed that judges should rule instead of kings, he said:

"' . . . if the time comes that the voice of the people doth choose iniquity, then is the time that the judgments of God will come upon you.' (Mosiah 29:26–27.) That time of iniquity came about sixty years later and at several other times. In the book of Helaman we read that 'they who chose evil were more numerous than they who chose good.' (Hel. 5:2.) If television viewing choices serve as a valid measure of our society, they who choose evil surely are more numerous than they who choose good."[6]

We maintain high moral standards regardless of what the world does. President Thomas S. Monson counseled: "Don't be afraid to walk out of a movie, turn off a television set, or change a radio station if what's being presented does not meet your Heavenly Father's standards. In short, if you have any question about whether a particular movie, book, or other form of entertainment is appropriate, don't see it, don't read it, don't participate."[7]

Helaman 5:5–12

President Spencer W. Kimball declared that "when you look in the dictionary for the most important word, do you know what it is? It could be *remember*. Because all of you have made covenants—you know what to do and you know how to do it—our greatest need is to remember."[8] We should write that down so we will remember it. The word *remember* appears fourteen times in these eight verses; it is actually a perfect summary teaching of the whole Book of Mormon in one word. Sometimes the Book of Mormon record repeats it by way of emphasis: "O remember, remember."

Helaman 5:6

Many Latter-day Saint parents have named their children after great scriptural personalities so that in thinking about their names, the children can reflect on those great lives and desire to pattern their lives after them.

Following is a great story illustrating that principle:

President George Albert Smith was named after his grandfather, known as George A. Smith, an apostle and a counselor to Brigham Young in the First Presidency of the Church. The fact that he was named after his grandfather had a great influence upon young George Albert Smith. Once, when ill, he had a dream in which his grandfather appeared to him. He reported:

"I saw a man coming towards me. I became aware that he was a very large man, and I hurried my steps to reach him, because I recognized him as my grandfather. In mortality he weighed over three hundred pounds, so you may know he was a large man. I remember how happy I was to see him coming. I had been given his name and had always been proud of it.

"When Grandfather came within a few feet of me, he stopped. His stopping was an invitation for me to stop. Then . . . he looked at me very earnestly and said:

"'I would like to know what you have done with my name.'

"Everything I had ever done passed before me as though it were a flying picture on a screen—everything I had done. Quickly this vivid retrospect came down to the very time I was standing there. My whole life had passed before me. I smiled and looked at my grandfather and said:

"'I have never done anything with your name of which you need be ashamed.'

"He stepped forward and took me in his arms, and as he did so, I became conscious again of my earthly surroundings. My pillow was as wet as though water had been poured on it— wet with tears of gratitude that I could answer unashamed."⁹

Helaman 5:10

The Lord would come to redeem his people—not *in* their sins but *from* their sins (Alma 11:34, 36–37).

Helaman 5:12

One of the most powerful promises in the Book of Mormon is that Christ, the Redeemer, God's own Son, is our rock, a sure foundation, a foundation whereon if we build we cannot fall. That is wonderful wording: if we center our lives on the rock, they *cannot* fall apart. It is true. If our lives are founded solidly on the Redeemer, when the mighty winds, whirlwind, hail, and storms beat on us—the temptations and trials of life—our lives *cannot* fall apart (see also commentary at 1 Nephi 15:24 and 3 Nephi 14:24–27; D&C 50:44).

The promise does not say we *may* not fall, or we *probably won't* fall; it says we *cannot* fall if our lives are founded solidly on him. The devil will try to "drag you down," or as we say, "beat you up," but when our lives are centered on Christ, the devil will have "no power" over us.

Helaman 5:14–22

Nephi and Lehi did remember the words their father taught them and went forth to teach the word of God, armed with "great power and authority." It is important to remember that priesthood *authority* comes from ordination, but priesthood *power* comes from righteousness. Like prophets and apostles before and after them, Nephi and Lehi were able to confound many and to witness the workings of God despite the prevalent wickedness.

Also like others before and after them, Nephi and Lehi were cast into prison; remember Abinadi (Mosiah 17:5); Alma and Amulek (Alma 14:17–18); the apostle Peter (Acts 12:5); and Joseph Smith (D&C 122:6). During the "many days without food" they had plenty of time to think about Abinadi's fate, who—for all his righteousness—did not escape the cruelest of deaths.

© Ronald Crosby. Used by permission.

Nephi and Lehi Encircled by a Pillar of Fire, *by Ronald Crosby.*

Helaman 5:23–50

The power of righteous servants of God is manifested in a miraculous way. The prophet-missionaries were encircled about "as if by fire." That was not our usual fire but the glory of the Lord and his messengers. His dwelling cloud (Hebrew *Shekhinah*) is depicted as "glory," "fire," "like lightning," "light," "exquisite whiteness," "brightness," "brilliance," and "radiance" (for more details, see commentary at 1 Nephi 1:6; 22:15–17; 3 Nephi 25:1).[10] Fire is an apt description. The Prophet Joseph Smith said that heavenly beings dwell in "everlasting burnings."[11] The experience of Nephi and Lehi recalls Shadrach, Meshach, and Abed-nego (Daniel 3:19–27).

While they were full of joy and glory, unspeakable manifestations of the Holy Spirit ensued. This is a supernal example of how the word of God is more powerful than the sword (Alma 31:5). Numerous Lamanites were convinced of the truth "because of the greatness of the evidences which they had received."

Helaman 5:40–42

"What shall we do, that this cloud of darkness may be removed from overshadowing us?" That is a good question for anyone who is feeling dark and depressed because of sin, the "despair [that] cometh because of iniquity" (Moroni 10:22). The answer is likewise true: "You must repent, and . . . have faith in Christ." The Light of the World can pull out of the darkness of sin anyone who really wants to get out of it. Importune him until the cloud of darkness disperses.

Helaman 5:50–52; 6:1–8

What a turn of affairs. The Lamanites sent missionaries to the Nephites, experiencing success telling their conversion stories. And how are the Lamanite disciples characterized? Their righteousness came "because of their firmness and their steadiness in the faith." It seems that the God of heaven greatly rejoices in his children being "firm" and "steadfast"; those terms appear frequently throughout the Book of Mormon record (see commentary at Jacob 3:1–2).

Notice the dramatic and transforming first-time experiences in the long history of the Lamanites (catalogued in Helaman 5:50–6:8):

1. The majority of the Lamanites were converted to the gospel.
2. The Lamanites laid down their weapons and their hatred and false traditions.
3. They freely yielded up the land that belonged to the Nephites.
4. The majority of the Lamanites became more righteous than the Nephites.
5. The Lamanites began to preach the gospel to the Nephites.
6. There was peace in all the land.
7. The Lamanites and Nephites had open travel and free trade with one another.[12]

Helaman 6:9–20

It is amazing, though not surprising, that both groups who were formerly antagonists could prosper so richly and thoroughly when peace prevailed. However, their strength became their weakness as riches corrupted the Nephites, and they set their hearts so much upon their riches that the cycle of apostasy began again. Just as important for our day, we see how secret combinations can exist imperceptibly, beneath the surface as it were, during periods of righteousness, peace, and prosperity, only to emerge again when society begins to decline and they see an opportunity.

Helaman 6:21–25

There is, indeed, an opposition in all things. Satan uses a righteous tool, *unity,* in his evil cause of secret combinations. Once again we see that the devil is a master counterfeiter; he specializes in cheap imitations or perversions of true and righteous principles and practices. Notice these imitations or perversions in some of the characteristics of gangs and other groups that terrorize societies: they use new, secret names, oaths and covenants, and secret signs and words; there is considerable criminal activity; they dress like robbers (see also 3 Nephi 4:7), mark themselves (Alma 3:13), and get their ideas from Satan.

Verse 25, as well as Alma 37:27, reminds us that those secret combinations, with their corrupted oaths and covenants, must not be revealed or passed on to others.

Helaman 6:26–30

The origins of secret combinations are described. Satan is the author of evil oaths. He has the power to inspire men and women to undertake abominable acts. He has done so since the beginning of time. However, every human being possesses "power to resist the devil."[13]

Helaman 6:34

The conditions described here occurred about 24 B.C. The great role reversal would continue even to the eighty-sixth year of the judges, or approximately 6 B.C., thus setting the stage for Samuel the Lamanite (see 13:1).

Helaman 6:37

Lamanite missionaries even ventured into the heart of the robbers' territory to preach the word of God among them. That is righteous boldness. And they were successful, through the word of God, in eradicating those evil forces from their entire society—without guns!

Helaman 7:1–10

The Gadianton band so thoroughly infiltrated every part of society that the government was in their control by about 23 B.C. In powerful imagery, Nephi's "heart was swollen with sorrow," wishing he could have lived in a different time. It is these very human kinds of expressions that make the Book of Mormon so believable and compelling. This lament was offered on Nephi's garden tower.

Helaman 7:11–13

Nephi poured out his soul in fervent prayer on his garden tower and attracted a large group of people anxious to know what could cause a man to vent such grief and personal affliction. His lamenting earned him a captive audience. For more on pouring out our souls in prayer, see commentary at Enos 1:3–4; Mosiah 24:10–15; and 26:13–20.

Helaman 7:14–29

Nephi's "tower sermon" is recounted. He speaks of "the good shepherd" (see the latter half of Alma's great discourse in Alma 5). It also confirms our understanding of priestcraft. The Lord inspired similar feelings in Joseph Smith: "Their hearts are set so much upon the things of this world, and aspire to the honors of men" that the Spirit of the Lord is withdrawn from men and they are liable to forfeit eternal life (D&C 121:35–38).

Nephi reminded his listeners that the Lamanites did not sin against the light as the Nephites did (compare Alma 24:30).

Helaman 8:1–9

We see how powerful but corrupt men in high places can and do incite others to rebel against prophets and principles of righteousness. We note the self-serving argument of Nephi's opponents: We are too powerful and our cities too great to stand in any real danger; it is you, Nephi, who has the problem. This is the same argument used by Laman and Lemuel when they were told Jerusalem was in big trouble. It seems axiomatic that thoroughgoing wickedness almost always brings a false sense of security (2 Nephi 28:20–22).

Helaman 8:10–28

This constitutes part two of Nephi's "tower sermon." In addressing the corrupt judges and those they incited, Nephi summoned the testimony and works of deceased prophets to stand as witnesses against his opponents. These prophets all testified of Christ.

Helaman 8:13–24

Here is one of the best passages in all of scripture on *proving Christ*. This later Nephi, along with all other prophets, rejoiced in the coming of Christ and delighted to show the evidence of his imminent mission and ministry.

The original Nephi (who left Jerusalem in the year 600 B.C.) wrote: "Behold, my soul delighteth in proving unto my people the truth of the coming of Christ. . . . God sendeth more witnesses, and he proveth all his words" (2 Nephi 11:4, 3). As with these Nephis and with the New Testament–period apostle Matthew (see Matthew 1–2), we also delight in proving the coming of Christ. "Can there any good thing come out of Nazareth?" it was asked. The answer was "Come and see" (John 1:46).

Alma and Amulek proved that "the word is in Christ unto salvation"; they called on the words of Zenos, Zenock, and Moses "to prove that these things are true" (Alma 34:6–7). Nephi and Lehi wrote about "the greatness of the evidences" (Helaman 5:50). Here this later Nephi gave us the most detailed list of those who testified of the coming of the Son of God: Moses, Abraham, Zenos, Zenock, Ezias, Isaiah, Jeremiah, Lehi and Nephi, "and almost all of our fathers . . . have testified of the coming of Christ." We have, indeed, received "so many evidences."

Helaman 8:13–15

On the serpent raised up as a type of the Messiah who would be raised up, see commentary at Alma 33:19–20.

Helaman 8:16

Regarding "all the holy prophets" testifying of Christ, see commentary at Mosiah 13:33 and "All the Prophets Prophesied of Christ," which follows it.

Helaman 8:21

The biblical record notes that the sons of King Zedekiah were killed before his eyes; then he was blinded and hauled off to Babylonian captivity (2 Kings 25:7; Jeremiah 39:6–7). The world is not aware, however, that one of Zedekiah's sons escaped from Jerusalem and helped lead another colony of immigrants to the New World. This verse and Helaman 6:10 identify that son as Mulek, who came to the Western Hemisphere to preserve the seed of Judah among the Israelites, who were, as prophesied, scattered upon *all* the face of the earth.

Helaman 9

Nephi's prophecy concerning the murder of the chief judge (8:27–28) is confirmed. Verse 2 implies that the people had at least a sense of the Mosaic test of a true prophet, even though they doubted Nephi was one. The great lawgiver said: "And if thou say in thine heart, How shall we know the word which the Lord hath not spoken? When a prophet speaketh in the name of the Lord, if the thing follow not, nor come to pass, that is the thing which the Lord hath not spoken, but the prophet hath spoken it presumptuously: thou shalt not be afraid of him" (Deuteronomy 18:21–22; see also Deuteronomy 13:1–3).

Helaman 9:21

The language of Nephi's chastisement sounds much like that of Jesus (compare Luke 24:25). We *are* fools if we do not believe the words of the prophets.

Helaman 9:25

The relationship between signs and belief is a crucial one for all of us to ponder and understand.

"And he that seeketh signs shall see signs, but not unto salvation.

"Verily, I say unto you, there are those among you who seek signs, and there have been such even from the beginning;

"But, behold, faith cometh not by signs, but signs follow those that believe.

"Yea, signs come by faith, not by the will of men, nor as they please, but by the will of God.

"Yea, signs come by faith, unto mighty works, for without faith no man pleaseth God; and with whom God is angry he is not well pleased; wherefore, unto such he showeth no signs, only in wrath unto their condemnation" (D&C 63:7–11).

Helaman 9:36

Nephi prophesied the murder of the chief judge and exposed the judge's brother as the murderer, thereby convincing some Nephites of his role as a true prophet. Every valiant elder or representative of the Lord Jesus Christ may declare as Nephi: "I am an honest man, and . . . I am sent unto you from God."

Helaman 9:40–41

Nephi was recognized as a true prophet by some. Others recognized that only God could know the thoughts and intents of a person's heart (D&C 6:16). Therefore, they reasoned, Nephi must be a god.

Helaman 10

Nephi had labored with such unwearyingness, selflessness, and diligence that the Lord promised him great power over the people and among the people. Nephi is a good example of what Paul later wrote: "Let us not be weary in well doing: for in due season we shall reap, if we faint not" (Galatians 6:9). As we sing,

> *Then don't stand idly looking on;*
> *The fight with sin is real.*
> *It will be long but must go on;*
> *Put your shoulder to the wheel.*[14]

The story about the handcart pioneers in the commentary at Mosiah 24:10–15 well illustrates the fact that we must keep putting our shoulders to the wheel, not allowing ourselves to give in to weariness but persevering with long-suffering and "unwearied diligence" (Helaman 15:6). Actually, we can get tired, and we may want to quit, but we don't—because we are valiant.

Helaman 10:1–11

Nephi demonstrated his absolute and uncompromising loyalty to the Savior of whom he prophesied. His life modeled the pattern of behavior of those who have their calling and election made sure, as revealed by Joseph Smith: "When the Lord has thoroughly proved him, and finds that the man is determined to serve Him at all hazards, then the man will find his calling and his election made sure."[15] Nephi did have his calling and election made sure.

As he went on his way toward his own house, perhaps dejected, he pondered the things that the Lord had shown him. Discourses could be written about the importance of pondering and the results that flow therefrom. Great and marvelous are the revelations that come to those who ponder the gospel plan and principles. See examples in commentary at 1 Nephi 11:1. Because of Nephi's pondering, the Lord declared four important truths to him:

1. He was to be blessed forever because of his unwearying loyalty.
2. All things that he desired for himself would be brought to pass.
3. The Lord formally acknowledged his identity in direct relationship to Nephi's valiance.
4. Nephi would receive the sealing powers of the priesthood, just as Elijah did, including control over the elements, power to bind and loose on earth and in heaven, and power to seal eternal relationships.

Taken together, these statements indicate that Nephi received a sacred and eternal blessing. Nephi had thoroughly proved himself and had served the Lord at all hazards. By identifying himself as God, the Lord was acknowledging in the presence of divine witnesses (the text says "angels") a special relationship of mutual love and respect between himself and Nephi. Scriptural parallels to Nephi's experience, where the

Lord called the person by name and identified himself, confirm this to be a moment when the Lord sealed upon Nephi his exaltation. To Alma, the Lord declared: "Blessed art thou, Alma. . . . Thou art my servant; and I covenant with thee that thou shalt have eternal life" (Mosiah 26:15, 20). To Joseph Smith, the Lord said: "I am the Lord thy God, and I gave unto thee, my servant Joseph, an appointment, and restore all things. Ask what ye will, and it shall be given unto you according to my word. . . . For I am the Lord thy God . . . ; for verily I seal upon you your exaltation" (D&C 132:40, 49).

The Lord's self-revelation to Nephi at this time may have reference to the Second Comforter. The Prophet Joseph Smith taught the following: "Now what is this other Comforter? It is no more nor less than the Lord Jesus Christ Himself; and this is the sum and substance of the whole matter; that when any man obtains this last Comforter, he will have the personage of Jesus Christ to attend him, or appear unto him from time to time, and even He will manifest the Father unto him, and they will take up their abode with him, and the visions of the heavens will be opened unto him, and the Lord will teach him face to face, and he may have a perfect knowledge of the mysteries of the Kingdom of God; and this is the state and place the ancient Saints arrived at when they had such glorious visions—Isaiah, Ezekiel, John upon the Isle of Patmos, St. Paul in the three heavens, and all the Saints who held communion with the general assembly and Church of the First Born."[16]

That Nephi also received the sealing powers of the holy priesthood indicates that he had entered into a state of sanctification. Modern revelation confirms that those who are endowed with power and taught from on high are those who are first sanctified (D&C 43:16; 88:68).

SEALING ON EARTH AND IN HEAVEN

The Lord said to Nephi, "I give unto you power, that whatsoever ye shall seal on earth shall be sealed in heaven; and whatsoever ye shall loose on earth shall be loosed in heaven" (Helaman 10:7), which is the same binding power he gave to Peter about fifty years later (Matthew 16:19; 18:18; D&C 128:10) and to Joseph Smith about eighteen hundred and fifty years later. To the latter-day prophet the Lord elaborated, "Whatsoever you seal on earth shall be sealed in heaven; and whatsoever you bind on earth, in my name and by my word, saith the Lord, it shall be eternally bound in the heavens; and whosesoever sins you remit on earth shall be remitted eternally in the heavens; . . . [and] whomsoever you bless I will bless" (D&C 132:46–47).

To seal means to bind, to create a bond—as in the bond of matrimony, or the seal of matrimony. Sealing means binding, validation, and ratification. This is authority and power that far surpasses that of earthly kings, presidents, magistrates, and rulers. With whom can God trust this awesome sealing power, which extends through all the universe and through all eternity? It is granted to those who, like Nephi, obey and serve the Lord with unwearyingness, selflessness, and diligence; to those who are totally committed to building the kingdom of God above all things; to those who covenant and dedicate themselves to promote God's work and glory.

King Benjamin urged his people to be steadfast and immovable, abounding in good works, "that Christ, the Lord God Omnipotent, may seal you his" (Mosiah 5:15). Along with the Prophet Joseph Smith, the Patriarch Hyrum Smith was given "the sealing blessings of my church, even the Holy Spirit of promise, whereby ye are sealed up unto the day of redemption" (D&C 124:124). When Elijah came, as promised by the prophet Malachi, he said to the latter-day prophet, "The keys of this dispensation [sealing power] are committed into your hands" (D&C 110:16).

An example of the use of sealing power is the performance of the ordinance of eternal marriage. When a man marries a wife "by my word, which is my law, and by the new and everlasting covenant, and it is sealed unto them by the Holy Spirit of promise," by someone who is "anointed" or "appointed this power and the keys of this priesthood," then he and she "inherit thrones, kingdoms, principalities, and powers, dominions, . . . exaltation and glory in all things, as hath been sealed upon their heads, which glory shall be a fulness and a continuation of the seeds forever and ever. . . . Then shall they be gods, because they have all power . . . and continuation of the lives" (D&C 132:19–20, 22).

The keys of Elijah, the powers of everlasting sealing, go far beyond genealogy and family history. John the Baptist brought back to the earth power, authority, and keys. Peter, James, and John brought back power, authority, and keys. But Elijah brought back the power to seal on earth and in heaven everything done in the kingdom of God for the exaltation of husbands, wives, and families.

It is almost overwhelming for mere mortals to contemplate the grandeur and scope of such far-reaching promises and powers, but for the worthy, prepared, and recommended, the sealing power is employed to bless the lives of the living and the dead in holy temples throughout the world.

Helaman 11

When there was no rain in ancient lands of the scriptures, it meant there would be famine. And famine often had a humbling effect on the people. As the saying goes, "a hungry stomach has a way of loosening up a stiff neck." McConkie and Millet wrote: "Famine is one of heaven's most eloquent sermons. When virtually all else has failed to get the attention of the rebellious and turn them to God, famines have succeeded. Famines can strip men of every sense of self-sufficiency and turn their eyes and ears to the voice of heaven."[17] Helaman 11:7 says the people "began to remember the Lord their God; and they began to remember the words of Nephi."

President Spencer W. Kimball taught in the April 1977 general conference, "The Lord uses the weather sometimes to discipline his people for the violation of his laws."[18]

Helaman 11:19

In this great narrative about the prophet Nephi and the dramatic events surrounding his ministry, there appears a little insert, an almost hidden comment, about his brother: "And behold, Lehi, his brother, was not a whit behind him as to things pertaining to righteousness."

Lehi is relegated to the wings, as it were, while his brother, Nephi, is the main actor on the stage of this part of history. So it was with Sam, brother of the earlier Nephi, and so it was centuries later with Hyrum Smith, while his brother Joseph took center stage. President Howard W. Hunter counseled: "If you feel that much of what you do . . . does not make you very famous, take heart. Most of the best people who ever lived weren't very famous either. Serve and grow, faithfully and quietly."[19]

The Savior taught that "thy Father which seeth in secret shall reward thee openly" (Matthew 6:6) and "inasmuch as men do good they shall in nowise lose their reward" (D&C 58:28).

Helaman 12:1–3

This whole chapter constitutes Mormon's commentary on the nature of fallen man. How quickly we forget God when things are easy and smooth in our lives. At the very moment that we bask in comfort and prosperity we tend to get hardened, we put our trust in our things, and we forget the real source of our prosperity (see also commentary at 1 Nephi 8:26). Therefore, the classic lesson: "And thus we see that except the Lord doth chasten his people with many afflictions, yea, except he doth visit them with death and with terror, and with famine and with all manner of pestilence, they will not remember him."

The Lord chastens his people because he loves them (Helaman 15:3), and he wants them to repent and return to him. Hundreds of years earlier Enos taught the same principle: "And there was nothing save it was exceeding harshness, preaching and prophesying of wars, and contentions, and destructions, and continually reminding them of death, and the duration of eternity, and the judgments and the power of God, and all these things—stirring them up continually to keep them in the fear of the Lord. I say there was nothing short of these things, and exceedingly great plainness of speech, would keep them from going down speedily to destruction" (Enos 1:23).

Modern prophets add a warning voice about the potential dangers of prosperity.

President Ezra Taft Benson: "Do you know what peace and prosperity can do to a people—it can put them to sleep."[20]

President Brigham Young: "The worst fear that I have about [members of this Church] is that they will get rich in this country, forget God and His people, wax fat, and kick themselves out of the Church and go to hell. This people will stand mobbing, robbing, poverty, and all manner of persecution, and be true. But my greater fear for them is that they cannot stand wealth; and yet they have to be tried with riches."[21]

President Harold B. Lee: "We are tested and we are tried, we are going through some of the severest tests today and we don't realize perhaps the severity of the tests that we're going through. . . . Today we are basking in the lap of luxury, the like of which we've never seen before in the history of the world. It would seem that probably this is the most severe test of any test that we've ever had in the history of this Church."[22]

Helaman 12:4

Why are the things of this world often labeled as "vain"? Because they are transitory; they are here today and gone tomorrow. Elder Dallin H. Oaks described them as follows: "The 'vain things of [the] world' include every combination of that worldly quartet of property, pride, prominence, and

THE BOOK OF MORMON

power. As to all of these, the scriptures remind us that 'you cannot carry them with you' (Alma 39:14)."[23]

Things of the world are also vain because they entice us away from our Father, our Savior, and our Comforter. Our hearts get attached to the unstable and temporary things of a very temporary world, and that is all in vain because they want our hearts on them and their eternal work.

Helaman 12:7

"How great is the nothingness of the children of men." King Benjamin taught that also (see commentary on "our own nothingness" as contrasted to "the worth of souls is great" at Mosiah 4:5, 11); so did Isaiah (Isaiah 40:15, 17). And Moses had poignant, personal experience with the "nothingness" of men (Moses 1:8, 10).

Helaman 12:14–15

"Reference is here made to the biblical account that shows Joshua commanding the sun and the moon to stand still so that his army might complete their rout of the Amorites (Joshua 10:12–14). Here a corrective note is added to that account, which supposed the sun to rotate around a stationary earth. . . . These verses provide a subtle but certain assurance that the prophet-editor Mormon, like many of the ancient spiritual leaders, was anything but primitive in his understanding concerning God, man, and the universe."[24]

Helaman 13–15

These chapters recount the prophetic work of Samuel the Lamanite, who prophesied the destruction of the Nephite people unless they repented. He predicted light and a new star at the time of Christ's birth and darkness and great tumults of nature at his death, and he commented on the Lord's chastening love as well as his mercy toward the Lamanites in the latter days.

Helaman 13:2–3

Samuel, the Lamanite prophet-missionary, was ill-treated and wanted to return home. The Lord told him to go back and preach again. Compare Alma 26:27.

Helaman 13:5, 9–10

A very specific prophecy was pronounced by Samuel: Within four hundred years the Nephite civilization would become extinct (compare Alma 45:10). Verse 10 notes that the "fourth generation" of Lamanites would live to see this fulfilled, thus equating one hundred years to a "generation." According to any English dictionary, the term *generation* may mean a race, kind, or class of people; we most often think of it in terms of a span of twenty to twenty-five years, but here it refers to a one-hundred-year period.

Helaman 13:21–22

The people's attitude toward riches is condemned, and the land is cursed. Riches and resultant pride are constantly recurring problems, back then and still today. Notice the cyclical phenomenon in Helaman 4:12; 7:21, 26; 13:31–33; 3 Nephi 6:15; Doctrine and Covenants 38:39; see also commentary at Jacob 2:12–16 and Jacob 2:17–19 and illustration at Ether 9–11.

Helaman 13:23–29

President Harold B. Lee counseled us to follow the living prophet:

"There will be some things that take patience and faith. You may not like what comes from the authority of the Church. It may contradict your political views. It may contradict your social views. It may interfere with some of your social life. But if you listen to these things, as if from the mouth of the Lord himself . . . the promise is that 'the gates of hell shall not prevail against you; yea, and the Lord God will disperse the powers of darkness from before you, and cause the heavens to shake for your good, and his name's glory.' (D&C 21:6.)"[25]

Helaman 13:38

What a frightening and tragic thought: "Your days of probation are past; ye have procrastinated the day of your salvation until it is *everlastingly too late,* and your destruction is made sure" (emphasis added). And another shameful and tragic thought: "Ye have sought for happiness in doing iniquity." Such a thing is impossible, for "wickedness never was happiness" (Alma 41:10).

Helaman 14

Signs were given of the birth of God's Son into the world (with references to their pronouncement in Helaman 14 and their fulfillment in 3 Nephi): in five years he will come to redeem all true believers (v. 2; 3 Nephi 1:13); a day and a night and a day with no darkness (vv. 3–4; 3 Nephi 1:15); a new star (v. 5; 3 Nephi 1:21); many signs and wonders in heaven (v. 6; Helaman 16:13; 3 Nephi 2:1); and people are amazed and fall to the earth (v. 7; 3 Nephi 1:16–17).

Signs were given of the Savior's death: there were great thunderings, lightnings, and earthquakes (v. 21; 3 Nephi 8:6–7); the earth was broken up (v. 22; 3 Nephi 8:12, 17–18); tempests howled, mountains were leveled, and valleys were lifted up (v. 23; 3 Nephi 8:5–6); highways and cities were destroyed (v. 24; 3 Nephi 8:8–11, 13–14); and graves were opened, and resurrected Saints ministered to many (v. 25; 3 Nephi 23:9–13).

One particularly unusual sign of the death of God's Son was three days of darkness (vv. 14, 20). The signs of light and darkness at his birth and death are appropriate: when the Savior comes into the world, there is more light; when he departs, there is more darkness.

The purposes of all these signs given in advance were "to

the intent that ye might believe on his name"; that the people might repent of their sins and have them remitted; and to reward their faith, "that they might know that their faith had not been in vain" (3 Nephi 1:8).

Helaman 14:3

"There shall be great lights in heaven." Could these lights be the angelic hosts who were present at their Master's entrance into mortality, appearing in glory? Compare Luke 2:9, 13–14.

Helaman 14:17

Resurrection is redemption! The resurrection of Christ redeems "all mankind, and bringeth them back into the presence of the Lord." Spiritual and physical death, the consequences of the Fall, are thereby overcome, and all of God's children are taken back to him who made them. Whether or not we may remain there, in his holy presence, depends on our faith and works here in this life. See further in commentary at 2 Nephi 2:8–10.

Helaman 14:18

The fire into which we are cast if we refuse to repent and turn to God is not fire as we know it; it is not a giant bonfire. President Joseph Fielding Smith explained, "It is not actual fire, but it is the torment of the mind."[26] There is yet another sense in which *fire* is used in the scriptures: referring to the glory of the Lord, which can either preserve and exalt or disintegrate and destroy. See commentary at Helaman 5:23–50 and 3 Nephi 25:1.

There are two spiritual deaths that some will experience: the first when they come to earth and are removed for a time from the presence of God, and the second when they depart this earth and are removed forever from the presence of God because of their disobedience and disinterest in repentance.

Helaman 14:20, 27

Darkness would cover this land "for the space of three days, to the time that he shall rise again from the dead." "Three days and three nights" is an idiom covering any parts of three days and nights. "According to early Jewish time-reckoning, any part of a day counted as a full day."[27] After his death Jesus did not remain in the earth three whole days and nights, else his rising from the dead would have been on the *fourth* day, but the scriptures mention his resurrection "on the third day" numerous times.

Helaman 14:21–27

At the time of the Savior's crucifixion and death, the earth suffered physical cataclysms. He had shown various prophets hundreds and even thousands of years in advance what physical catastrophes would transpire at his mortal death. For example, he had said to Enoch, "Look, and he looked and beheld the Son of Man lifted up on the cross, after the manner of men; and he heard a loud voice; and the heavens were veiled; and all the creations of God mourned; and the earth groaned; and the rocks were rent" (Moses 7:55–56; see also 1 Nephi 19:12).

Samuel prophesied the very thing that Matthew would record a few decades later: that many graves of the righteous dead would open up immediately after Jesus' resurrection, and they, too, would be resurrected and appear and minister unto many people (Matthew 27:52–53).

Notice that Samuel said he received his information as an independent revelation from an angel. Could that messenger have been Gabriel, who also announced the Savior's ministry to other mortals?

Helaman 14:30–31

A two-verse discourse on the doctrine of agency, an indispensable principle of eternal life. It is our choice: we choose good or evil, and life or death. We are not victims of our genes or our environment. We can obey despite what we may have been born with (or without) or despite the homes into which we came. Whatever we choose, we get the corresponding natural consequence, the blessing or the punishment. It is the law of the harvest, or the law of restoration. See Alma's treatment of the same subject in Alma 41.

Helaman 15:3–4

God loves us, so he will chasten us. "Chasten" connotes disciplining to make one "chaste," or pure. It is not the same as "chastise," though God will do that, too. Both are needed—chastening usually for our transgressions, and trials because we learn and grow from being tried and tested. "They [the Saints] must needs be chastened and tried. . . . For all those who will not endure chastening, but deny me, cannot be sanctified" (D&C 101:4–5). Read and ponder Proverbs 3:12; Hebrews 12:5–11; Revelation 3:19; Doctrine and Covenants 95:1.

"The people of Nephi hath he loved. . . . The Lamanites hath he hated." There are other scriptural uses of the strong word *hate*. Genesis 29:30–31 says that Jacob loved Rachel and hated Leah. Luke 14:26 records Jesus saying, "If any man come to me, and hate not his father, and mother, and wife, and children, and brethren . . . he cannot be my disciple." In none of these cases is the word *hate* to be taken literally, of course; nowhere in all of scripture is there evidence that the Lord hates any of Heavenly Father's children, and nowhere is found a command that disciples of Christ are to hate any of their fellow human beings. Rather, this is an example of the ancient literary device we call hyperbole, which intentionally exaggerates and strongly contrasts emotions for emphasis. The intent of the Genesis passage is to show that Rachel was favored and loved and Leah was cared for less, and likely neglected, in comparison with her sister. The passage from Luke features an intentional exaggeration for effect. We cannot love someone else *more* than we love God; we must place

107

our greatest affection on him. "Hate" is merely an idiomatic way of saying "love less." Here in Helaman we are told that in times past God had loved Nephites because they were obedient, and he had loved Lamanites less because their deeds had been evil continually. Compare commentary at 1 Nephi 17:35, 40.

Helaman 15:7–16

Scriptures lead to faith in the Lord, repentance, change of heart, firmness, steadfastness, and "fear to sin," that is, strict obedience—all of which are accompanied by blessings.

The Lamanites, like the Jews, are promised that "in the latter times," after their many afflictions through the centuries, the Lord will be merciful unto them and help bring them back to the knowledge of their Redeemer.

Helaman 16

Here are ways in which one can oppose a prophet: ascribe his power to Satan; explain away miracles; teach people to rationalize; teach that faith is a product of ignorance and tradition; question his motives; and enlist followers to spread opposition.

Elder Richard L. Evans, a member of the Quorum of the Twelve Apostles, taught that "a prophet is seldom popular, and the cost of being a prophet is always great, for he may be called upon to say those things which are not pleasing, . . . and he may find himself fighting against a tide of mass-misconception, and, as history records, be stoned, crucified, banished, ridiculed, shunned, or rejected. For the truth is not pleasing unto all men, and time has proved that majorities are not always right. . . .

"It is not important that a prophet should say those things with which you and I are in full accord. But it is important that you and I should bring ourselves into full accord with those things which a prophet speaks by virtue of his office and calling."[28]

THIRD NEPHI
THE BOOK OF NEPHI

3 Nephi 1

"It was six hundred years from the time that Lehi left Jerusalem; and it was in the year that Lachoneus was the chief judge and the governor over the land"—the historical report is similar to the beginning of Luke's account in the same year: "there went out a decree from Caesar Augustus, that all the world should be taxed. (And this taxing was first made when Cyrenius was governor of Syria.)" (Luke 2:1–2).

Nephi's son Nephi now guarded the records. The father was not heard from again; we suspect he was translated, as Alma had been (Alma 45:19). The prophecies began to be fulfilled "more fully" (3 Nephi 1:4). Some antagonists, however, claimed that the widely publicized prophecies were not being fulfilled and began to mock and ridicule the believers. They even dared set a date when the one grand sign (the day-night-day with continuing light) had better happen or the foolish believers would be killed. The Lord reassured his faithful that he would come into the world, with the sign being fulfilled, that very night. When it actually happened, unbelievers fell to the earth in shock and fear.

3 Nephi 1:4

Some of the greatest signs would understandably accompany the greatest event in history, the coming into mortality of Earth's Creator himself.

In many dispensations, the Lord's Saints have had the promise of signs—gifts of the Spirit given to those who believe and obey the gospel of Jesus Christ (Mark 16:16–18;

On the Morrow Come I into the World, *by Robert Barrett.*

Mormon 9:24–25; D&C 68:9–11). Signs flow from and strengthen faith but do not generate it out of nothing (D&C 63:7–11). Signs are manifestations of God's love. Of course Satan has his counterfeits, "signs and lying wonders," to try to deceive our Heavenly Father's children who do not love the truth (2 Thessalonians 2:9; see verses 9–12).

3 Nephi 1:9

Referring to the designated day for the believers to be killed for their foolish belief, Brigham Young University professors McConkie, Millet, and Top wrote: "Here we witness a phenomenon which is repeated ad nauseam in the Book of Mormon: the wicked who refuse to believe dare not allow others to believe. There is no room in their tightly controlled . . . system for faith or spirit or revelation or hope. They do not know, so they conclude that no one else knows. They cannot feel, so they dare not allow others to feel."[1]

3 Nephi 1:12–13

The destiny of the universe centered on this night, and yet, with all that was happening, God cared enough to answer one man's prayer! The voice of the Lord came to Nephi,

assuring him that he, the Lord, was coming into the world
that very night. But wasn't the Lord's spirit already in Mary's
womb? How could the same spirit be talking with Nephi on
the other side of the world? We have no definitive, revealed
answer to the question of when a spirit enters its develop-
ing body: at conception, during pregnancy when movement
is first felt, or at the very moment of birth—or if a spirit can
even come and go during pregnancy. If Jesus' spirit was already inside his mortal body within Mary's womb and his
birth was imminent, then another authorized being—the
Holy Ghost or some other angelic ministrant—could speak
on behalf of Jesus, by divine investiture of authority. Angels
and prophets often speak the very words of Jesus Christ, authorized by him to be his spokesmen on earth.

Part of 3 Nephi 1:14 may sound confusing, but it makes
sense when we understand that the Being who is speaking fills
two roles and speaks from both perspectives: as Jehovah (who
is the Father by divine investiture of authority) and as Jesus
Christ, the soon-to-be mortal Messiah. Thus, to Nephi he
says with perfect propriety and accuracy that when he comes
to earth on the morrow as Jesus Christ, he is fulfilling the
will of the Father and of the Son—"of the Father because of
me," because of his role as Jehovah, and "of the Son [Jesus
Christ] because of my flesh." In other words, this verse says
that Jehovah sent Jesus Christ. God the Father did indeed
send his Son, Jesus Christ, and Jesus sent himself when he was
speaking as Jehovah.

Regarding Jesus Christ speaking as the Father when fulfilling his role as the great Jehovah, President Joseph Fielding
Smith stated: "All revelation since the fall has come through
Jesus Christ, who is the Jehovah of the Old Testament. In
all of the scriptures, where God is mentioned and where he
has appeared, it was Jehovah who talked with Abraham, with
Noah, Enoch, Moses and all the prophets. He is the God of
Israel, the Holy One of Israel; the one who led that nation
out of Egyptian bondage, and who gave and fulfilled the Law

of Moses (1 Ne. 19:10; 3 Ne. 11:10, 14; 15:2–9). The Father [Elohim] has never dealt with man directly and personally since the fall, and he has never appeared except to introduce and bear record of the Son."[2]

Jesus Christ is both the Father and the Son, the Father because he is Jehovah, and as such he spoke with the authority of Elohim, and the Son because he was the spirit Son as well as the earthly Son of Elohim. (For further discussion of Jesus as the Father and the Son, see commentary at Mosiah 15:2–9.)

3 Nephi 1:15–21

As prophecies and signs were fulfilled, unbelievers fell to the earth, filled with astonishment and fear. A similar scene will unfold at the Savior's Second Coming to these lands.

Why was there no darkness? Because the literal Light of the World was entering the physical world (D&C 88:5–12). Similarly, darkness would dominate at the death of Jesus because the Light of the World had left the physical world. Verses 15 and 19 describe the fulfillment of the first of Samuel the Lamanite's prophecies regarding the birth of the Messiah (compare Helaman 14:3–4). The appearance of the new star is the fulfillment of the second prophecy by Samuel the Lamanite (compare Helaman 14:5). Verse 16 recounts the fulfilling of Samuel's third prophecy (compare Helaman 14:7).

3 Nephi 1:22–30

Even with miraculous events happening all around, some hardened hearts once again began propagating Satan's lyings and deceivings, trying to undermine others' faith. A few believers started disseminating a distorted doctrine of discontinuance of the law of Moses but were quickly set straight. The law of Moses was not totally fulfilled until the Atonement was completed. The next challenges were an infestation of robbers and the "wickedness of the rising generation," some of whom split off and joined the robber gangs.

3 Nephi 2:1–3

How quickly people forget! The tragedy of September 11, which in 2001 dramatically galvanized the United States of America into a unity of patriotism and a turning to God not seen since World War II, was also quickly forgotten in the succeeding months and years, as many people returned to their worldly concerns and false sense of security.

Hardened hearts and blinded minds tend to ignore God and disparage, malign, and discredit his doctrine, at the same time supporting and promoting the ways of wickedness—and the message here is that it can happen quickly in any society.

3 Nephi 2:5–8

Three different calendar systems were used during Nephite history: (1) total years since Lehi left Jerusalem (Mosiah 29:44–46), (2) total years since King Mosiah established the rule of judges (3 Nephi 2:5–7), and (3) total years since the coming of Christ into mortality (3 Nephi 2:8; 8:2). Most of the western world today still measures time by the same method the Nephites adopted here: reckoning time since the birth of Christ—the meridian, or high point, of all time.

3 Nephi 2:9

Nephi, father of the present Nephi who continued keeping the record, disappeared. He may have been taken up by the Spirit, or translated, as was his great-grandfather, Alma the Younger (Alma 45:19).

3 Nephi 2:11–19

Security in Nephite homelands became so precarious that all law-abiding citizens had to take up arms against the out-of-control gangs and fight to maintain their rights, privileges,

and constitutionally protected freedoms—religious and political. Their sovereignty as a nation was threatened.

Citizens of all political and racial backgrounds united to
take a stand against the robber gangs and other criminal elements, but because of the people's sinful lives, they failed to
contain the evil forces threatening them.

Brothers McConkie, Millet, and Top commented on the
change in skin color noted in verse 15: "The mark of God's
curse, the dark skin (see 1 Nephi 2:23; 2 Nephi 5:21–23)
was taken away. This was consistent with the prophetic word
which declared that when the Lamanites are restored to the
knowledge of Jesus Christ and his gospel, 'their scales of darkness shall begin to fall from their eyes; and many generations
shall not pass away among them, save they shall be a pure and
a delightsome people' (2 Nephi 30:6)."[3]

3 Nephi 3:1–10

The secret combination—the band of robbers—brazenly
regarded itself as strong enough to demand capitulation from
the Nephite government. The governor of the band, using
flattery, false accusation, intimidation, and threats, demanded
that the head of the government give up, join the secret society, and partner with the robbers in their works, which, as
the robber chief said, "I know to be good" (recall Isaiah's
warning of woe to those who call evil good; 2 Nephi 15:20).

3 Nephi 3:11–26

Mormon provided valuable insight to us today. A key requirement for good government among the Nephites, including their deliverance, lay in the personal righteousness and
courage of political and military leaders. Lachoneus, the governor, and Gidgiddoni, the chief captain of Nephite armies,
were just men and great prophets. They encouraged their
people to make temporal and tactical preparations to confront
the opposition in a defensive war and especially to repent and
turn to God for help in this time of crisis (see D&C 98:32–38

on the Lord's law of warfare). They did unite and prepare, and they did repent and plead with God for deliverance.

The parallels between these conditions in the days before the Lord's first coming to ancient America and the conditions shaping up in these last days—just before the Lord's Second Coming to the Americas—are striking.

3 Nephi 4

The united Nephites, having prepared temporally and spiritually to overcome their enemies, with the help of the Lord are able to utterly rout and annihilate the opposing forces. Siege warfare was an established tactic. In ancient times, capture of a stronghold or fortified position (an out-post, town, or city) was usually accomplished by encircling it with a powerful armed force and preventing both escape and importation of supplies. This often hastened disease, starvation, or social disintegration. Examples of siege warfare in the ancient Near East are numerous. In the old Israelite home-land they include Jericho (Joshua 6), Samaria (2 Kings 17:5), Lachish (2 Chronicles 32:9), and Jerusalem (2 Kings 24:10). Patterns of warfare in the Book of Mormon fit perfectly within this authentic milieu, especially the great Gadianton siege of Nephite lands, including Zarahemla (3 Nephi 3:23; 4:16–17). Noteworthy is the defeat of the Gadianton armies, lead by Zemnarihah precisely because "it was impossible for the robbers to lay siege sufficiently long to have any effect upon the Nephites, because of their much provision which they had laid up in store" (3 Nephi 4:18).

3 Nephi 5:1–6

Here is a message to all freedom-loving nations: Wage an unrelenting war and put an end to all "wicked, and secret, and abominable combinations"—any organizations and individuals who oppose truths revealed from heaven. And how is that done? The unrelenting war we Latter-day Saints fight is through dissemination of gospel truth. Only repentance and covenant making lead to true rehabilitation of combatants and of criminals in society.

3 Nephi 5:8–9

Mormon, the historian and abridger, noted that in this record he could not include even "a hundredth part" of all that his predecessors wrote (see also commentary at Words of Mormon 1:5 and 3 Nephi 26:6–11), though interestingly he attested that "there are records which do contain all the proceedings of this people." Someday we will have all those records the Lord has preserved.

3 Nephi 5:12–20

Mormon inserted some personal comments about his life and labors: he was named after a place, the land of Mormon, where Alma established the first church "after their transgression"—after their wicked living during the days of King Noah.

Mormon described his calling, using words that modern missionaries love to quote in reference to themselves: "I am a disciple of Jesus Christ, the Son of God. I have been called of him to declare his word among his people, that they might have everlasting life." And he was called to make a written record by way of fulfilling the faith and prayers of all the holy ones who preceded him.

Mormon testified that his record is true, although "there are many things which, according to our language, we are not able to write"—meaning either that the language in which they wrote didn't have the capacity to express certain things adequately or that some things were too sacred to include in the written record (see 3 Nephi 19:32; Mormon 9:33; Ether 12:25; see also commentary at 3 Nephi 26:16–18).

Mormon defined himself as "a pure descendant of Lehi" who had been blessed with "so much knowledge" unto the salvation of his soul.

3 Nephi 5:21–26

These powerful verses are centered on the latter-day gathering of Israel and the tribe of Joseph. The Lord's latter-day gatherer, Joseph Smith, is prophesied of, and an allusion to Jacob's allegory can be seen.

Commenting on the gathering in the last days, Elder Dallin H. Oaks said: "In the early years of this last dispensation, a gathering to Zion involved various locations in the United States: to Kirtland, to Missouri, to Nauvoo, and to the tops of the mountains. Always these were gatherings to prospective temples. With the creation of stakes and the construction of temples in most nations with sizeable populations of the faithful, the current commandment is not to gather to one place but to gather in stakes in our own homelands. There the faithful can enjoy the full blessings of eternity in a house of the Lord. There, in their own homelands, they can obey the Lord's command to enlarge the borders of His people and strengthen her stakes (see D&C 101:21; 133:9, 14). In this way, the stakes of Zion are 'for a defense, and for a refuge from the storm, and from wrath when it shall be poured out without mixture upon the whole earth' (D&C 115:6)."[4]

President Dieter F. Uchtdorf reemphasized the counsel for members of the Lord's Church to stay in their homelands: "As the members will stay in their countries and build the Church, despite economic challenges and hardships, future generations will be grateful to those courageous modern-day pioneers. They abide by the loving invitation of the First Presidency given in 1999:

"'In our day, the Lord has seen fit to provide the blessings of the gospel, including an increased number of temples, in many parts of the world. Therefore, we wish to reiterate the long-standing counsel to members of the Church to remain in their homelands rather than immigrate to the United States. . . .

"'As members throughout the world remain in their homelands, working to build the Church in their native countries, great blessings will come to them personally and to the Church collectively' (First Presidency letter, Dec. 1, 1999)."[5]

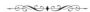

WHY DOES GOD HAVE A COVENANT PEOPLE?

Mormon spoke of the covenant the Lord made with the house of Jacob, or Israel (3 Nephi 5:25; see also *"Israel* and *Zion* in Latter-day Saint Usage" in commentary at 2 Nephi 8:9–10). Actually, we often speak of the "Abrahamic covenant," named after Jacob's grandfather, the great patriarch Abraham, but did the covenant begin with Jacob, or even with Abraham?

The scriptures indicate that the covenant has been on the earth beginning with Adam (Moses 5:58–59) and was then passed on through—

- Enoch (Genesis 6:18, footnote *a,* quoting JST, Genesis 8:23; Moses 7:50–52),
- Methuselah and Noah (Genesis 9:9, footnote *a,* quoting JST, Genesis 9:15; 9:11, footnote *c,* quoting JST, Genesis 9:17; Moses 8:2–3),
- Melchizedek and Abraham (Genesis 13:14, footnote *a,* quoting JST, Genesis 13:13),
- Isaac (Genesis 26:3–5), and
- Jacob (Genesis 28:13–15).

The covenant then became part of the mission of all the house of Jacob, or Israel.

It is a practice in scriptural history to name various powers and privileges after specific individuals who were exceptional examples of the use of those powers and privileges. For instance, we speak of the Adamic language, the Order of Enoch, the Melchizedek Priesthood, the Aaronic Priesthood, the law of Moses, the Spirit of Elijah, the Book of Mormon, and the Abrahamic covenant. To be sure, none of those things belongs to any of those individuals; they all belong to the Lord Jesus Christ. But to avoid too frequent repetition of his holy name, we label many things in his gospel after outstanding mortal models or prototypes. The special covenant relationship of God with his people Israel has been called after Abraham because he was a classic exemplar of its use, even though it is truly the covenant of Jesus Christ.

What does the covenant of Jesus Christ with his people consist of? Marvelous blessings are promised as his disciples comply with his eternal laws. To illustrate, we have blessings promised to Abraham and his descendants (Abraham 2:9–11; Galatians 3:26–29; D&C 132:29–37, 49–50; see also LDS Bible Dictionary, "Abraham, Covenant of," and Topical Guide, "Abrahamic Covenant"):

1. Become a great nation through whom all the families of the earth will be blessed
2. Everlasting covenant of celestial marriage
3. A prolific posterity
4. Blessings of the gospel and the priesthood
5. Blessings on those who bless; curses on those who curse
6. Land inheritance
7. Kings
8. The Messiah
9. The great latter-day Prophet Joseph Smith (D&C 124:58)
10. Adoption into the covenant lineage of those born outside the covenant.

That sounds remarkable, to be on the receiving end of all those promised blessings! Why wouldn't everyone on earth want to accept and enjoy all those blessings? Because there is something more to the covenant. It entails not only blessings but also *responsibilities*. The covenant also includes serious expectations of duties to perform as God's elect or chosen lineage. His people are chosen not only to have blessings poured down on them but to fulfill the covenant responsibilities of disseminating the truths of the gospel of Jesus Christ to all the rest of the world. Moses wrote about God's covenant people as a "holy people, . . . a peculiar people . . . above all the nations" (Deuteronomy 14:2), and Isaiah wrote about them being "a light to the Gentiles" (Isaiah 49:6). Jesus himself taught: "I give unto you to be the light of this people. . . . Therefore let your light so shine before this people, that they may see your good works and glorify your Father who is in heaven" (3 Nephi 12:14, 16). Covenant people are obligated to "bear this ministry and Priesthood" (Abraham 2:9) to all others and invite them to join in—to be "grafted in" or "adopted" into God's family. What they had to bear is often referred to in the Old Testament as a "burden," because they recognized that to be a covenant person carried weighty responsibilities.

"Take my yoke upon you," Jesus said (Matthew 11:29). Animals were yoked together to harness their energy and strength and increase their productivity. Though a yoke was, in a sense, a weight or a burden, it was a useful, positive, desirable thing—as is the yoke of submission and obedience to God and its consequent freedom from the burden of sin. "My yoke is easy" (Matthew 11:30). The Savior's burden, carrying the responsibility of a covenant person, is certainly easier than carrying the heavy burden of the sinner. "My burden is light" (Matthew 11:30). "Light" is the opposite of heavy, and it is the opposite of dark. Those who emulate Christ discover that the work of God is not so much wearisome as it is joyous to the soul, and their reward is "peace in this world, and eternal life in the world to come" (D&C 59:23).

3 Nephi 6

The chapters of 3 Nephi 6–11 constitute a fascinating parallel to our own time: Nephites before the Lord's first coming to America, and Latter-day Saints before the Lord's Second Coming.

President Ezra Taft Benson stated: "The record of the Nephite history just prior to the Savior's visit reveals many parallels to our own day as we anticipate the Savior's second coming. The Nephite civilization had reached great heights. They were prosperous and industrious. They had built many cities with great highways connecting them. They engaged in shipping and trade. They built temples and palaces.

"But, as so often happens, the people rejected the Lord. Pride became commonplace. Dishonesty and immorality were widespread. Secret combinations flourished because, as Helaman tells us, the Gadianton robbers 'had seduced the more part of the righteous until they had come down to believe in their works and partake of their spoils.' (Helaman 6:38.)"[6]

Consider the parallels between that ancient time and our own time:

1. Blessings from God bring tremendous prosperity, increased construction, commerce, and social interchange (vv. 4–8). But prosperity often precipitates pride.

2. Incessant disputations; some lifted up in pride and boastings because of riches (v. 10).

3. Numerous businessmen and businesswomen, lawyers, and officers causing the disputations and boastings in pride (v. 11).

4. People distinguished by ranks, according to their riches and their chances for learning (v. 12).

5. Some were proud while others were humble and penitent (v. 13).

6. Great inequality of riches, and relatively few Church members remaining firm, steadfast, and immovable (v. 14).

7. Many acquiescing to the power of Satan: proud, seeking for power, authority, riches, and the vain things of the world (v. 15).

With constant problems because of pride and riches, is it any wonder that the Lord looks back on this time in Nephite history with a stern warning to us modern Saints: "If ye seek the riches which it is the will of the Father to give unto you, ye shall be the richest of all people, for ye shall have the riches of eternity; . . . but beware of pride, lest ye become as the Nephites of old" (D&C 38:39).

3 Nephi 6:12

There is a godly place where we are not distinguished by ranks, according to our riches and our chances for learning—the holy temple. There, in the Lord's university, with the most exalting curriculum on earth, it doesn't matter what executive positions we have, what titles we may have earned, or how much money we have. There, in God's classroom, we are all dressed alike, in white, and we present ourselves united before the Father and the Son, with the Holy Ghost also teaching us.

3 Nephi 6:16–18

Why is righteousness so short-lived? "They had enjoyed peace but a few years" and now "they did wilfully rebel against God," or, as King Benjamin put it, they were in "open rebellion against God" (Mosiah 2:37).

3 Nephi 6:20–30

The Lord always provides plenty of warning to those who need to repent and change their wicked ways (Amos 3:7; 2 Chronicles 36:15–16; 2 Nephi 25:9). Holy men were called up as messengers from God to boldly testify of the people's sins (v. 20), but judges, lawyers, and priests—those from the legal and religious establishments—led the opposition to the inspired messengers and arranged secretly for their assassination. The devil administers his own secret covenant, around which secret combinations and conspiracies thrive—always to set at defiance the laws which guarantee the rights and freedoms of everyone. Self-centered elitism is the devil's priority.

3 Nephi 7:1–14

The Nephite government fell with the murder of the chief judge, Lachoneus II. An apostate then became king over the secret combination responsible for disintegration, and society fragmented into tribes. All this happened because the people "did yield themselves unto the power of Satan" and allowed a secret combination to flourish. Years ago, President Ezra Taft Benson raised a warning: "I testify that wickedness is rapidly expanding in every segment of our society. (See D&C 1:14–16; 84:49–53.) It is more highly organized, more cleverly disguised, and more powerfully promoted than ever before. Secret combinations lusting for power, gain, and glory are flourishing. A secret combination that seeks to overthrow the freedom of all lands, nations, and countries is increasing its evil influence and control over America and the entire world. (See Ether 8:18–25.)"[7]

3 Nephi 7:15–20

This Nephi, son of Nephi, was one of the greatest prophets of all time. The voice of the Lord came to him, as did angels—ministering to him daily. He performed many miracles, including raising his brother Timothy from the dead (also 3 Nephi 19:4). He was keeper of the Nephite records and later was chosen as one of Jesus' twelve apostles in the Americas, even baptizing the others who were called (3 Nephi 19:12). It appears that he served the same role as did Peter in the original Quorum of the Twelve Apostles—president of the quorum.

3 Nephi 7:25

Another of the purposes of baptism is revealed: as a witness and testimony that the individual has repented and received a remission of his or her sins.

3 Nephi 8:1

The Lord gives his criterion for when a miracle can be done in his name: when the miracle worker is cleansed from all sin. Heaven's standard of worthiness, and the only way any teacher, missionary, or leader can effectively function in God's kingdom, is to *be clean.*

3 Nephi 8:5–25

The greatest storm ever known arose, along with great and terrible tempests and whirlwinds, earth-shaking thunderings, sharp lightnings, submerging of cities, burning of cities, earthquakes, and other violent convulsions of nature—lasting for a total of three hours. [8]

"The whole face of the land was changed" and "the face of the whole earth became deformed" suggest to some researchers that no one would ever be able to identify the specific location of any particular city or feature of the landscape in Book of Mormon lands. The prophet-historian Mormon, however, living in these same lands centuries after these disastrous cataclysms described in considerable detail the location of numerous cities and other geographical features—suggesting that perhaps the upheavals and displacements may not have been so wide-scale and extensive as some have supposed.

Verses 20–23 emphasize the fact that, at the crucifixion of Jesus on the other side of the world and the massive destruction on this side of the world, there was thick darkness everywhere—total darkness, because there was no light. The Light of the World had been extinguished, and until he came again—or at least until his voice was heard again—there would be much less light. It seems only natural that the earth should be in such tumult and turmoil after the death of Christ because it too is a living entity and was mourning the suffering of its Creator (Moses 7:39–40, 48). This was all foreseen much earlier (1 Nephi 12:4–5). Remember, Jesus is in all things and through all things (D&C 88:5–12).

Notice how the darkness is described as a "vapor of darkness" that could be felt. A similar kind of darkness prevailed in ancient Egypt during the plagues (Exodus 10:21).

3 Nephi 9:1–14

God himself gave a damage report, a description of the extent of the destruction at the crucifixion. What would a survivor be thinking after suffering such cataclysms and then hearing a voice saying that he, the speaker, did all that: "I burned with fire . . . I caused to be sunk . . . I covered with earth . . . I buried up . . . I caused to be burned . . . I did send down fire" and, last but not least, your very survival is because I allowed it. Such a graphic pronouncement of power could not help but rivet the attention of all listeners on the next declarations: "Will ye not now return unto me . . . that I may heal you?" There could have been no doubt that this voice, whoever he was, had the power to do so.

God invites all to "return and repent" (on this significant combination of words, see commentary at Alma 34:34). His message, then and now, is look to God and live (as Moses' serpent in the wilderness: just look and be healed; see commentary at Alma 33:19–20).

3 Nephi 9:15–21

The One who caused all the cleansing damage then announced who he is. There can be no mistaking who he is: "I am Jesus Christ the Son of God. I created the heavens and the earth, and all things that in them are." The Creator of the world is the Son of the Father in heaven. He is the Redeemer. The law of Moses is fulfilled in him. He is the One who originally gave the law; in fact, he *is* the law (3 Nephi 15:4–9). He exclaimed, "I am the light and the life of the world" and "I am Alpha and Omega, the beginning and the end." He was crucified and then resurrected.

3 Nephi 9:20

The law of sacrifice is an eternal law. It has been on the earth from the beginning and will continue forever. One aspect of this eternal law—the sacrificial offering of animals—was performed for centuries to point the minds of the people to the ultimate sacrifice of the Savior, but when Jesus died for us, he adjusted our focus to higher aspects of the law. Now, instead of blood sacrifices, he wants us to sacrifice, or give up, worldliness and dedicate our hearts and spirits to him and his work (see further commentary about sacrifice at 1 Nephi 2:11–24; Omni 1:26; Alma 34:13–14).

Whoever comes unto Jesus "with a broken heart and a contrite spirit, him will I baptize with fire and with the Holy Ghost, even as the Lamanites, because of their faith in me at the time of their conversion, were baptized with fire and with the Holy Ghost, and *they knew it not*" (emphasis added). The last phrase clearly suggests that true conversion is often a calm, quiet, even unnoticeable experience.

President Ezra Taft Benson described the process in these words: "We must be careful, as we seek to become more and more godlike, that we do not become discouraged and lose hope. Becoming Christlike is a lifetime pursuit and very often involves growth and change that is slow, almost imperceptible. The scriptures record remarkable accounts of men whose lives changed dramatically, in an instant, as it were: Alma the Younger, Paul on the road to Damascus, Enos praying far into the night, King Lamoni. Such astonishing examples of the power to change even those steeped in sin give confidence that the Atonement can reach those deepest in despair.

"But we must be cautious as we discuss these remarkable examples. Though they are real and powerful, they are the exception more than the rule. For every Paul, for every Enos, and for every King Lamoni, there are hundreds and thousands of people who find the process of repentance much more subtle, much more imperceptible. Day by day they move closer to the Lord, little realizing they are building a godlike life. They live quiet lives of goodness, service, and commitment. . . .

"We must not lose hope. Hope is an anchor to the souls of men. Satan would have us cast away that anchor. In this way he can bring discouragement and surrender. But we must not lose hope. . . . We must remember that most repentance does not involve sensational or dramatic changes, but rather is a step-by-step, steady, and consistent movement toward godliness."[9]

It is tremendously significant that Jesus asks all disciples from this point on to offer as a sacrifice to him "a broken heart and a contrite spirit." By so doing, we emulate the Savior in very deed, for Jesus experienced both a broken heart and a contrite spirit. He died of a broken or ruptured heart, as Elder James E. Talmage indicated: "While, as stated in the text, the yielding up of life was voluntary on the part of Jesus Christ, for He had life in Himself and no man could take His life except as He willed to allow it to be taken (John 1:4; 5:26; 10:15–18), there was of necessity a direct physical cause of dissolution. . . . The strong, loud utterance, immediately following which He bowed His head and 'gave up the ghost,' when considered in connection with other recorded details, points to a physical rupture of the heart as the direct cause of death. If the soldier's spear was thrust into the left side of the Lord's body and actually penetrated the heart, the outrush of 'blood and water' observed by John is further evidence of a cardiac rupture; for it is known that in the rare instances of death resulting from a breaking of any part of the wall of the heart, blood accumulates within the pericardium, and there undergoes a change by which the corpuscles separate as a partially clotted mass from the almost colorless, watery serum. . . . The present writer believes that the Lord Jesus died of a broken heart. The psalmist sang in dolorous measure according to his inspired prevision of the Lord's passion:

'Reproach hath broken my heart; and I am full of heaviness: and I looked for some to take pity, but there was none; and for comforters, but I found none . . . ' (Ps. 69:20, 21; see also 22:14)."[10]

In addition, a contrite spirit was also the Savior's experience. *Contrite* is defined as "crushed in spirit by a feeling of remorse for guilt."[11] This Jesus experienced for all of us as well (Moses 6:54). Mark implied Jesus was crushed in spirit in Gethsemane when he reported that Jesus entered the garden and began to feel "very heavy" and "sorrowful unto death" (Mark 14:33–34). The crushing weight of sin, sorrow, and suffering for the universal family of God progressed to the point where Jesus began to bleed from every pore (Luke 22:44; D&C 19:16–19). And so the great Redeemer asks us, in return for his vicarious suffering on our behalf, to experience vicariously and symbolically what he experienced.

3 Nephi 10:1–2, 12

Only righteous people were spared through all the physical devastation. Ponder what might have been going through their minds "for the space of many hours." After what the Lord had taught in his few introductory statements, they had much to think about.

3 Nephi 10:4–6

A hen watches over and protects her young, gathering them under her wings to ensure their safety. The Lord says that if his people are obedient, he will be their guard and protector; he will fight their battles; he will hold them close and keep them safe.

3 Nephi 10:12

The great destructions that preceded Jesus' coming were due, in large part, to the people rejecting, casting out, and killing the prophets. The righteous receive and follow the prophets. The Lord promised:

"If my people will hearken unto my voice, and unto the voice of my servants whom I have appointed to lead my people, behold, verily I say unto you, they shall not be moved out of their place.

"But if they will not hearken to my voice, nor unto the voice of these men whom I have appointed, they shall not be blest" (D&C 124:45–46).

President Boyd K. Packer testified of the leaders of the Church: "If we follow them we will be saved. If we stray from them we will surely be lost."[12]

3 Nephi 10:14

Will this also be said at the Second Coming? They had been warned, and we have been warned.

3 Nephi 10:18

"Soon after the ascension of Christ into heaven he did truly manifest himself unto them." The text does not clearly define the exact time of Jesus' coming to the Western Hemisphere. Did this occur after his forty-day, postresurrection ministry in the Holy Land? Or after the resurrection on the first day of the week? Though different ideas have been put forward regarding the time frame, Elder James E. Talmage stated: "Christ had risen; and following Him many of the righteous dead on the western continent rose from their graves, and appeared as resurrected, immortalized beings among the survivors of the land-wide destruction; even as in Judea many of the saints had been raised immediately after the resurrection of Christ [Helaman 14:25; 3 Nephi 23:7–13; compare Matthew 27:52, 53]. . . . *About six weeks* or more after the events last considered, a great multitude of the Nephites had assembled at the temple in the land called Bountiful, and were earnestly discoursing with one another over the great changes that had been wrought in the land. . . . While thus congregated they heard a sound as of a Voice from above; but both a first and a second utterance were to them unintelligible. As they listened with rapt intentness, the Voice was heard a third time, and it said unto them: '*Behold my beloved Son, in whom I am well pleased, in whom I have glorified my name: hear ye him.*' [emphasis in original; see 3 Nephi 11:7; compare Matthew 3:17; Mark 1:11; Luke 9:35; JS–H 1:17.]"[13]

The righteous always have the promise, if not of being spared, at least of having "great favors" and "great blessings" poured out upon their heads—the most desirable and the most lasting of all heaven's favors and blessings.

3 Nephi 11–28:11

In the 34th year (3 Nephi 8:2, 5), the Lord Jesus Christ appeared and taught his people in ancient America. His teachings comprise, in the English Book of Mormon, thirty-four pages, and they are the most precious and valuable teachings in the most precious and valuable book in the world.

3 Nephi 11:1

Once again, in the state of Utah in 1994, a great multitude was able to gather together and marvel and wonder at a temple in the land (city) of Bountiful.

3 Nephi 11:3

How will we recognize his voice when he speaks to us? It is not a mysterious, mystical, magical voice, nor harsh, nor loud. If we have dedicated ourselves to studying his words, we have heard his voice (D&C 18:34–36). The quiet impressions, the perceptible revelations, are the voice of God speaking to us. We also hear him speaking to us in the temple. What we hear there is most certainly the voice of God and the will of God for us to hear and obey. Someone said, "Make time for the quiet moments, as God whispers and the world is loud."

3 Nephi 11:7

The voice of the Father is heard on rare and sacred occasions in this telestial world. When the Father does come, he comes to say one specific thing: "This is my Son." Why does he testify of this one, single fact? Because that is the most important thing he could say, the most needed testimony he could bear. Jews do not believe God, Elohim, would have a Son (the *Shema* proclaims, "Hear, O Israel: the Lord our God is one Lord"; Deuteronomy 6:4). Muslims—between one and two billion of them on the earth now—do not believe God, Allah, would have a Son who would come to live with the rest of us groveling humans in this world ("Far is it removed from His transcendant majesty that he should have a son"; the Qur'an, Sura IV:171). Neither do many Christians these days believe that God the Father literally had a Son in this world. It is a unique and powerful witness of the divinity of that Son; his own Father bears solemn testimony of that fact at each momentous occasion in the Old World and in the New World, in ancient times as well as in modern times.

3 Nephi 11:8

"They saw a Man descending out of heaven." Tribes of ancient America believed in Quetzalcoatl, whose name means "bird-serpent." He descended out of the sky like a bird, and he was as the serpent raised up on a pole to heal the people (see further in commentary at Alma 33:19–20).

Jesus' descent to the Nephites provides a pattern for how he will come at his second coming. When he ascended into heaven from the Mount of Olives after his resurrection, two angelic witnesses said: "Ye men of Galilee, why stand ye gazing up into heaven? this same Jesus, which is taken up from you into heaven, shall so come in like manner as ye have seen him go into heaven" (Acts 1:11).

CHRIST'S COMING TO AMERICA AS A PATTERN FOR THE SECOND COMING

Scripture References to Christ's Coming to the Nephites	Events	Scripture References to the Future Coming of Christ
3 Nephi 2:14–16	Lamanites become righteous	D&C 49:24
3 Nephi 3:4	There are wars and rumors of wars	D&C 49:24
3 Nephi 3:22	The righteous gather together	D&C 45:26
3 Nephi 6:17–18; 7:7	Increased wickedness	D&C 115:6
3 Nephi 7:14	People reject the prophets	Joseph Smith–Matthew 1:30
3 Nephi 8:4	Increased skepticism concerning his coming	D&C 1:14
3 Nephi 8:6, 10–19	Earthquakes and other disturbances accompany his coming	D&C 45:26, 48
3 Nephi 8:20–23	Darkness covers the earth	D&C 45:42
3 Nephi 8:24–25	Christ comes as a thief in the night	2 Peter 3:10
3 Nephi 11:8	Christ comes from heaven in glory	D&C 29:11; 133:42–49
3 Nephi 9:1–13; 10:12	The wicked are destroyed at his coming; the righteous are preserved	D&C 5:19; 29:11

3 Nephi 11:1–11	Christ appears at his temple(s)	Malachi 3:1–2
3 Nephi 11:14	Christ shows the wounds in his body	Zechariah 13:6; D&C 45:51–52
3 Nephi 23:9–11	Christ's coming begins a resurrection of the righteous	D&C 88:96–98
3 Nephi 10:12	Those prepared for Christ's coming are those who sustain the prophet	D&C 45:32; 124:45–46

3 Nephi 11:10

Once again the man speaks some defining names and titles to identify clearly who he is: "I am Jesus Christ, whom the prophets testified shall come into the world."

3 Nephi 11:11

"I am the light and the life of the world." The identification of Jesus as the light of the world is metaphorical but also literal (D&C 88:6–13).

The Savior had just drunk from a very bitter cup. President James E. Faust described how we can follow His example: "Many members, in drinking of the bitter cup that has come to them, wrongfully think that this cup passes by others. In His first words to the people of the Western continent, Jesus of Nazareth poignantly spoke of the bitter cup the Father had given Him (see 3 Ne. 11:11). Every soul has some bitterness to swallow. Parents having a child who loses his way come to know a sorrow that defies description. A woman whose husband is cruel or insensitive can have her heart broken every day. Members who do not marry may suffer sorrow and disappointment. Having drunk the bitter cup, however, there comes a time when one must accept the situation as it is and reach upward and outward."[14]

There is nothing any of us will ever suffer that our Savior has not also suffered. He descended not only *to* our condition but *below* all things (D&C 88:6; 122:8). When we cry out, "But you don't understand!" he is the only One who actually does understand—all things, and his understanding is accompanied by compassion. The same applies, of course, to our Father.

3 Nephi 11:14

A beautiful lesson comes from the wounds in the Savior's side, wrists, hands, and feet. Elder Jeffrey R. Holland wrote: "However dim our days may seem, they have been a lot darker for the Savior of the world. As a reminder of those days, Jesus has chosen, even in a resurrected, otherwise perfected body, to retain for the benefit of His disciples the wounds in His hands and in His feet and in His side—signs, if you will, that painful things happen even to the pure and the perfect; signs, if you will, that pain in this world is *not* evidence that God doesn't love you; signs, if you will, that problems pass and happiness can be ours."[15]

Elder Tad R. Callister, a member of the Seventy, explained the effects of Jesus' physical wounds: "In his resurrected state, Jesus retained the prints of nails in his hands and feet as a special manifestation to the world. Such marks, however, are only temporary. After all have confessed that he is the Christ, his resurrected body will, like those of all mankind, be restored to its 'proper and perfect frame' (Alma 40:23)."[16]

"I am the God of Israel, and the God of the whole earth." He was not appearing as a great moral teacher or even as our elder brother. He is above all others who live on this planet. He is God.

3 Nephi 11:15–17

One by one, all the people—twenty-five hundred of them (3 Nephi 17:25)—saw with their eyes, felt with their hands, bore testimony of him, praised him, and worshipped him.

Jesus could simply have shown himself to the whole multitude, but this is a poignant illustration of his care for the one.

During his ministry—on both sides of the world—Jesus touched people, both physically and spiritually. His priesthood ordinances also involve touch, both physically and spiritually. Touch was an important element in lasting conversion: the people, one by one, touched his body for two reasons: (1) to know and testify forever that the living Christ is a real, corporeal being, to avoid what later happened to apostates who claim that God is without body, parts, or passions; and (2) to experience the wounds of the Atonement—to be personal eyewitnesses of the dramatic, tangible evidence of his pure love.

Hosanna is a Hebrew word (*Hosha-na*) meaning "Save us, we pray" or "Save us, we beseech thee."

3 Nephi 11:19

Nephi "bowed himself before the Lord and did kiss his feet." After a long and influential ministry, Elder Bruce R. McConkie of the Quorum of the Twelve Apostles said during his final general conference address: "I am one of his witnesses, and in a coming day I shall feel the nail marks in his hands and in his feet and shall wet his feet with my tears.

"But I shall not know any better then than I know now that he is God's Almighty Son, that he is our Savior and Redeemer, and that salvation comes in and through his atoning blood and in no other way."[17]

3 Nephi 11:21–12:2

Once true conversion takes place, baptism follows. Baptism is a simple act, lasting only a few seconds, but it shows faith and humility. With firm belief in Christ, and after repenting of one's sins, the symbolic act of total immersion in the baptismal waters signals cleansing and coming forth to newness of life—being born again, this time spiritually. The importance of this ordinance is evident by its frequent mention: in these twenty-three verses, baptism is referred to nineteen times. The righteous Nephites were no longer under the old law, but part of a new Church organization, so they were baptized again to enter the kingdom of God on earth.

3 Nephi 11:22, 28–30

These people had obviously had a problem with contention. The Savior kept reminding them, "There shall be no disputations among you, . . . *as there have hitherto been*" (emphasis added). The Lord explained, "He that hath the spirit of contention is not of me"; it is the devil who "stirreth up the hearts of men to contend with anger."

The Spirit of God, on the other hand, promotes unity and harmony. President Henry B. Eyring, then a member of the Quorum of the Twelve Apostles, explained: "Where people have that Spirit with them, we may expect harmony. The Spirit puts the testimony of truth in our hearts, which unifies those who share that testimony. The Spirit of God never generates contention (see 3 Ne. 11:29). It never generates the feelings of distinctions between people which lead to strife. . . . It leads to personal peace and a feeling of union with others. It unifies souls. A unified family, a unified Church."[18]

3 Nephi 11:25

Today's baptismal prayer is exactly the same as given anciently in the Book of Mormon, with only one alteration. Instead of saying "Having authority given me of Jesus Christ," we say "Having been commissioned of Jesus Christ" (D&C 20:73). Daniel H. Ludlow wrote: "One possible explanation for this difference . . . is that the disciples in the Book of Mormon received their authority *directly* from Jesus Christ; therefore, they rightfully could say 'having authority given me of Jesus Christ.' However, in this dispensation priesthood bearers have been given the power to baptize from John the Baptist, who was commissioned by Jesus Christ to come to earth and restore this authority. Therefore, in this dispensation we use the words 'having been commissioned of Jesus Christ.'"[19]

3 Nephi 11:27

On the Father, Son, and Holy Ghost being one, see commentary at Mosiah 15:2–9.

3 Nephi 11:38

"Become as a little child." Elder James E. Talmage wrote: "Christ would not have had His chosen representatives become childish; far from it, they had to be men of courage, fortitude, and force; but He would have them become childlike. The distinction is important. Those who belong to Christ must become like little children in obedience, truthfulness, trustfulness, purity, humility, and faith."[20]

3 Nephi 11:31–41

Jesus defined and elaborated on exactly what his doctrine is. For clarity and emphasis, he repeated three times "this is my doctrine." His doctrine is simple: Believe in him (faith); return to him (repentance); immerse ourselves in him (baptism); and be guided by him (through the Holy Ghost). Anything more or less than this "cometh of evil"; in other words, it can be dangerous to go beyond the pure and powerful doctrine he has given and on which the missionaries always focus in helping others to become genuinely converted. Keep it pure and simple!

Doing that, we are building on his "rock," that is, on him (see commentary at 3 Nephi 14:24–27), and the "gates of hell" will not prevail against us. Have you ever thought about the gates of hell? It is curious how many times the Lord refers to them. In 3 Nephi 18:13 he warns that "the gates of hell are ready open to receive [you]." These days the gates of hell are pornography, aberrant sexual relationships, selfishness, greed, pride, and other forms of severe worldliness.

These gates of hell are gaping wide open to swallow up anyone who gets close enough and is spiritless enough to be
snatched. Knowing and living the Lord's doctrine is absolutely urgent in order to escape the current bombardment of
worldliness surrounding us. The doctrine of Christ, including
his principles, ordinances, and covenants, becomes our shield
and protection against the powers of darkness.

This doctrine, Christ says, must be declared unto "the
ends of the earth" (also D&C 112:4).

TO THE ENDS OF THE EARTH

The phrase "the ends of the earth" appears fifty-nine times
in scripture. The Lord emphasizes that his words shall "hiss forth
unto the ends of the earth" (2 Nephi 29:2). The gospel shall "roll
forth unto the ends of the earth" (D&C 65:2); "the revelations"
including "great and glorious tidings" are extended to "the ends
of the earth" (D&C 72:21; 109:23). "The voice of the Lord is
unto the ends of the earth" (D&C 1:11; see also 45:49); "this
promise [the covenant] is unto all, even unto the ends of the
earth" (Mormon 9:21). "Salvation [is] unto the ends of the earth"
(1 Nephi 21:6; Acts 13:47); "all the ends of the earth shall see
the salvation of God" (3 Nephi 16:20; see also Isaiah 52:10;
Mosiah 15:31; 3 Nephi 20:35; D&C 133:3). Describing the
scope of the great latter-day gathering, Doctrine and Covenants
58:45 says "they shall push the people together from the ends of
the earth." And speaking to the Prophet Joseph Smith, the Lord
declared, "The ends of the earth shall inquire after thy name"
(D&C 122:1).

Through his prophets the Lord has commanded, "Repent, all
ye ends of the earth," calling on *the people* far and wide, over
the whole length and breadth of the earth, to repent and return
to him (3 Nephi 27:20; Ether 4:18; Moroni 7:34). Mormon said,
"I write unto all the ends of the earth" (Mormon 3:18), meaning to all *the people* who live throughout the earth; "I would
that I could persuade all ye ends of the earth" (Mormon 3:22),

desiring to convince and convert souls to the far-flung reaches of the globe.

"To the ends of the earth" also means to every "corner" of the earth. Joseph Smith admonished, "Don't let a single corner of the earth go without a mission."[21]

Anyone who watches the hand of the Lord move throughout the earth will testify that his words, his glad tidings, the revelations of salvation, the new and everlasting covenant, meaning the fulness of the gospel (D&C 66:2), are indeed penetrating to the farthest reaches of this planet. In the Western Hemisphere, for example, the names of Jesus Christ and Joseph Smith are known and loved to the northernmost stake of the Church (Fairbanks, Alaska, with its northernmost branch in North Shore) and to the southernmost stake of the Church (Punta Arenas, Chile, with its southernmost branch in Puerto Williams).

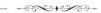

3 Nephi 12–14

Jesus taught the Nephites the same eternal truths that he had given his Jewish disciples (Matthew 5–7), only with greater clarity and specific additions. Like the Ten Commandments, which he has repeated to all peoples in all dispensations—to ancient Israelites in the Holy Land (Exodus 20; Deuteronomy 5) and in the New World (Mosiah 13) and to modern Israel in the Doctrine and Covenants (section 42)—these verities are also timeless. Whether given on a mount (Matthew 5–7) or on a plain (Luke 6) or at the temple (3 Nephi 12–14), these teachings constitute what President Harold B. Lee called the "Constitution for a Perfect Life." The main theme is "how to reach the kingdom of heaven" or "how to overcome the flesh." Elder Melvin J. Ballard said, "A man may receive the priesthood and all its privileges and blessings, but until he learns to overcome the flesh, his temper, his tongue, his disposition to indulge in the things God has forbidden, he cannot come into the celestial kingdom of God."[22] These magnificent principles teach how to overcome the natural man and achieve that celestial glory.

Some may wonder why this Book of Mormon text of Jesus' great teachings is so similar—in some parts identical—to Matthew's version of the Sermon on the Mount (Matthew 5–7). Did Joseph Smith simply copy Matthew's text, with occasional alterations or revisions? Possibly the best scriptural response to that interrogatory is 2 Nephi 29:8–9, 11:

"Know ye not that the testimony of two nations is a witness unto you that I am God, that I remember one nation like unto another? Wherefore, I speak the same words unto one nation like unto another. And when the two nations shall run together the testimony of the two nations shall run together also.

"And I do this that I may prove unto many that I am the same yesterday, today, and forever. . . .

"For I command all men, both in the east [Bible lands] and in the west [Book of Mormon lands]."

3 Nephi 12:1–2

The first instruction was given to the Twelve. They are usually called "disciples" in 3 Nephi, but they were also apostles (Moroni 2:1–2). Jesus began by pronouncing what in English have come to be known as the "Beatitudes" (or as one Primary child called them, "The Beautiful Attitudes"), which are, in a sense, Jesus' character in words. The English word *Beatitude* derives from the Latin *beatus,* which means "to be blessed" or "to be happy or fortunate." It is the equivalent of the Hebrew *ashrei,* "blessed is/blessed are . . ." This ancient form of instruction is especially prevalent in the Psalms: "Blessed is the man that walketh not in the counsel of the ungodly" (Psalm 1:1; see also 2:12; 32:1–2; 40:4; 41:2; 84:4; 106:3; 119:1–2; 128:1; and others). Thus Jesus used this ancient Israelite method of teaching to describe the characteristics and attributes we must possess if we desire membership in the kingdom of God—citizenship in the celestial kingdom. Perhaps that is why President Harold B. Lee stated that the Beatitudes embody "the constitution for a perfect

140

life," and that in them "the Master has given us somewhat of a revelation of his own character, which was perfect, or what might be said to be 'an autobiography' . . . and in so doing has given us a blueprint for our own lives."[23]

In addition, the Beatitudes are particularly well-suited to the temple setting of this entire sermon in 3 Nephi (remember they were at the temple in Bountiful). Several of the Beatitudes are based on the Psalms, and many of the ancient Israelite Psalms were composed in or for the temple or adapted to the ancient Israelite temple service.[24] The Lord gave four beatitudes to the Nephites before beginning the well-known collection in the New Testament (Matthew 5:3–12).

1. "Blessed are ye if ye shall give heed unto the words of these twelve."

2. "Blessed are ye if ye shall believe in me and be baptized."

3. "More blessed are they who shall believe in your words because that ye shall testify that ye have seen me."

4. "Blessed are they who shall believe in your words, and come down into the depths of humility and be baptized."

Elder Spencer J. Condie reminded us: "President Harold B. Lee . . . suggested that the Beatitudes represent a recipe for righteousness with incremental steps, beginning with 'the *poor in spirit* who come unto [Christ]' (3 Ne. 12:3; emphasis added). The next step in the celestial direction is to *mourn*, especially for our sins, for 'godly sorrow worketh repentance to salvation' (2 Cor. 7:10). One then becomes *meek* and begins to *hunger and thirst for righteousness.* A natural sequel is a greater inclination to be *merciful,* an increased desire to become *pure in heart,* and a stronger desire to be a *peacemaker* (see 3 Ne. 12:5–9). But even the proper and inspired use of our moral agency has a price indicated in the next beatitude: 'And blessed are all they who are *persecuted* for my name's sake, for theirs is the kingdom of heaven' (3 Ne.

12:3–10; emphasis added). As we climb the steps outlined in the Beatitudes, we soon humbly recognize that our lives are on a higher plane than those who love the things of this world. And notwithstanding our attempts to share with them gospel truths that can also elevate their lives, many of them will begin to persecute us and scoff at our lifestyle and point mocking fingers at those who have partaken of the fruits of the gospel (see 1 Ne. 8:26–27).

"The Savior reserved a special blessing for those who would be reviled and persecuted and falsely accused for His sake: 'Ye shall have great joy and be exceedingly glad, for great shall be your reward in heaven; for so persecuted they the prophets who were before you' (3 Ne. 12:11–12)."[25]

3 Nephi 12:3

"Blessed are the poor in spirit," that is, the "poor in pride, [but] humble in spirit" (Matthew 5:3, footnote *b*). The Nephite record makes a significant addition: "Blessed are the poor in spirit *who come unto me*" (emphasis added). We are willing to be dependent on our Savior.

In fact, all of the Beatitudes may be read more profitably by inserting the phrase "who come unto me," for in truth that is the implication in all of them (those who mourn who come unto me, the meek who come unto me, the peacemakers who come unto me, and so forth). We are dependent on Jesus for exaltation and lasting happiness.

We must be willing to be dependent on our Savior. Here in mortality we are nothing of ourselves (Mosiah 4:11). Recognizing our nothingness should lead not to hopelessness but to willing dependence on the only Person in the universe who can rescue us from our fallen condition. The nothingness we refer to here is our incapacity and helplessness to get ourselves out of this fallen, mortal condition; we are not suggesting that we are worthless—nothingness is not worthlessness—because we know each soul is worth a great deal in the sight of God.

The opposite of dependence is pride, which always drives us away from God. When we feel independent, we may think we don't need God. Doctrine and Covenants 56:18 tells us, "Blessed are the poor who are pure in heart, whose hearts are broken, and whose spirits are contrite, for they shall see the kingdom of God coming in power and great glory unto their deliverance."

An example of those who are poor or humble in spirit but pure in heart is the people who hearkened to King Benjamin: "They had viewed themselves in their own carnal state, even less than the dust of the earth. And they all cried aloud with one voice, saying: O have mercy, and apply the atoning blood of Christ that we may receive forgiveness of our sins, and our hearts may be purified; for we believe in Jesus Christ, the Son of God" (Mosiah 4:2).

Other examples of those with clean and pure hearts are the men we sustain today as prophets, seers, and revelators.

3 Nephi 12:4

Those who mourn and try to keep God's commandments will eventually be comforted; their sorrow shall be turned into joy (John 16:20).

One sign of a true Saint is that he or she is "willing to mourn with those that mourn; yea, and comfort those that stand in need of comfort" (Mosiah 18:9).

Jesus' ministry perfectly illustrates this godly quality of character; we often read that he was "moved with compassion" (Matthew 9:36; 14:14; Mark 1:41; 6:34; compare Matthew 15:32; 20:34; Mark 5:19; Luke 7:13). The English word *compassion* derives from the Latin *com* ("with") plus *pati* ("to bear, to suffer"). Thus having compassion means "to bear or suffer with." A synonym that derives from the Greek is *sympathy* (*sym*, "with," plus *pati*, from which we get *pathos*). Other related terms are *commiseration* ("to lament with, to have pity for") and *condolence* ("to feel pain with").

When the scriptures speak of Jesus' compassion, therefore,

we can visualize him understanding someone's misery or suffering, experiencing deep feeling for that person's pain, and desiring to relieve it. Being moved with compassion is a spiritual consciousness of someone's personal tragedy and a feeling of selfless tenderness toward it.

In the Beatitudes, in this great sermon at the temple, and in his whole life, we learn of Jesus' character, the way he lived. He said, "I am the way," and this is the way he wants us to live—to be willing to feel for others' burdens and be willing to help carry them.

3 Nephi 12:5

"Blessed are the meek." This is a direct quotation of Psalm 37:11. Meekness is the quality of character that may be defined as poise under pressure and patience in the face of provocation. President Harold B. Lee taught: "A meek man is defined as one who is not easily provoked or irritated and forbearing under injury or annoyance. Meekness is not synonymous with weakness."[26] President Gordon B. Hinckley observed: "The meek and the humble are those who are teachable. They are willing to learn. They are willing to listen to the whisperings of the still, small voice for guidance in their lives. They place the wisdom of the Lord above their own wisdom."[27] The Prophet Joseph Smith taught that "we should cultivate a meek, quiet and peaceable spirit."[28] Mildness, humbleness, and gentleness are meekness, and meekness is power under control.

An excellent example of meekness in the New Testament is John the Baptist. He was bold and rigorous in denouncing evil and hypocrisy, but at the same time he was humble and meek. Speaking of the Savior, the great prophet said, "He must increase, but I must decrease" (John 3:30).

As this verse from the Beatitudes indicates, the meek will inherit this celestialized earth (D&C 130:9).

3 Nephi 12:6

Matthew recorded, "Blessed are they which do hunger and thirst after righteousness: for they shall be filled" (Matthew 5:6), but here the Nephite record adds with what we may be filled: "with the Holy Ghost." When we are spiritually hungry and thirsty there is nothing more desirable, rich, and satisfying than being filled up with the Spirit of God.

3 Nephi 12:7

The law of the harvest is that what we send out comes back to us. If we are merciful, compassionate, tolerant, and patient with the foibles or weaknesses of others, then that merciful treatment will be given us, too.

President Gordon B. Hinckley encouraged: "Let us be more merciful. Let us get the arrogance out of our lives, the conceit, the egotism. Let us be more compassionate, gentler, filled with forbearance and patience and a greater measure of respect one for another. In so doing, our very example will cause others to be more merciful, and we shall have greater claim upon the mercy of God who in His love will be generous toward us."[29]

3 Nephi 12:8

This beatitude has a direct temple connection and is based on Psalm 24, one of the psalms of ascent or procession sung by the Levites and priests as devotees went up to the temple in Jerusalem to worship and participate in the sacrifices. Part of this psalm reads:

"Who shall ascend into the hill of the Lord? or who shall stand in his holy place?

"He that hath clean hands, and a pure heart; who hath not lifted up his soul unto vanity, nor sworn deceitfully.

"He shall receive the blessing from the Lord, and righteousness from the God of his salvation.

"This is the generation of them . . . that seek thy face, O Jacob. . . .

"Who is this King of glory? The Lord of hosts, he is the King of glory" (Psalm 24:3–6, 10).

Though the King James Version of Psalm 24:3 uses the words "hill of the Lord," the Hebrew is more directly related to the temple: "who shall go up to the mountain of Jehovah," which is a reference to the Lord's mountain-house or temple, as we see in Isaiah 2:2. And the phrase "who shall stand in his holy place" directly refers to the temple because a section of the Jerusalem temple was explicitly called "the Holy Place." The implication of the King James Version of Psalm 24 is that one could encounter God in the temple. The Septuagint (Greek version of the Old Testament abbreviated as LXX) is much more explicit (especially verse 6) in pointing out that the ultimate intent of going up to the temple was to "seek the face of the God of Jacob":

"Who shall go up to the mountain of the Lord, and who shall stand in his holy place?

"He that is innocent in his hands and pure in his heart; who has not lifted up his soul to vanity, nor sworn deceitfully to his neighbour.

"He shall receive a blessing from the Lord, and mercy from God his Saviour.

"This is the generation of them that seek him, that seek the face of the God of Jacob. . . .

"Who is this king of glory? The Lord of hosts, he is this king of glory" (LXX, Psalm 23:3–6, 10).

All those whose hearts are clean and pure have the promise that they shall see God. The same requirement of purity was and always will be in effect for anyone to enter a temple of the living God, his earthly home, where he might be seen. "It shall come to pass that every soul who forsaketh his sins and cometh unto me, and calleth on my name, and obeyeth my voice, and keepeth my commandments, shall see my face and know that I am" (D&C 93:1). Thus, the pure in heart are those who forsake their sins, call on the Savior's name, obey his voice, and keep his commandments—and then they can see God. That is a literal promise. Those who are pure, as he is pure, not only will see him but will remain and live with him forever. That promise is not just for our postmortal life, however. In the Doctrine and Covenants the Lord explains one way that God can be seen in this life: "And inasmuch as my people build a house unto me in the name of the Lord, and do not suffer any unclean thing to come into it, that it be not defiled, my glory shall rest upon it; yea, and my presence shall be there, for I will come into it, and all the pure in heart that shall come into it shall see God" (D&C 97:15–16).

To see God, according to Elder Royden G. Derrick, means to come to know God, discover him, visualize him, recognize him, and understand him.[30] To see him is to recognize the divine in his children.

3 Nephi 12:9

Those who eventually become the children of God—that is, those who become permanently part of the eternal family of God—are those who have learned to make peace. They have learned, for example, to get rid of pride and have stopped stirring up contention and spawning criticism in favor of more charitable relationships. They guide themselves and others to the Prince of Peace.

3 Nephi 12:10–12

Peter wrote, "If ye suffer for righteousness' sake, happy are ye: and be not afraid of their terror, neither be troubled" (1 Peter 3:14). Being persecuted while bearing the name of Jesus Christ and while trying to be Christlike is nothing new. It has happened to many people greater than we throughout the ages. Paul wrote, "All that will live godly in Christ Jesus shall suffer persecution" (2 Timothy 3:12). And we will be blessed for it. How great is our reward? "All that my Father hath shall be given unto [you]" (D&C 84:38). How do we endure the painful persecution? "He also gave them strength, that they should suffer no manner of afflictions, save it were swallowed up in the joy of Christ" (Alma 31:38).

3 Nephi 12:13

In an age before refrigerators, salt was the great preservative. In this memorable metaphor, the Savior calls his disciples salt. They would preserve his teachings and lifestyle among the peoples of the earth, but if they failed in their conscientious following of his example, they would be worthless in his kingdom and would be cast out, as useless salt is cast out.

Salt is plentiful. The evaporation of one cubic mile of seawater leaves about 140 million tons of salts, most of which would be sodium chloride, or common salt. It could also be extracted from the seawaters themselves but with care to remove impurities and poisonous elements in those waters, which are heavy with various minerals.

Salt does not lose its savor with age. Rather, its savor is lost through mixture and contamination. The Lord's metaphor in this passage may be a warning to avoid any alteration of God-given teachings or any admixture with the philosophies of men or the corrupting influences of those who love evil. The encouragement is for disciples to maintain a pure and undefiled gospel and to season the world with their tasteful living.

In Leviticus, the handbook for Levitical priests, the Lord commanded that "every oblation of thy meat offering shalt thou season with salt; neither shalt thou suffer the salt of the covenant of thy God to be lacking from thy meat offering" (Leviticus 2:13). Salt was a token of the covenant that the Lord had made with his people and was part of Israel's sacrificial system. That sacrificial system was a type, shadow, and symbol of the great and last sacrifice that Jesus himself would offer (see Hebrews 9–10). Salt ultimately points to the Savior.

Jesus perpetuated the symbol by labeling the people themselves as the possessors and promulgators of his covenant. As the salt would season the meat offering, so the disciples of the Lord Jesus Christ would season the world and preserve his truth in it.

3 Nephi 12:14–16

Just as the Savior gave unto us to be the salt of the earth—to preserve his word and his work in the world—so he gives unto us to be the light of this people. We are many lights now, a large city, and we cannot be hid. We are conspicuous lights in this world of darkness. As a candle or lamp is put up on a candlestick or lamp stand, so we must set our light to shine throughout our communities and nations: "Let your light so shine before this people." Jesus Christ is our Light, for he said, "I am the light which ye shall hold up" (3 Nephi 18:24). In other words, our objective is to let him, our Light, shine through us to the glory of the Father, not for our own glory.

As Jesus said, we are the light of the world but only in the sense that we allow him to shine through us. In the ultimate sense, he is the light of the world to illuminate the darkened minds and lives of those who live without God in the world. There is no switch to turn off the darkness, but we do have him to turn on the light, which dispels the darkness. We may not be able to turn off all the darkness of sin in the world— the drunkenness, the pornography, the abuse, the immorality, the violence, the hate—but we can turn on the light of Christ, any time and any place, to help dispel the evil influences that surround us.

3 Nephi 12:17–48

The Savior shifted to a crucial theme that he would teach and illustrate: "Think not that I am come to destroy the law or the prophets." The Law and the Prophets are two of the three major parts of the holy scriptures that the people then possessed. The Jews called them the *Torah* (the Law) and the *Nevi'im* (the Prophets). The other was called the *Ketuvim,* the Writings, or poetical works, such as Psalms, Proverbs, and Ecclesiastes.

Jesus was not destroying or canceling out all those sacred writings any more than a university professor is destroying basic arithmetic by teaching integral calculus.[31] He came not to abolish but to complete. That is the meaning of the Greek term used in the New Testament version of this beatitude. As the Latter-day Saints say to other Christians—or to Jews, Muslims, or anyone else—we do not come to erase any truth you already have but to fulfill, to complete, to add to what you have with the fulness of the everlasting gospel. We say, as the Lord said, "I do not bring it to destroy that which [you] have received, but to build it up" (D&C 10:52). And Joseph Smith declared, "We don't ask any people to throw away any good they have got; we only ask them to come and get more."[32]

3 Nephi 12:18–20

A "jot" is the smallest letter in the Hebrew alphabet (*yod*). A "tittle" is the English word representing a small stroke or mark used to distinguish one letter from another. It could also represent a tiny decorative flourish that the calligrapher adds to a letter of a word in the Hebrew Bible as he writes it out by hand.

Jesus is referring to two of the smallest things known to ancient Israelites to show that not even the minutest detail of the old law (and the prophetic writings) is negated or voided, but all is now accomplished and fulfilled in him.

The text of Matthew suggests future fulfillment; 3 Nephi 1:25 also indicates "the law was not yet fulfilled"; but 3 Nephi 12:18 uses the past perfect tense, meaning the law had now been fulfilled.

The purpose of the old law was to lead the people of Israel to Christ, and his commandments are now before us to save us. Keeping them is the only way any of us will enter into the kingdom of heaven.

3 Nephi 12:21–45

Specific examples are given of how the Savior came not to destroy but to fulfill. He did not do away with the old law, especially the basic commandments, but rather added higher laws. These examples illustrate a basic theme of the sermon: how to overcome the flesh—that is, how to learn to control the body. We came to earth not just to obtain a physical body but to learn to control it, to achieve self-mastery. The examples Jesus gave teach us that we must learn to control our emotions (especially anger), our sexual desires (any immoral thoughts and actions), our food intake (through fasting), and our tongue (our verbal communication).

3 Nephi 12:21–22

Included in the old law was a commandment not to kill (the Hebrew verb *ratzakh* means "to murder, to slay with premeditation"; Exodus 20:13). That law, of course, still stands. But the higher law is to refrain from even getting angry. The Savior charges us not to allow the feelings of anger to get started that could lead to murder. Anger is a very strong emotion. It is beyond irritation, annoyance, disgust, or other such feelings, which are also contrary to the spirit of the gospel; it is a deep, passionate wrath or rage that could lead one to commit murder. Even Nephi, son of Lehi, a noble, righteous prophet, struggled with feelings of anger toward his enemies (his older brothers), and he knew that such intense feelings were wrong, sinful, and damaging to his own spirituality (2 Nephi 4:17–31, especially vv. 17–19, 27–29). Nephi knew that such intense anger was forbidden by the gospel of Jesus Christ, as is plainly expressed here in verse 22. The Joseph Smith Translation of Ephesians 4:26 asks the relevant question: "Can ye be angry, and not sin?"

"We have seen that anger against another can only result after we commit sin (think unrighteously), but there is something in the nature of anger itself and its consequences that is also sinful. *Anger itself is a sin* when sin is defined as anything that retards the growth or progress of an individual."[33]

"President Spencer W. Kimball, in his excellent book *The Miracle of Forgiveness,* tells us in effect that anger is 'a sin of thought' which, if not controlled, may be the forerunner of vicious and violent acts."[34]

Elder Theodore M. Burton taught: "Whenever you get red in the face, whenever you raise your voice, whenever you get 'hot under the collar,' or angry, rebellious, or negative in spirit, then know that the Spirit of God is leaving you and the spirit of Satan is beginning to take over. At times we may feel justified in arguing or fighting for truth by contentious words and actions. Do not be deceived."[35]

One sister missionary learned through experience to avoid anger. She wrote: "I had one companion that I regret very much getting angry with. That was twenty-five years ago, when I knew nothing about it being a sin to criticize and even let something get to the point of anger. No one got along with this sister. . . . We just walked to a different drumbeat. She was very philosophical in an emotional way. She was all heart. I was all head and hard work. She wanted to disobey the rule that we should be in at 1 P.M. every afternoon, to study and allow the people their siesta time until 3 P.M. I desperately needed that study time. I loved studying the scriptures and Spanish. She was bored with that and really didn't know the discussions. She loved talking to the people all day long. She would cry and get emotional at almost every door. It was so embarrassing to me. I refused to stay out with her. It made us both hardhearted towards one another to the point that we wouldn't even walk down the same side of the street together. Now, when I look back on it with the maturity and gospel knowledge I have about anger and contention, I wish I had let her have her way now and then and not been so rigid. Keeping the Spirit would have been so much more important than having all that contention. . . . She wasn't asking that we break any covenants or commandments; she was just happier teaching than studying. . . . I could have loved her anyway. She wasn't asking me to go to movies or break those kinds of rules; she just wanted to rearrange the proselyting. I could have done that and lived with fewer regrets. I wish someone had taught me about anger back then. I thought I was justified. I wasn't." She spoke further about uncontrolled emotions: "Do I repent daily and frequently, especially of improper and unkind feelings such as anger, impatience, sarcasm, and cynicism? Do I understand that anger and irritation are wrong, even when I am in the right—that anger is an offense to the Spirit and is not the Lord's way of solving differences and frustrations?"[36]

"Anger, irritation, annoyance—all from below. My, how the devil loves to separate people: spouses from each other, children from parents, ward members from each other, brothers and sisters, etc. [BYU colleague] Catherine Thomas said that the reason we have abrasive people in our lives is so we can learn to develop divine love. This life is a laboratory for practicing divine love. And until we get the hang of it, we will have one irritating person after another come into our lives to give us plenty of practice."[37]

Every disciple of Christ is expected to learn to control his or her strong feelings. Some people these days consider themselves victims of their own anger. Elder Lynn G. Robbins explained that each of us can choose whether or not to react with anger:

"A cunning part of [Satan's] strategy is to dissociate anger from agency, making us believe that we are victims of an emotion that cannot control. We hear, 'I lost my temper.' Losing one's temper is an interesting choice of words that has become a widely used idiom. To 'lose something' implies 'not meaning to,' 'accidental,' 'involuntary,' 'not responsible'— careless perhaps but 'not responsible.'

"'He made me mad.' This is another phrase we hear, also implying lack of control or agency. This is a myth that must be debunked. No one makes us mad. Others don't make us angry. There is no force involved. Becoming angry is a conscious choice, a decision; therefore, we can make the choice not to become angry. *We* choose!

"To those who say, 'But I can't help myself,' author William Wilbanks responds: 'Nonsense.'

"'Aggression, . . . anger, . . . screaming and yelling,' are all learned strategies in dealing with anger. 'We *choose* the one that has proved effective for us in the past. Ever notice how seldom we lose control when frustrated by our boss, but how often we do when annoyed by friends or family?' ('The New Obscenity,' *Reader's Digest,* Dec. 1988, 24; emphasis added)."[38]

The text of Matthew 5:22 reads, "Whosoever is angry with his brother without a cause." The latter phrase is deleted in this purer rendition by the Savior as recorded among the Nephites (3 Nephi 12:22), because there is no cause, no justification, ever, to become really angry with a brother. The phrase was also deleted by the Prophet Joseph Smith in his inspired revision of the biblical text (JST, Matthew 5:22). The Spanish Bible (Casiodoro de Reina, dating from a half-century earlier than the English King James Version) also omits that phrase.

Raca is an Aramaic term that Joseph Smith adopted from the English Bible as an adequate rendering of a certain concept in the language of the Book of Mormon plates. *Raca* means an "empty" or "worthless" person (interestingly, the modern Hebrew cognate *ravak* means "bachelor"). Labeling someone as a *raca* or as a fool is forbidden by the Lord because we must not tell another child of Heavenly Father that he is worthless or "good for nothing" (on the value of every soul, see D&C 18:10; Topical Guide, "Worth of Souls"). It was, colloquially speaking, the ancient Aramaic way of calling someone an "airhead" or an "empty fool." A person may be doing foolish things, but he or she is not inherently a "fool" but a child of the God of heaven.

In the Greek New Testament, "the council" referred to

the Jewish Sanhedrin (Matthew 5:22; 3 Nephi 12:22). A person charged with denunciation, castigation, or condemnation of a brother could be arraigned before that council. In a larger sense, one guilty of such sinful name-calling in a future day may be arraigned before a heavenly council, at the judgment bar of God.

"Hell fire" in Hebrew is *esh Gei Hinnom,* "fire of the Hinnom Valley," or, in the Greek transliteration, *Gehenna.* The hell to which people are cast down or cast out, the place of punishment by ever-burning fire, is represented by the Greek word *Gehenna.* The Hinnom Valley was the border between the Israelite tribes of Judah and Benjamin (Joshua 15:8; 18:16). The valley lay to the southwest just outside the original City of David. Centuries before the Roman period, the Hinnom Valley was used for burning the trash of the city and for the burning of incense (2 Chronicles 28:3). The valley was also the scene of the burning of children as sacrifices to idols (2 Kings 23:10; 2 Chronicles 33:6; Jeremiah 7:31); prophets warned of fiery judgments upon all those involved in such a repulsive practice.

The burning came to be symbolic in the New Testament of the devouring fire of judgment, representing the concept of hell as a place of continual burnings and eternal punishment. The book of Revelation describes hell as a lake of fire and brimstone (see commentary at Mosiah 3:27). There are twelve occurrences of *Gehenna,* translated as "hell" or "hell fire." The most famous is Jesus' teaching in the Sermon on the Mount (Matthew 5:22), repeated here among the Nephites.

3 Nephi 12:23–24

If there are strained relations or friction between us and anyone else, before going to the temple or to sacrament meeting and renewing covenants with God, we should first be reconciled with that person—talk things over, work it out, resolve differences, forgive and forget. Then we can approach the Lord and his sacred things with full purpose of heart and, as he says, "I will receive you."

3 Nephi 12:25–26

"Agree with thine adversary quickly" means "Quickly have kind thoughts for, or be disposed toward" (Matthew 5:25, footnote *a*). The adversary in this case means an opponent in a lawsuit. There would be far fewer lawsuits if people would be disposed to agreeing, or working things out, before going to court.

President Joseph F. Smith taught: "Be reconciled to each other. Do not go to the courts of the Church nor to the courts of the land for litigation. Settle your own troubles and difficulties; . . . there is only one way in which a difficulty existing between man and man can be truly settled, and that is when they get together and settle it between them. The courts cannot settle troubles between me and my brother."[39]

3 Nephi 12:27–30

Included in the old law was a commandment not to commit adultery (Exodus 20:14, one of the Ten Commandments). That law, of course, still stands. But the higher law is for individuals never even to lust after another. If they do, they have already committed adultery in their hearts. We must not allow the lustful feelings that could lead to adultery to get started, and we will never have to worry about that great sin. As Alma encouraged his son, "Bridle all your passions, that ye may be filled with love" (Alma 38:12; see also commentary at Alma 38:12). If we are filled with genuine love, there is no room for lust. If we control the first tempting urges to accommodate physical desires, then we will not follow through and succumb to the serious sexual sin. The Savior reiterated the same commandment in our day, with added warnings of consequences for violating it:

"Verily I say unto you, as I have said before, he that looketh on a woman to lust after her, or if any shall commit adultery in their hearts, they shall not have the Spirit, but shall deny the faith and shall fear" (D&C 63:16).

Larry E. Dahl, a professor in Religious Education at Brigham Young University, wrote: "In the scriptures, the heart has to do with the core or essence of a person—his real intent and unfeigned desires. (See Prov. 23:7.) If one would in fact commit adultery with the object of his lust if the opportunity were present, he is an adulterous person. Although taught in terms of a man lusting after a woman, the principle applies to all, male and female.

"But what if one really wouldn't commit the act of adultery, yet suffers real temptation? In a world saturated with immoral aural and visual stimuli, such thoughts and temptations can be daily fare.

"Although we cannot avoid all the stimuli, we can plead with the Lord to help us control and channel our thoughts. We can consciously avoid compromising situations and forthrightly resist temptation. Rather than allowing improper thoughts to linger—and enhancing and savoring them—we can dismiss them with a prayer or an uplifting hymn or song, and deliberately channel our thoughts into positive paths.

"If we imagine ourselves involved in improper things, our thoughts may influence our heart's inclination and perhaps even our future behavior. Dr. Maxwell Maltz underscores the connection between our thoughts and our body's nervous system: 'Experimental and clinical psychologists have proved beyond a shadow of a doubt that the human nervous system cannot tell the difference between an "actual" experience and an experience *imagined vividly and in detail*.'"[40]

The Lord commands us to not allow the lusts of the flesh to enter into our heart. Though our physical bodies normally contain strong sexual desires—which are good, wholesome, and proper when used at the right time and under the right conditions for divinely approved purposes—it is better to deny ourselves any improper, lustful desires. That is, in a figurative sense, a way of "taking up our cross," denying ourselves certain forbidden pleasures to avoid being cast into hell and losing the opportunity to enjoy those sacred sexual powers forever. Moroni wrote: "Touch not the evil gift, nor the unclean thing. . . . Come unto Christ . . . and deny yourselves of all ungodliness" (Moroni 10:30, 32; see also Matthew 16:24, footnote *d*, from JST, Matthew 16:26).

President Spencer W. Kimball taught: "Many acknowledge the vice of physical adultery, but still rationalize that anything short of that heinous sin may *not* be condemned too harshly; however, the Lord has said many times: 'Ye have heard that it was said by them of old times, Thou shalt not commit adultery:

"'But I say unto you, That whosoever looketh on a woman to lust after her hath committed adultery with her already in his heart.' (Matt. 5:27–28.)

"And to paraphrase and give the modern version: 'And she that looketh upon a man to lust after him shall deny the faith, and shall not have the Spirit; and if she repents not she shall be cast out [or excommunicated].' (See D&C 42:23.) The commands of the Lord apply to women with equal force as to their husbands, and those scriptures come with the same sharpness and exactness to both sexes, for he has but a single standard of morality. It is not always the man who is the aggressor. Often it is the pursuing, coveting woman, and note that for both, *all* is lost if there is not true, sustained, and real repentance.

"Home-breaking is sin, and any thought, act, or association which will tend to destroy another's home is a grievous transgression."[41]

3 Nephi 12:31–32

The old law permitted the option of divorce when a marriage partner was unfaithful and committed a sexual transgression with another person. A writing of divorcement was issued (Deuteronomy 24:1). Divorce is "permitted under some circumstances because of the hardness of the people's hearts, but as explained by Jesus, 'from the beginning it was not so'" (LDS Bible Dictionary, "Divorce"). At the time of Jesus and in the modern Church of Jesus Christ, divorce is likewise permitted. But the higher law of God makes no allowance for divorce. In celestial realms there is no such thing as making an eternally binding covenant and then breaking it. The higher law of celestial marriage is now available and encouraged, though the full penalties for marriage failure are not currently exacted, due to human shortcomings.

President Gordon B. Hinckley wrote: "There may be now and again a legitimate cause for divorce. I am not one to say that it is never justified. But I say without hesitation that this plague among us, which seems to be growing everywhere, is not of God, but rather is the work of the adversary."[42]

3 Nephi 12:33–37

In the old law was a commandment not to "forswear thyself" but follow through on all oaths to the Lord (Leviticus 19:12; Numbers 30:2; Deuteronomy 23:21). Not to "forswear thyself" means not to break your oath or perjure yourself (Matthew 5:33, footnote *a*). The higher law advised against swearing by heaven, or by the earth, or by our head, and so on. It is best to keep our communication plain and simple. Oaths, vows, and covenants of eternal import are made between a person and the Father or the Lord, in sacred ways and in sacred places.

3 Nephi 12:38–42

In the old law was the notion of an eye for an eye and a tooth for a tooth (Exodus 21:24; Leviticus 24:20). The higher law of the gospel of Jesus Christ requires forbearance in striking back when we are harmed or deprived in any way. "Ye shall not resist evil" is an injunction against setting ourselves against the evil one; in other words, we are not to return evil for evil but submit, with forbearance and not vengeance, to any injustice against us. This is not *passive* submission to injury but *pacific,* or meek, response to it.

Joseph Smith's translation of Luke 6:29–30 gives the proper sense of the teaching: "Unto him who smiteth thee on the cheek, offer also the other; *or, in other words, it is better to offer the other, than to revile again. . . . For it is better that thou suffer thine enemy to take these things, than to contend with him.*" Go the extra mile to be "submissive, meek, humble, patient, full of love" (Mosiah 3:19). Being willing to live the gospel makes us willing to go beyond what the law requires.

"The Lord requires sacrifice, meaning something above and beyond the minimum. The Master spoke of the 'second mile' and told us to go there. . . . Why? Because He wants to bless us. So He put all the blessings in the second mile."[43]

3 Nephi 12:43–45

Included in the old law as understood by some of the ancients was the notion that we could love our friends but hate our enemies (compare 4 Nephi 1:39). The group known as Essenes, for example, who lived during Jesus' mortal life in Jerusalem and in Qumran near the Dead Sea, openly taught as a fundamental tenet of their brand of Judaism that one should love the children of light but hate the children of darkness.[44] But the higher law of the gospel of Jesus Christ teaches us a better way to respond to opposition and persecution: "Love your enemies, bless them that curse you, do good to them that hate you, and pray for them who despitefully use you and persecute you."

Heavenly Father and the Savior are our example. An essential attribute of God is love. And we have a mortal example: Joseph Smith, who said: "I have no enemies but for the truth's sake. I have no desire but to do all men good. I feel to pray for all men."[45]

Thus Jesus commands his audience to love their enemies, bless those who hurl curses at them, and pray for those who despitefully use them. The reason? "That ye may be the

children of your Father who is in heaven." After all, God the
Father is kind and loving toward all his children, even those
who forsake or ignore him. He is patient and long-suffering.
"He maketh his sun to rise on the evil and on the good." It
is no accident that Jesus concludes this section of his great
sermon by commanding his listeners to be perfect, as their
Father in Heaven and he are perfect. Loving kindness and
tolerant restraint are hallmarks of God's perfection.

3 Nephi 12:46–47

The Lord gave six specific examples of how things in old
time, under the law, were fulfilled in him. The old things are
now "done away" by adding a higher, more excellent standard of expectation among God's holy ones or Saints. He
goes on to say that he expects perfection in his true disciples.

3 Nephi 12:48

President Hugh B. Brown said, "We take seriously and
literally the injunction of the Savior to be perfect."[46] In fact,
the Old Testament also teaches that we should be perfect
(Deuteronomy 18:13). But what is the perfection that God
expects of us here on the earth? We often think perfection
is defined as "flawless" or "sinless." But there has been only
One in the history of this world who was in every way flawless
and sinless. Yet the scriptures say that "Noah was a just man
and perfect" (Genesis 6:9); Job was "perfect and upright"
(Job 1:1); and Seth was "a perfect man" (D&C 107:43).

Apparently the scriptural definition of perfection is different from our usual one. In the Bible three Hebrew
words and two Greek words are translated into King James
English as "perfect." They are *shalem* (1 Kings 8:61; 15:14;
2 Kings 20:3), *tam* (Job 1:1), *tammim* (Genesis 6:9; 17:1;
Deuteronomy 18:13), *teleios* (Matthew 5:48; 19:21; Ephesians
4:13; Colossians 4:12; James 3:2), and *artios* (2 Timothy
3:17). None of these five words means "flawless" or "sinless." They are otherwise rendered as "whole," "upright,"

"undefiled," "just," or "complete." A person who is whole, complete, upright, and so forth, is one who, upon sinning, as all mortals do, immediately and thoroughly repents and is again reconciled to God and becomes whole, complete, and upright once more. It is an ongoing process of repenting and improving throughout this life.

Elder Bruce R. McConkie explained: "We don't need to get a complex or get a feeling that you have to be perfect to be saved. You don't. There's only been one perfect person, and that's the Lord Jesus, but in order to be saved in the Kingdom of God and in order to pass the test of mortality, what you have to do is get on the straight and narrow path— thus charting a course leading to eternal life—and then, being on that path, pass out of this life in full fellowship. . . . If you're on that path and pressing forward, and you die, you'll never get off the path. There is no such thing as falling off the straight and narrow path in the life to come, and the reason is that this life is the time that is given to men to prepare for eternity. . . .

"You don't have to live a life that's truer than true. You don't have to have an excessive zeal that becomes fanatical and becomes unbalancing. What you have to do is stay in the mainstream of the Church and live as upright and decent people live in the Church—keeping the commandments, paying your tithing, serving in the organizations of the Church, loving the Lord, staying on the straight and narrow path. If you're on that path when death comes—because this is the time and the day appointed, this the probationary estate— you'll never fall off from it, and, for all practical purposes, your calling and election is made sure."[47]

As this verse indicates, the Father and the Son are our supreme examples of the perfection that we eventually and ultimately want to achieve. By becoming one with our Savior (that's the meaning of the word *at-one-ment*) we may eventually become perfect in him. Note the words of Moroni: "Come unto Christ, and be perfected in him, and deny yourselves of all ungodliness . . . that by his grace ye may be perfect in Christ" (Moroni 10:32).

3 Nephi 13:1–4

Jesus spent a good deal of the next part of his sermon teaching about the nature of our Father in heaven by discussing private daily devotions. Do not, he said, make a public show of doing that which is better done in private—almsgiving, welfare relief, fasting, and personal prayer—for "thy Father who seeth in secret, himself shall reward thee openly."

A central message of several teachings in 3 Nephi 13 is to be careful not to do good things just *to be seen of men*. Satan always sponsors his own imitation of righteous principles; for example, we should seek glory but not the glory of men. Our immediate and ultimate objective is to have our eye single to the glory of God. We should "do [our] alms," all our righteous acts, secretly and quietly.

Latter-day Saints are some of the most generous people in the world; they give a high percentage of their time, labor, and resources to do the work of God and bless the lives of others. It is part of the gospel of Jesus Christ to share, but we should do so without fanfare and without seeking public recognition.

3 Nephi 13:5–8

As with almsgiving, so with praying. No ostentation. If we pray in order to parade our piety, we are revealing our lack of the same. Those who "sound a trumpet" (3 Nephi 13:2) or give alms to be seen of men are being hypocritical.

As with other religious acts, prayer should be done privately and quietly. "Enter into thy closet" (compare Alma 33:7) may indeed mean our bedrooms and their closets, or— as the New Testament Greek term connotes—our "places of privacy," whether in our houses, our offices, or our "wilderness" (Alma 34:26).

We are warned against "vain repetitions." There is

nothing wrong with repetition itself. In fact, God teaches us more often than not through repetition. He continually teaches and reteaches, iterates and reiterates, all through the scriptures. And in the holiest classroom on earth, in the house of God, the main method used is repetition. "Vain" repetition is what we are encouraged to avoid.

Are Latter-day Saints guilty of using vain repetitions? Consider the following standard clichés used in Latter-day Saints' prayers:

"We're thankful for this day."

"We're thankful for the building we have to meet in."

"We're grateful for all our many blessings."

"Bless those who aren't here this week that they'll be here next week."

"Bless the sick and afflicted."

"Bless us that no harm or accident will befall us."

"Bless us with all the blessings we stand in need of."

"Bless the missionaries that they'll be guided to the honest in heart."

"Bless us that we'll strive to incorporate these things into our daily lives."

"Take us all home in peace and safety."

Is there anything inherently wrong with any of these phrases? Absolutely not, *as long as voicing them is sincere, genuine, and heartfelt.* If we will, we can pray, even a long prayer, without multiplying words (3 Nephi 19:24). Heavenly Father knows what we are grateful for and what we need before we ever kneel down. He does not necessarily need to hear it, but we need to say it. We need to express ourselves to him verbally—frequently and regularly.

One day in the Holy Land, Brother Ogden learned an unforgettable lesson about sincere prayer. When his daughter Sara was four years old, he took her on an overnight campout and fishing trip with the Jerusalem Branch Boy Scouts to the northeastern corner of the Sea of Galilee, near the site of ancient Bethsaida, where the Jordan River enters the lake and which from 1948 to 1967 was the border between Israel and Syria. While the boys were out fishing, pulling in some big catfish and maybe a St. Peter's fish or two, Sara and her father went for a walk about a quarter of a mile west from the camp to find the precise place where the Jordan River flows into the lake.

After some time spent fighting their way through the thick jungle of reeds and tangled undergrowth, knowing that they must be very close to the river, they found it simply impossible to move forward. They were stuck in the middle of the tall thickets of reeds, about eight to ten feet high, unable to see in any direction and hardly able to move.

Brother Ogden was carrying Sara on his shoulders and had by then grown tired, out of energy, and perplexed. Sara suggested, "Daddy, why don't we pray?"

They folded their arms and prayed, asking Heavenly Father to help them find their way safely out of the thick tangle of vegetation.

They forged on in the general direction of the camp until they came to a barbed-wire fence. Having maneuvered their way over the fence, they looked back. Hanging on the fence was the international triangular sign for a minefield. *They had just made their way through a minefield!*

Needless to say, Brother Ogden was thankful for a daughter who suggested they pray and to a Father in Heaven who answered their prayer.

The scriptures say this world is a field. These days it is a minefield. How do we avoid stepping in the wrong places, risking getting tangled up in the world's thick undergrowth or blown to bits by hidden weapons? We make sure we are staying morally clean, avoiding improper reading material and films, studying the scriptures, worshipping in the temple, fasting, keeping the Sabbath Day holy, serving others, and especially praying—frequently and regularly. If we are not doing all those things, we can be sure that we will be stepping into dangerous situations. If we are doing all those things, then we will be "worthy to stand."

3 Nephi 13:9–13

Jesus gave an example of how to pray to the Father: "after this manner," not that these exact words should be repeatedly uttered. Verse 10 omits one phrase contained in the biblical text (Matthew 6:10), "Thy kingdom come," likely because it had come. One phrase in verse 12 is curious: "Lead us not into temptation." God does not, of course, lead anyone into temptation, but the sense may be "Don't bring us into the *control* or *power* of temptation" greater than we can bear. That is what the Hebrew rendering of the New Testament phrase means.

3 Nephi 13:14–15

Can we expect Heavenly Father to forgive us of all our sins if we refuse to forgive others? To be forgiven, we must forgive (Mosiah 26:31; D&C 64:8–10). The Prophet Joseph Smith showed us how a mortal can do it. He once remarked that "all was well between him and the heavens; that he had no enmity against any one; and as the prayer of Jesus, or his pattern, so prayed Joseph—'Father, forgive me my trespasses as I forgive those who trespass against me' [see Matthew 6:12, 14], for I freely forgive all men. If we would secure and cultivate the love of others, we must love others, even our enemies as well as friends."[48]

A most poignant example of this kind of forgiving power in modern times is the experience of Corrie ten Boom during and after World War II.

"In modern history perhaps no more atrocious crime has been committed than the Holocaust, the systematic murder of millions of Jews, political prisoners, handicapped persons, and others by Hitler's Nazi regime. Corrie ten Boom, a Christian political prisoner, survived the concentration camp at Ravensbruck, but her beloved sister, Betsie, did not. After the war Corrie traveled the world preaching sermons of reconciliation, peace, and forgiveness. Then it happened. She was called upon to practice what she preached. She records in her autobiography, *The Hiding Place,* the defining moment of her Christian discipleship:

"'It was at a church service in Munich that I saw him, the former S.S. man who had stood guard at the shower room door in the processing center at Ravensbruck. He was the first of our actual jailers that I had seen since that time. And suddenly it was all there—the roomful of mocking men, the heaps of clothing, Betsie's pain-blanched face.

"'He came up to me as the church was emptying, beaming and bowing. "How grateful I am for your message, Fraulein," he said. "To think that, as you say, He has washed my sins away!"

"'His hand was thrust out to shake mine. And I, who had preached so often . . . the need to forgive, kept my hand at my side. Even as the angry, vengeful thoughts boiled through me, I saw the sin of them. Jesus Christ had died for this man; was I going to ask for more? Lord Jesus, I prayed, forgive me and help me to forgive him.

"'I tried to smile. I struggled to raise my hand. I could not. I felt nothing, not the slightest spark of warmth or charity. And so again I breathed a silent prayer. Jesus, I cannot forgive him. Give me Your forgiveness.

"'As I took his hand the most incredible thing happened. From my shoulder along my arm and through my hand a current seemed to pass from me to him, while into my heart sprang a love for this stranger that almost overwhelmed me.

"'And so I discovered that it is not on our own forgiveness any more than on our goodness that the world's healing hinges, but on His. When He tells us to love our enemies, He gives, along with the command, the love itself' (Corrie ten Boom, with John and Elizabeth Sherrill, *The Hiding Place* [New York: Bantam Books, 1971], p. 238)."[49]

3 Nephi 13:16–18

As with prayer, so with fasting. No ostentation. If we do it to parade our piety, we are revealing our lack of the same. As with other religious acts, fasting should be done privately and quietly. By our sad, distorted facial expressions, we should not suggest, "Oh, look, world, I've fasted now for twenty-*five* hours!" The Lord actually encourages us to "appear not unto men to fast." Quiet devotion brings open blessings.

Here are some suggestions for fasting. Plan and prepare a schedule. Have a particular purpose. Start the fast with a private prayer. Keep the Spirit by using Saturday evening as part of the fasting period, and fast a full twenty-four hours, refraining from all food and also drink, if possible. Plan specific activities: Study the scriptures, write in a journal, and attend church meetings; maybe even participate in a *family* testimony meeting. Pay a generous fast offering. Set aside some time to ponder and meditate. Consider Moroni 7 or 10, or Mosiah 4, or Isaiah 53, or some other particularly powerful chapter of scripture. And finally, end the fast with a private prayer.

The combination of fasting and praying can cause humble followers of the Savior to "wax stronger and stronger in their humility, and firmer and firmer in the faith of Christ, unto the filling their souls with joy and consolation, yea, even to the purifying and the sanctification of their hearts, which sanctification cometh because of their yielding their hearts unto God" (Helaman 3:35).

3 Nephi 13:19–21

Whatever we consider our "treasure," that is where our hearts will be. That is where our thoughts and affections will be placed. The Savior warns: Be careful about accumulating earthly treasures; they are all transitory and apt to be stolen. You will take none of them with you when you depart from this earth (Psalm 49:16–17; 1 Timothy 6:7; Alma 39:14). But do lay up treasure in heaven. Those are treasures that will endure forever.

3 Nephi 13:22–23

The eye is the light of the body and the window to the soul. If our eye is single (and Joseph Smith later added to the phrase "single *to the glory of God*"; Matthew 6:22, footnote *b*, from JST, Matthew 6:22; see also D&C 4:5), that is, if we are dedicated to our Savior's glorious cause, then our whole body will be full of light (D&C 88:67). He is our light, so our whole life can be filled with his influence, and no darkness will persist in us. There is no life without Light.

3 Nephi 13:24

Mammon is an Aramaic term referring to worldly riches or wealth. It is true that we cannot have one foot in the kingdom and one foot still in the world. It is not possible to walk that way. No man can serve two masters. Service to God and the pursuit of worldly wealth are mutually exclusive enterprises for those called to the holy apostleship or any other full-time Church service. *La'avod* in Hebrew means "to serve"; it also means to work and to worship. It is certainly not possible to serve or worship two opposite lords at the same time. We must choose, just as the original Twelve and Seventy had to choose. We either prove ourselves a true child of God or we become a child of the devil (Alma 5:41). We must hold to the one, the Holy One, only.

3 Nephi 13:25–34

Jesus changed the focus of his instruction, as well as his audience, for the concluding section of his great sermon (3 Nephi 13:25–14:27). He turned his attention to the Twelve and other leaders whose calling was to go out and teach and testify—and by extension today to all authorities and missionaries, anyone in full-time service to the kingdom. "Take no thought for" means "don't worry about" or "don't be overly anxious about." Those in full-time service to the Lord must not be burdened with the daily cares of food, drink, and clothing (compare Alma 31:37–38). Others can help provide for their temporal needs so they can dedicate themselves completely to his work, without distractions.

Jesus' illustrations are refreshing. Look at the birds and the flowers, how the God of heaven cares for their needs (compare D&C 84:81–82). Notice, he said, the fowls of the air; they do not plant, cultivate, and harvest the fields; they do not store up great quantities of supplies in barns; but God takes care of them. The lesson is one of faith and trust. Jesus encouraged his disciples to divest themselves of constant pre-occupation with worldly survival, though he did not intend for people to abandon their mortal labors and wait for God to provide.

Consider the example of a young, newly married couple. The world suggests that before they start bringing babies into the world, they should wait until they have a house and a good, stable, full-time job, the car paid for, and all the clothes and amenities that the baby will need upon arrival and for the first months of his or her life. The Lord says that even though they don't have everything in place, they are not yet finan-cially secure—and, in fact, are still struggling to finish school and working full time—and yes, the schedule is exhausting, still, they should not put off bringing children into the world. If we are faithful and do what we can, then we can have con-fidence that God will take care of us. God wants his children to be submissive and dependent, to look to him and live. We work hard, do all we can, and God provides.

Can any of us add, just by thinking about it, even one cubit (about eighteen inches) to our height? A foot and a half is a significant addition to one's height, and it takes time. The answer must be no. We are quite dependent on God for our growth—but consider the lilies of the field; they grow with-out thinking about it.

"Consider the lilies of the field how they grow." Lilies are flowers that grow from a bulb, like iris, crocus, hyacinth, and tulip. By saying that the once-wise king in all his glory was not arrayed like one of the lilies, we are to understand that the flush of colorful spring flowers scattered over all the hills, valleys, and plains would produce in the eyes of the beholder genuine admiration and awe for the elegant beauty of one of God's simple creations. If God cares for the smallest works of his hands, surely he will care for and provide for humankind, his crowning creation.

God's own children are of greater value than all the flora and fauna; surely he will care for our needs, too. Heavenly Father knows all our needs; he can provide (D&C 84:83). One of his divine efforts is "providence" for his children (Jacob 2:13; D&C 78:14; Joseph Smith–History 1:75).

Our priority must be to seek "first the kingdom of God and his righteousness, and all these things shall be added unto you." Joseph Smith, as was his prerogative as a prophet, later made significant additions to the teachings of verse 33: "*Wherefore, seek not the things of this world,* but seek ye first *to build up* the kingdom of God, *and to establish* his righteousness" (Matthew 6:33, footnote *a*, from JST, Matthew 6:38; emphasis added). "Do many things of [your] own free will, and bring to pass much righteousness" and you shall "in nowise lose [your] reward" (D&C 58:27–28).

Seek first the kingdom of God. He is always first; our fellowman is second; we are third. We get in trouble spiritually when we put ourselves in first place. God and his work and glory must always be our number one priority.

President Ezra Taft Benson said:

"Why did God put the first commandment first? Because He knew that if we truly loved Him we would want to keep all of His other commandments. . . .

"We must put God in the forefront of everything else in our lives. . . .

" . . . Our love of the Lord will govern the claims for our

affection, the demands on our time, the interests we pursue, and the order of our priorities.

"We should put God ahead of *everyone else* in our lives."⁵⁰

"Take therefore no thought for the morrow"—again, the idea is "don't worry about" or "don't be overly anxious about" the things of tomorrow. "Let the morrow take thought for the things of itself" (D&C 84:84). There is enough to be concerned about each day—one day at a time—without piling on all future concerns. That does not negate, however, the need to prepare for the future, but that is what we do when we live fully and properly each day. Daily, righteous living quietly and automatically provides for the morrow.

3 Nephi 14:1–5

The Lord's people are commanded not to judge others. The danger in judging others is that we are never in possession of all the facts. We can never really know what is happening in others' lives, in their homes, with their families or friends. Tragic, stressful, or anxiety-producing events may bring out negative, evil, or hateful reactions and words. If we knew and understood the background causes of such undesirable behavior or unkind words, we might feel more compassion towards a person who perpetrated or spoke such things.

What blessings, joy, and peace come as we avoid unrighteously judging others. If we do misjudge others, we can repent. If others misjudge us, we can forgive.

A danger in judging others is that our inclination is to judge them by their *actions*, whereas we would like to be judged by our *intentions*. It is wise to leave judgment to the great Judge of us all. He is in possession of all the facts and the intentions, and he is just and merciful.

In one sense we should be constantly judging what is good for us and what is not. We must be careful to judge what to read and what not to read, what to watch on TV and in movie theaters and what not to watch, what music we should listen to and what would be damaging to our spiritual sensitivities, what we should wear and what we should not wear, what we should eat or drink and what we should not eat or drink, and what we should say and what we should avoid saying.

Knowing that we should and must judge in some ways, the Lord has clarified the command: "Judge not *unrighteously, that ye be not judged: but judge righteous judgment*" (Matthew 7:1, footnote *a*, from JST, Matthew 7:1–2; emphasis added). He has given us definitive guidelines on how to judge righteously. We may know with a perfect knowledge whether something is good for us or bad for us, as Moroni 7:15–17 teaches us (see commentary at Moroni 7:15–17).

An incentive to our judging righteously and compassionately is the warning that whatever measure of judgment we use on someone else, that same measure of judgment will be used on us (see also Alma 41:14–15; Mormon 8:19–20; Moroni 7:18; D&C 1:10).

A "mote" is a tiny splinter; a "beam" is a large board used in construction. We are quick to notice the tiny weaknesses and flaws in others and yet slow to recognize large debilities in ourselves.

This message is vividly rendered in the hymn "Let Each Man Learn to Know Himself":

> *Let each man learn to know himself;*
> *To gain that knowledge let him labor,*
> *Improve those failings in himself*
> *Which he condemns so in his neighbor.*
> *How lenient our own faults we view,*
> *And conscience' voice adeptly smother,*
> *Yet, oh, how harshly we review*
> *The self-same failings in another!*
>
> *And if you meet an erring one*
> *Whose deeds are blamable and thoughtless,*

Consider, ere you cast the stone,
If you yourself are pure and faultless.
Oh, list to that small voice within,
Whose whisperings oft make men confounded,
And trumpet not another's sin;
You'd blush deep if your own were sounded.

And in self-judgment if you find
Your deeds to others' are superior,
To you has Providence been kind,
As you should be to those inferior.
Example sheds a genial ray
Of light which men are apt to borrow,
So first improve yourself today
And then improve your friends tomorrow.[51]

3 Nephi 14:6

"Give not that which is holy unto the dogs" is a behest that was given in a parallelism; the second phrase is "neither cast ye your pearls before swine." The parallel clearly defines ancient Israelites' regard for the dog. Unlike in modern Western society, the dog in Israelite culture was not "man's best friend" but an ill-respected scavenger. Jesus said in the New Testament record, "It is not meet to take the children's bread, and to cast it to dogs" (Matthew 15:26), a hyperbolic statement of the priority of gospel dissemination and of the care with which the mysteries of the kingdom should be reserved for the spiritually attuned. Figuratively, then, dogs represent unworthy persons, or, as in another case, persons who are not prepared for sacred things (Matthew 15:21–28).

The delicate structure of pearls is implied in Jesus' warning not to cast pearls before swine, since, unlike other gems, pearls are relatively soft, and trampling on them could destroy them. Our most precious and sacred gems of the gospel must be shared only with those who are prepared to receive them. The Lord later added another dimension to this admonition:

"And the mysteries of the kingdom [for example, sacred teachings, covenants, and ordinances of the temple] ye shall keep within yourselves; for it is not meet to give that which is holy unto the dogs. . . . for the world cannot receive that which ye, yourselves, are not able to bear; wherefore ye shall not give your pearls unto them" (JST, Matthew 7:10–11, in Bible appendix; compare D&C 41:6).

3 Nephi 14:7–12

Here is one of the most powerful promises ever given to humankind and the most often repeated. There are conditions to this promise, of course. We must ask in faith (James 1:6), we must seek persistently (Luke 11:5–10; 18:1–5), and we must knock with rigor. We must also ask, seek, and knock obediently and not improperly ("ask not amiss"; 2 Nephi 4:35; Helaman 10:5), else we have no promise from the great Benefactor (D&C 82:10). Elder Richard G. Scott taught: "His invitation, 'Ask, and ye shall receive' (3 Ne. 27:29) does not assure that you will get what you *want*. It does guarantee that, if worthy, you will get what you *need,* as judged by a Father that loves you perfectly."[52]

In verse 12 the law and the prophets are summarized in one idea, known widely as the "golden rule": whatever we would like people to do to us, we do that to them. Elder Marvin J. Ashton said, "The best and most clear indicator that we are progressing spiritually and coming unto Christ is the way we treat other people."[53]

3 Nephi 14:13–14

Baptism is not the *door* to our heavenly mansion but the *gate* to the path that leads to the mansion. Relatively few are genuinely interested in entering the gate and walking that path (1 Nephi 14:12; 2 Nephi 31:17–20; 3 Nephi 27:33; D&C 132:25).

The words *strait* and *narrow* mean about the same thing:

constricted, tight. The juxtaposition of synonyms is a familiar ancient literary technique.[54]

A modern use of the word *strait* is the Strait of Magellan (in Patagonia, at the southern tip of South America), which connects the Pacific and Atlantic Oceans. It is not a straight line between two points—one cannot see one ocean from the other. So with us: we cannot see the other side (of heaven), but if we persevere in the strait path, we will arrive there.

Note the scriptural difference between "strait" and "straight"; they are two different words. Our path is described as "strait"; the Lord's path is "straight" (Alma 7:9; 37:12; D&C 3:2). Jesus Christ is the only one who never had to make course corrections. Our Savior's paths are always straight because "he cannot walk in crooked paths; neither doth he vary from that which he hath said; neither hath he a shadow of turning from the right to the left, or from that which is right to that which is wrong" (Alma 7:20).

3 Nephi 14:15–20

Jesus warned his listeners to beware of false prophets who are among the sheep (the members of the Church), but they are dangerous wolves in disguise. How can we recognize them? "Ye shall know them by their fruits" (compare Moroni 7:5). The words and works of men and women are compared to fruit, good works being good fruit, and evil works, bad fruit. Whether in the world of plant life or human life, God wants good produce, good fruit.

There grew in scriptural lands a formidable abundance of thorns and thistles, and they could not escape the figurative eye of the prophets and the Savior. Thorns and thistles served only to afflict, distract, and annoy. They never symbolized anything good or positive.

Trees, because of their essential role in providing food, material for buildings, shelter, occupational tools and implements, and shade, and for preventing deterioration of the landscape, enjoyed respect and near reverence from the inhabitants of scriptural lands. Trees were also among the favorite objects of imagery and symbolism. Trees usually represent people.

From Jesus and his disciples came many examples of trees as object lessons. Bad trees produce ill will, negativism, criticism, accusation, cynicism, and all kinds of destructive thinking and sinful behavior. Good trees produce good fruit. Joseph Smith was a good tree. The Book of Mormon is a good tree. The Church of Jesus Christ of Latter-day Saints is a good tree. Jesus Christ himself is the best tree of all—the Tree of Life. We can know the trees; that is, we can know the hearts and souls of people perfectly by what comes out of their minds and mouths. In a sense, we seldom speak or act truly impulsively; we say and do what we are.

3 Nephi 14:21–23

President John Taylor declared: "'We are told that "Many will say to me in that day, Lord, Lord, have we not prophesied in Thy name and in Thy name have we cast out devils, and in Thy name done many wonderful works?" Yet to all such he will say; "Depart from me, ye that work iniquity." You say that means the outsiders? No, it does not. Do they do many wonderful works in the name of Jesus? No; if they do anything it is done in the name of themselves or of the devil. Sometimes they will do things in the name of God; but it is simply an act of blasphemy. This means you, Latter-day Saints, who heal the sick, cast out devils and do many wonderful things in the name of Jesus. And yet how many we see among this people of this class, that become careless, and treat lightly the ordinances of God's house and the Priesthood of the Son of God; yet they think they are going by and by, to slide into the kingdom of God; but I tell you unless they are righteous and keep their covenants they will never go there. Hear it, ye Latter-day Saints!'"[55]

To live eternally with our Father in Heaven, we must

learn his will and do it. We must obey the Father and know the Son, too. Joseph Smith made an interesting change in the concept expressed in verse 23, "I never knew you" (compare Mosiah 26:27). He reversed the pronouns to read: "Ye never knew me" (JST, Matthew 7:33). In essence, the Savior was saying that his listeners knew that he was born in Bethlehem, that he carried on his ministry around the Sea of Galilee, chose twelve apostles, died and was resurrected, visited and taught his disciples in the ancient Americas, and even that he would come in this last dispensation to restore his gospel and his Church to the earth—but his listeners *did not really know him.* They did not pay the price to become personally acquainted with him to the point that they understood well his plan and purposes and were willing to sacrifice anything to accomplish his will.

3 Nephi 14:24–27

The parable that concludes Jesus' great sermon is a classic illustration from nature. Whoever hears the words of life and obeys them is like a wise man who built his house (his life) upon a rock. And how do we define "rock" in this case? It is the Lord Jesus Christ. He is the Rock of our salvation, the Stone of Israel. The image of rock or stone is commonly used in scripture to denote something firm, solid, and immovable. The Savior is our Rock, a sure foundation whereon if we build, we cannot fall.

"And now . . . remember, remember that it is upon the rock of our Redeemer, who is Christ, the Son of God, that ye must build your foundation; that when the devil shall send forth his mighty winds, yea, his shafts in the whirlwind, yea, when all his hail and his mighty storm shall beat upon you, it shall have no power over you to drag you down to the gulf of misery and endless wo, because of the rock upon which ye are built, which is a sure foundation, a foundation whereon if men build they cannot fall" (Helaman 5:12; see also 2 Nephi 28:28).

That is wonderful wording: if we found our lives on the Rock, they *cannot* collapse. If our lives are founded solidly on the Redeemer, when the mighty winds, whirlwind, hail, and storms—the temptations of life—beat down upon us, our lives cannot fall apart.

The rains come down from above, the floods come up from below, the winds blow from the sides; that is the way temptations come (D&C 90:5). They come at us from above, from below, and from all sides, trying to weaken and destroy our houses (our lives), but again, the promise is sure: if our lives are centered in, or founded on, the Savior Jesus Christ, they *cannot* fall apart.

President Howard W. Hunter explained this teaching: "The words of the Master regarding the house without a foundation say to me that a man cannot have a shallow and reckless notion that he is sufficient to himself and can build his own life on any basis that happens to be easy and agreeable. As long as the weather is fair, his foolishness may not be evident; but one day there will come the floods, the muddy waters of some sudden passion, the rushing current of unforeseen temptation. If his character has no sure foundation in more than just lip service, his whole moral structure may collapse."[56]

It seems significant that Nephi's report of this sermon does not end in the same way as Matthew's does. In Matthew's version we read, "And it came to pass, when Jesus had ended these sayings, the people were astonished at his doctrine: For he taught them as one having authority, and not as the scribes" (Matthew 7:28–29). The Nephites had no real encounter with the scribal or rabbinic method of teaching, which was based on citing previous rabbinic authorities. Therefore, Jesus does not mention that rabbinic tradition here.

3 Nephi 15:1–10

When he had concluded his instruction, Jesus scanned the crowd with his all-seeing and penetrating eye, told them they had received the same teachings as his Old World disciples, and reminded them of the holy promise for obedience— "him will I raise up at the last day." Perceptively, like all great teachers, he noted individual questions, which centered on the religious system that had been in operation for the last several centuries.

The old law that all the branches of the house of Israel had been living, the law given to Moses centuries earlier by this same Person—known as Jehovah back then but called Jesus in mortality—was now fulfilled, completed, ended (also 3 Nephi 9:16–17). The elaborate system of performances and ordinances, of types, signs, and shadows of his coming, was now fulfilled when he actually came. He was teaching them a higher law, as illustrated in the Sermon at the Temple. The law of Moses could not provide salvation; only the atonement, or redemption, of Jesus Christ can save and exalt (Mosiah 13:27–32).

The Savior makes a distinction between the law and the covenant. The law given to Moses was fulfilled and ended, but the great covenant was still in force and indeed always would be. It is an everlasting covenant, given originally to Adam and Eve and perpetuated by righteous patriarchs and prophets through all generations. The covenant, always part of the gospel of Jesus Christ, was on the earth from the beginning, with Adam and Eve.[57] It was renewed with Enoch (Genesis 6:18, footnote *a*, from JST, Genesis 8:23; 9:9, footnote *a*, from JST, Genesis 9:15; 9:11, footnote *c*, from JST, Genesis 9:17; JST, Genesis 9:21–24, in Bible appendix; Moses 7:51–69; 8:2), Noah (Genesis 6:18; 9:9), and Abraham (Abraham 2:9–11). It was included in the law given to Moses, but unlike the ritual laws given through Moses, the covenant was not later discontinued. The covenant consisted of all the commandments plus the promises and responsibilities of a covenant people.

3 Nephi 15:12–13

One responsibility of a covenant people is to be a light to other people (3 Nephi 12:14–16; Isaiah 42:6), and one of the blessings of the covenant is a land inheritance, the right to claim property for an eternal possession. The Americas, the land of Zion, is the Father's possession to give to others as he sees fit. The scattering and gathering of Israel to their lands of inheritance is the work of the Father (3 Nephi 20:10).

3 Nephi 15:14–24

The Jews in the Old World did not know of Israelites on the American continent because God the Father commanded his Son, the Good Shepherd, that they should not know, owing to their obstinacy and unbelief. The Good Shepherd has many sheep. His sheep in ancient Israel, the Jewish nation, failed to understand what he taught them concerning other sheep (as recorded in John 10:16). Their unbelieving attitude kept them from receiving further instructions. When he mentioned other sheep who should hear his voice, some of them thought he was referring to the Gentiles (non-Jews in the Mediterranean world). But no, those Gentiles would not hear his voice directly, as did the Nephites; rather, he was manifested to them through the ministration of the Holy Ghost and the apostles. How that happened can be studied in the New Testament books of Acts through Revelation.

The pattern of the Savior teaching only certain groups in person was followed in the spirit world immediately after his death. He did not visit the wicked, ungodly, unrepentant, or rebellious who rejected the truth. Rather, he organized and commissioned a missionary force among the righteous to go forth among the unrighteous. This is certainly a manifestation of God's great justice (D&C 138:20, 29–34).

The "other sheep" referred to in these verses and the first verses of chapter 16 are the Nephites, who were Israelites guided by the hand of God to the Western Hemisphere, as well as other groups of Israelites among the "lost tribes" of Israel. The revelations—ancient and modern—do not give us much information regarding the whereabouts of these "other sheep," nor details about exactly who they are. We patiently await additional instructions on the subject. No doubt God has had various groups of righteous "sheep" on this planet and on many other worlds.

In fact, toward the end of the first day of his visit, the Savior commanded his New World audience to go to their homes and ponder the things he had said while he went to show himself "unto the lost tribes of Israel, for they are not lost unto the Father, for he knoweth whither he hath taken them" (3 Nephi 17:3–4).

3 Nephi 16

The term *Gentiles* has a variety of meanings, each occurrence depending on the context. For instance, in the Old Testament *Israel* represented God's covenant people and *Gentiles* represented the unbelieving neighbors outside the covenant. *Israel* has a number of other uses also: it can refer to the man Jacob, whose name was changed to Israel, and it can refer to the direct, lineal descendants of that prophet-patriarch. In addition it can refer to the land inheritance of the covenant people, the Holy Land, which in ancient times as well as modern times adopted the title *Israel*.

Gentiles in the Book of Mormon may refer to those who belong to another branch of the house of Israel, distant in time and place from the ancient peoples of the Book of Mormon; to those who come (even Israelites) from Gentile nations; or, to all those who live without the gospel. It can also be a cultural designation for Jacob's descendants who live in non-Israelite cultural settings. See further definition of *Gentiles* in the commentary at 1 Nephi 10:11.

At this point it may be helpful to define some other terms: *Hebrews, Israelites,* and *Jews.* It is important to understand the distinction. For example, all Israelites are Hebrews, but not all Hebrews are Israelites; all Jews are Israelites, but not all Israelites are Jews:

Hebrews are those who descend from the great father of nations, Abraham. Israelites are one important branch of his posterity, but there were others: Ishmaelites, from Abraham and Hagar and Ishmael's twelve sons; Midianites, from the son of Abraham and Keturah, his later wife, plus the descendants of other sons of that later wife. Therefore, some of those other sons' descendants, today known as Arabs, could also be designated as among the Hebrew peoples. Thus, all Israelites, the covenant branch of Abraham, are Hebrews, but not all Hebrews are Israelites.

Israelites are those who descend from the man Israel, or Jacob, and his twelve sons. The scriptural records particularly follow the posterity of two of those sons, Judah and Joseph, whose descendants inherited promised lands in the Old World and in the New World. Descendants of Judah were known as Jews, though some from other tribes were in later centuries included in the national use of the term. In the final centuries of the Old Testament record and in New Testament times, descendants of any of the tribes of Israel then living in the land of Israel, or the land of Judah, were generically known as *Jews*.

Jews are those who—strictly speaking—are literal descendants of Judah, but in later times those descended from such tribes as Ephraim and Manasseh (as Lehi, early prophet in the Book of Mormon record) and Levi (as Zacharias and John the Baptist of that sacerdotal lineage) were also known generically as Jews. Thus, all Jews were Israelites, but not all Israelites—by strict definition—were Jews. It is important to recognize that the Book of Mormon does sometimes refer to the entire house of Israel as "Jews."

3 Nephi 16:5–16

The Savior's prophecy of the gathering of scattered Israel speaks of both Jews and Lamanites. Unbelieving Gentiles scattered the Lamanites upon the face of "this land," the Americas, and caused them to be smitten, slain, and hated (compare Helaman 15:12). But in the latter days, when the Gentiles shall sin against the Savior's gospel, become lifted up in pride above all other nations, and filled with all kinds of iniquity, then the Lord will remember his covenant and promises to Israel, including the Lamanites, and show them that the Gentiles shall have no more power over them. This warning is aimed directly at America. However, the Lord still promises the blessings of the covenant to the Gentiles if they repent and accept the gospel.

3 Nephi 16:17–20

These verses from the writings of Isaiah are quoted four times in the Book of Mormon. Watchmen are those who publish the good tidings—the gospel of Jesus Christ. They are the prophets and all servants of the Lord who are called to teach, testify, and bring people to Christ.

Two Jerusalems are spoken of: the first is the famous Old Jerusalem in the Holy Land and the second is the New Jerusalem, also called Zion. New Jerusalem, or Zion, will be built in Independence, Jackson County, Missouri. Joseph Smith wrote:

"I received, by a heavenly vision, a commandment in June [1831], to take my journey to the western boundaries of the State of Missouri, and there designate the very spot which was to be the central place for the commencement of the gathering together of those who embrace the fullness of the everlasting Gospel. Accordingly I undertook the journey, with certain ones of my brethren, and after a long and tedious journey, suffering many privations and hardships, arrived in Jackson County, Missouri, and after viewing the country, seeking diligently at the hand of God, He manifested Himself unto us, and designated, to me and others, the very spot upon which he designed to commence the work of the gathering, and the upbuilding of an 'holy city,' which should be called Zion—Zion, because it is a place of righteousness, and all who build thereon are to worship the true and living God, and all believe in one doctrine, even the doctrine of our Lord and Savior Jesus Christ. 'Thy watchmen shall lift up the voice; with the voice together shall they sing: for they shall see eye to eye, when the Lord shall bring again Zion' [Isaiah 52:8]."[58]

The words of the song that will be sung have been revealed (D&C 84:99–102). On the Lord's coming to the New Jerusalem and all the earth seeing his salvation, see Doctrine and Covenants 133:2–5.

3 Nephi 17:3

Jesus did not need a break, but the people did. He instructed them to do four vital things, highlighted by the four verbs: *ponder, ask, understand,* and *prepare.*

We all need to do more pondering. It can have great benefits. To ponder is to weigh mentally, to think deeply about something. Pondering is a form of prayer and a form of worship. Note the instructive examples detailed in the commentary at 1 Nephi 11:1. If we will ponder, meditate, and reflect more on the things of eternity, the Lord can also show us great things (1 Nephi 18:3).

3 Nephi 17:6–24

These are tender scenes of a compassionate God wanting to heal all the crippled, diseased, and afflicted bodies and souls—because their faith was sufficient that he could do it. Where faith was lacking, the Savior could do no mighty miracles among the people of the Old World, and he even marveled at their unbelief (Mark 6:5–6). Note how he could "see" the strength of their faith. The people fell to the earth and worshipped him; then their little children were brought to him, and he himself knelt down and prayed things too powerful and sacred to record—things that eyes have never seen, ears have never heard, tongues have never spoken, "neither can the hearts of men conceive so great and marvelous things as we both saw and heard Jesus speak; and no one can conceive of the joy which filled our souls at the time we heard him pray for us unto the Father." The fulness of joy caused an outpouring of tears. Even Jesus was so full of emotion that he wept. Undoubtedly one of the reasons that God himself was so emotional was his joy in placing his hands on the head of each of the children and pronouncing blessings upon each, one by one. Imagine the scene, as heaven and earth connected, the veil was lifted, and the fire or glory of God enveloped every soul!

One day at the Provo Utah Temple, Brother Ogden stopped by the office of his friend, temple recorder Kurt Jensen. Brother Jensen looked up and asked: "You're a grandfather. When one of your grandchildren is blessed or baptized, where do you want to be?"

"There at the ordinance, of course."

"Well," Brother Jensen said, "I was reading in 3 Nephi 17, where the children are surrounded by fire, and angels came down and ministered to them. Who do you think those angels were? Wouldn't they be the grandparents and great-grandparents? Who in all the universe would most want to be there for such a sacred occasion?"

That the things that were said and done were so sacred as to prohibit them from being recorded suggests the kind of ordinances and promises that occur in latter-day temples—sealings of husbands and wives, sealings of children to parents, sealings that guarantee exaltation to committed disciples, and promises of inexpressible power. No wonder divine messengers, including family members of the children, came in the midst of fire. God himself dwells in everlasting fire (see commentary at Helaman 5:23–50).

3 Nephi 18:1–14

At the first Nephite sacrament meeting, with twenty-five hundred in attendance (3 Nephi 17:25), the Savior himself administered the emblems of his body and blood. The people ate and drank and "were filled"—filled not so much with those physical elements but with the Holy Ghost (3 Nephi 12:6). The sacrament is one of the most sacred public ordinances we have in the Church, and it must be partaken of worthily, remembering the body and blood of the Lord.

The instructions he gave as he administered the sacramental elements constitute the very points of the sacrament prayers: we partake to show our willingness to keep his commandments, to always remember him, and to have his Spirit be with us. Doing these things, we are building upon his rock, able to withstand the rains, floods, and winds of temptation, and avoid entering the gates of hell (see also commentary at 3 Nephi 11:31–41; 14:24–27).

The instruction to remember his body as the Nephites partook of the bread would have been particularly stunning and powerful because they had just felt the wounds in his hands, feet, and side. In our day as well, we partake of the bread and so remember the Bread of Life. By our remembering his body, our bodies may be raised to exaltation (John 6:35, 51–57).

3 Nephi 18:15, 18–23

"Watch and pray always"; see commentary at 2 Nephi 32. Be sure to pray for that "which is right," have family prayer, and pray specifically for others.

3 Nephi 18:16, 24

The Savior is the light we should hold up and allow to shine unto the world (see commentary at 3 Nephi 12:14–16). He shows us the way to pray to the Father. Elder Jeffrey R. Holland elaborated: "The praying Christ. That is the example to which we are to point others. The Christ of humility. The Christ of spiritual communion. The Christ who is dependent upon his Father. The Christ who asks for blessings upon others. The Christ who calls down the powers of heaven.

The Christ who submits, yields, and obeys the will of the Father. . . . That is the light we are to show to the world. It is the image of Christ praying such unspeakable things."[59]

3 Nephi 18:22, 28–32

"While of these emblems we partake . . . , / Let us re-member and be sure / Our hearts and hands are clean and pure."[60] If we participate in the sacrament unworthily, pre-tending to take upon us the name of Christ and promising to remember him and obey him—and we are not serious about that covenant nor really intending to keep it—we are taking the name of the Lord *in vain,* and "the Lord will not hold him guiltless that taketh his name in vain" (Exodus 20:7; Mosiah 13:15).

If we know someone is living in sin and is not worthy to partake of the sacrament, we should encourage him not to participate in the sacred ordinance but we should not ex-pel him and reject him; we should work with him, encourage him, minister to him. It may be that he will return, repent, and be healed and saved.

Priesthood leaders—those who preside—are responsible for monitoring the worthiness of participants in sacred ordi-nances. No one else may forbid someone to take the sacra-ment.

3 Nephi 18:36–39

Jesus touched his leader-disciples, one by one, authoriz-ing them to bestow the gift of the Holy Ghost on others once he departed (Moroni later recorded a fuller description of this conferral of power; see Moroni 2:1–3). All ordinances are physical; they all involve touch. Touch can provide a tangible transmission of power and love. When we experience a scene like this in our own lives, it is, as we say, "touching," because it affects us emotionally and spiritually. As with the ancient leaders, we hope Jesus will continue to touch our souls and symbolically place his hands upon our lives, so that we may live.

For further explanation about the cloud in which the Lord appeared and disappeared, see commentary at Helaman 5:23–50.[61]

3 Nephi 19:1–5

At the end of the first day's instruction, Jesus ascended into heaven, and families dispersed to their own homes to fulfill the Savior's instruction to ponder the meaning of events just witnessed. Throughout the night notice was sent forth, and people from all over toiled to be in place the next day. Originally only twenty-five hundred of the most righteous were in attendance at the temple site, where Jesus would show himself again. Can we imagine that there would have been any who would not have expended every effort to be there? Why do some today not extend even modest effort to be in appointed places designated by the same Savior through his authorized servants? The next day the multitude was so expansive they had to be separated into twelve bodies.

The names of Jesus' twelve disciples (apostles; Moroni 2:2) are given. As with the original Quorum of the Twelve Apostles in the land of Israel, there are sets of brothers and other relatives.[62]

3 Nephi 19:6–9

The first thing the Twelve taught the people was to kneel down and pray to the Father in the name of Jesus. And the foremost thing the people prayed for—that which they most desired—was to receive the gift of the Holy Ghost. Because Jesus would soon leave them, they wanted the gift of constant companionship of one of the Gods while in this frail existence far from their heavenly home.

3 Nephi 19:10–14

Two baptisms followed their fervent praying: the baptism of water, to symbolically wash away their sins—burying the old man of sin and rising to newness of life, in the likeness of the Resurrection—and the baptism of fire, to symbolically burn away their sins to provide a worthy vessel for the Spirit of the Lord to reside in. The two baptisms feature two great cleansing agents—water and fire—to purify and sanctify souls to become holy as God is holy.

The symbol of the Holy Ghost is fire. The people were encircled about "as if it were by fire"—again not our usual fire, but the radiance, brilliance, light, or glory that accompanied angelic ministrants from heaven (see commentary at Helaman 5:23–50, especially verse 45, and 3 Nephi 25:1).

3 Nephi 19:18, 22

The question often arises: Why would the disciples pray to Jesus when he had so recently instructed them to pray to the Father in his name? The Savior himself answered that question: "They pray unto me because I am with them." One of the Godhead, the Holy One of Israel, was there present, in person, with them; when he departed they would continue to pray, as instructed, to the Father in his name.

3 Nephi 19:19–20, 27–28

Jesus provided another extraordinary example for us. While in the middle of his work, he departed out of the midst of the people, "went a little way off from them and bowed himself to the earth," and thanked his Heavenly Father for a particular blessing.

Jesus did the same during his mortal ministry in the Holy Land. The four Gospels record several occasions when he stepped aside, away from the crowds, and talked personally with his Father. Everything Jesus did and said was a lesson, a message to all mortals. By way of illustration, before the miracle of raising his friend Lazarus from the dead, Jesus paused to talk with his Father, to give him thanks (John 11:41–42). He intentionally did that to remind those listening to him that he was in constant touch with the One who sent him here—as we also should be in constant touch with the same One who sent us here. What Jesus was saying and doing was teaching and strengthening his faithful disciples, so that they would always give credit, praise, and honor to the Father.

3 Nephi 19:23, 29

Jesus prayed for the leaders and for all those who believe in him through their teaching, that they might be one, that they might be united—the same salient doctrine he taught his disciples in the Old World, as recorded in his great intercessory prayer (John 17).

The concept of oneness is both important and urgent in the gospel of Jesus Christ. It is the vital message inherent in the English word *atonement* (at-*one*-ment), the idea of becoming one.

Note how the Lord uses various parts of the Father's crowning creation, the physical body for each of his children, to illustrate the desirability of one-ness: the children of God lived "with *one eye* . . . having their *hearts knit together* in unity" (Mosiah 18:21; emphasis added); "them that believed were of *one heart* and of *one soul*" (Acts 4:32; emphasis added); "his people ZION . . . were of *one heart* and *one mind*" (Moses 7:18; emphasis added); "we, being many, are *one body* in Christ" (Romans 12:5; emphasis added); "stand fast in *one spirit*, with *one mind*" (Philippians 1:27; emphasis added). One eye, one mind, one heart, one body, one spirit, and one soul. Every member of the body is needed; all members must unite together in order for the body of Christ to function perfectly.

To establish Zion, then, we must become of one heart and one mind. God does not seem to be celebrating diversity but unity. That may not be too popular a notion in the world, but the Godhead is encouraging us to become like they are— to feel and to think and to act as they do.

"I and my Father are one," Jesus proclaimed (John 10:30; see also D&C 50:43; 93:3). So much alike are they that if we know one, we know the others. The Father, the Son, and the Holy Ghost are *one God* (2 Nephi 31:21; Alma 11:44; 3 Nephi 11:36; D&C 20:28). Of us the Savior said, "They may become the sons of God, even one in me as I am one in the Father, as the Father is one in me, that *we may be one*" (D&C 35:2; emphasis added).

Is all this "three are one" merely theological doubletalk, or is there something profoundly significant and sacred in this doctrine?

Surely the three Gods are teaching us mortals the fundamental and indispensable principle that will lead us to become as they are. In that great intercessory prayer, our Advocate with the Father pleaded with him: "Holy Father, keep . . . those whom thou hast given me, that they may be one, as we are . . .

"That they *all may be one;* as thou, Father, art in me, and I in thee, that they also may *be one in us:* . . .

"And the glory which thou gavest me I have given them; *that they may be one, even as we are one:*

"I in them, and thou in me, that they may be *made perfect in one*" (John 17:11, 21–23; emphasis added).

There is the foundational reason for us to be united, as one: to become perfect. "I say unto you, *be one;* and if ye are not one ye are not mine" (D&C 38:27; emphasis added). In all the above passages we see the basic meaning of that otherwise abstract word *atonement;* the great sacrificial offering of the Lamb is meant to help us become as one—one with him and the Father and one with each other.

3 Nephi 19:24

This is one of our best descriptions of mighty prayer: without ceasing—determined to keep praying until Heaven responded. As Joseph Smith taught, "Come to God [and] weary him until he blesses you"—not multiplying many words, being inspired what to pray, and being filled with desire.[63] Indeed, the purest prayers are those in which the Spirit reveals to the petitioner the actual words that should be used (D&C 50:29–30).

3 Nephi 19:25, 30

What a joyful moment! Certainly the Savior of the world is a happy Person. He knows and lives a fulness of joy. So finally—for the first and only time in all of scripture—we read that Jesus "did *smile* upon them," and he "did *smile* upon them again." And they were radiant, with his glory enveloping them with a whiteness and brilliance exceeding anything earthly, for surely they had transcended the bounds of earth, penetrated the veil, and basked in heavenly light.

3 Nephi 19:31–36

What a remarkable scene! We would love to have been there (perhaps we were, watching afar off). How would it be to see the Savior of the world kneeling and hear him talking so personally with his Father—words that cannot even be spoken or written, they were so powerful and marvelous. Sadly, he lamented that his mortal friends and disciples on the other side of the world never did attain to so great faith and deep spirituality as to open the heavens and see and hear such miraculous and unspeakable things.

3 Nephi 20:1–9

Standing up to take a break from the intense spiritual outpouring, the people joined Jesus in another sacrament meeting, as he miraculously provided the emblems of his body and blood, and they "gave glory to Jesus." That the ordinance of the sacrament was conducted two times in as many days by the very Being to be remembered in the ordinance ought to teach us something about its true significance. Of the many ordinances we participate in for ourselves during our lifetime, most are only done once in our behalf, but the sacrament is not one of those.

3 Nephi 20:10–46

The rest of chapter 20 contains some quotation and explanation of what Jehovah (Jesus) had revealed centuries earlier to Isaiah, as recorded in Isaiah 52—the most frequently cited chapter of Isaiah in the Book of Mormon (see also 2 Nephi 8:24–25; Mosiah 12:20–24; 15:13–18; Moroni 10:31).

Jesus again encourages his faithful ones to search the writings of Isaiah and to notice that when his prophecies are fulfilled, they will know that the Father's covenants to all Israel—including them—are being fulfilled.

Isaiah's prophecies include a great gathering to lands of inheritance—including Lehi's posterity in the Americas—and a gathering to the knowledge of the Lord their God.

3 Nephi 20:15–21

Two passages from the Old Testament prophet Micah were also referred to by the Savior when he appeared to his people in the land Bountiful. The first is from Micah 4:12–13 (cited in 3 Nephi 20:18–19), where the Lord, after bringing the exiles back from Babylon and finding other nations gathering against Jerusalem and eyeing her as prey, assured his people of ancient Israel that his purposes would be fulfilled. They will return from exile; they will be planted again in their land; they will exert their strength (as iron, brass, beating in pieces, etc.) with the protection of the Lord, because his people Israel must continue in the land in order to realize the promises to the fathers—for instance, that the Messiah would be born in Bethlehem (Micah 5:2) and would minister to his people in their land. The other passage from Micah is 5:8–15 (cited in 3 Nephi 20:16–17 and in 21:12–21), similar in tone to the previous one.

Contrary to the threatening, forceful imagery of the above verses, the previous verse in Micah states that "the remnant of Jacob shall be in the midst of many people as a dew from the Lord, as the showers upon the grass" (Micah 5:7). In biblical imagery dew and showers always suggest nourishment, peace, relief, and blessing. Apparently the remnant of Jacob in the latter days will also be a blessing to the Gentiles and promote the righteous life.

In ancient America, however, the Savior focused on the terror that he, through a remnant of Jacob, would strike in the hearts of their adversaries among the Gentiles (see 20:16–19; 21:12–21).

Note that many of the predictions of the ancient prophets of Israel like Micah, Isaiah, and others have multiple fulfillment or multiple adaptation. Prophetic utterances are sometimes used in different contexts in different dispensations. For example, Hosea's words "When Israel was a child, then I loved him, and called my son out of Egypt" (Hosea 11:1), besides applying to the Israelite exodus from Egypt, were adapted by Matthew to another sense: "[Joseph] took the young child and his mother by night, and departed into Egypt: and was there until the death of Herod: that it might be fulfilled which was spoken of the Lord by the prophet, saying, Out of Egypt have I called my son" (Matthew 2:14–15). Micah's words about the remnant of Israel could very well apply both to antiquity and futurity, but the Lord has not chosen to make the intent of these verses any clearer to us at the present time.

3 Nephi 20:22

For more on the New Jerusalem, see Moses 7:62–64 and the commentary in this volume at Ether 13:3–11 (all entries). For a detailed study of Zion, the New Jerusalem—where,

when, how, why, and by whom it is established—see
Galbraith et al., *Jerusalem, the Eternal City,* 491–93, 536–50.

3 Nephi 20:23

One like unto Moses would come (Deuteronomy 18:15–
19). Moses was a great deliverer and lawgiver. To fulfill
Moses' prophecy, the Mighty One of Israel, the Lord Jesus
Christ, did come, and he was *the* great Lawgiver and Deliverer
(see Joseph Smith–History 1:40). There are few passages that
are quoted as many times in as many books of scripture and
in as many contexts as Deuteronomy 18:15 (15–19). It is one
of the most powerful testimonies of Christ in the scriptures.
The Savior himself quoted it. And yet we do not seem to use
it much in our day. We wonder why not.

3 Nephi 20:24

See commentary at Mosiah 13:33 about all the prophets
testifying of Christ.

3 Nephi 20:25–27

Descendants of Father Abraham—the people of Israel—
have this great promise as children of the covenant: "In thy
seed shall all the kindreds of the earth be blessed." Upon all
the peoples of the earth the blessings of the covenant will be
poured out—through the covenant people—namely, blessings of the fulness of the gospel, the priesthood, the Holy
Ghost, eternal posterity, land inheritance, and more. See further in "Why Does God Have a Covenant People?" in commentary at 3 Nephi 5:21–26.

3 Nephi 20:29–33, 46

For a detailed study of Old Jerusalem in the Holy
Land—when, how, why, and by whom it is established—see
Galbraith et al., *Jerusalem, the Eternal City,* 349–64, 491–93,
524–36.

In verse 29, Jesus Christ quotes his Father saying that "in [his] own due time," he would again give the covenant people of Israel, specifically the Jews, "the land of their fathers for their inheritance, which is the land of Jerusalem, which is the promised land unto them forever."

More remarkably, verse 30 proclaims that "the time cometh, when the fulness of my gospel shall be preached unto them." Brother Ogden has written in the margin of his Book of Mormon at verse 30: "not yet—1988," "not yet—1994," "not yet—2001," "not yet—2005," and "not yet—2010."

Most remarkable of all, verse 31 says, "and they shall believe in me, that I am Jesus Christ, the Son of God," and at that point, the exclamation: "*Then* will the Father gather them together again, and give unto them Jerusalem for the land of their inheritance" (emphasis added). Those are the events that will occasion the lifting up of the voice, and singing and rejoicing, for "the Father hath comforted his people, he hath redeemed [Old] Jerusalem."

Verse 46 hints at the only way the Near East peace process will ever be concluded equitably. Jerusalem and surrounding lands will be given to those who are "*his* people" (emphasis added). This is what the Lord said to Father Abraham approximately four thousand years ago: "I, Abraham, and Lot, my brother's son, prayed unto the Lord, and the Lord appeared unto me, and said unto me: Arise, and take Lot with thee; for I have purposed to take thee away out of Haran, and to make of thee a minister to bear my name in a strange land which I will give unto thy seed after thee for an everlasting possession, when they hearken to my voice" (Abraham 2:6). The key words are: "I will give [the land] unto thy seed . . . *when they hearken to my voice.*"

3 Nephi 20:32, 34–35

See commentary on these same verses, quoted previously at 3 Nephi 16:17–20.

3 Nephi 20:36–38

This passage is quoted three different times in the Book of Mormon. Explanation is given in Doctrine and Covenants 113:7–10. Zion, the New Jerusalem, is to "put on thy strength" and "put on thy beautiful garments," which represent the authority of the priesthood. Doctrine and Covenants 113:10 indicates that the remnants are exhorted to return to the Lord. Recall that Isaiah's son was named *Shearjashub*, meaning "the remnant shall return"—return not only to the land but to the Lord. Hebrew *lashuv* means both "return" and "repent," the idea being that backsliding Israel will come back to her God. The bride, the Lord's wife, will return from playing the harlot and repent and adorn herself with beautiful, clean wedding garments as she prepares for the coming of the bridegroom, her husband, the Savior (Jeremiah 3:14; Matthew 22:1–14; 25:1–13; D&C 133:10, 19).

Israel is to rise up from her dejected position and sit down in a more glorious and honored place, the New Jerusalem, the redeemed Zion.

To loose herself from the bands of her neck means to repent and remove herself from "the curses of God upon her . . . [in her] scattered condition among the Gentiles" (D&C 113:10); in other words, to flee Babylon, the wicked world, and free herself from the captivity of the devil.

Israel had sold herself as a harlot, having prostituted her sacred relationship with her Husband, "for naught"; that is, she had betrayed her God, searching for the worthless lusts of the flesh and pleasures of worldliness. Nevertheless, she can be "redeemed without money" through the atonement of her Savior, whose loving invitation comes "without money and without price" (2 Nephi 9:50).

3 Nephi 20:39

Some seem to think that God's existence depends on people's belief in him. This means that if someone believes in him, then he is real for that person. If another person does not believe in God, however, he is as unreal to that person as he is real to the first. In this verse, however, the Lord teaches us that whether or not we choose to believe in him and follow him, the time will come when we will have to acknowledge him as our Lord.

3 Nephi 20:40

Those who bring good tidings, who publish peace and salvation, who testify, "Thy God reigneth!" or "God lives!" are, particularly, the missionaries of The Church of Jesus Christ of Latter-day Saints. See further in commentary at Mosiah 15:14–18.

Medical doctors assisting missionaries throughout the world conclude that of all the parts of the body that they treat for ailments, the *feet* are among the most frequent victims. Over the ages, and again in this last dispensation, many tired, blistered, and swollen feet have carried the glad tidings of great joy.

"How beautiful" is Hebrew *mah nauvoo*. This is the source of the name *Nauvoo,* the city the Saints built on the banks of the Mississippi River. The name was probably first seen by the Prophet Joseph in his study of Professor Joshua Seixas's grammar *A Manual Hebrew Grammar for the Use of Beginners,* from which he studied in the School of the Prophets in Kirtland, January–March 1836.[64]

"Him that bringeth good tidings" is one word in Hebrew (*m'vaser*), containing the same root word as *besora,* which is "gospel."

Once again, "salvation" is Hebrew *Yeshua*—in English, "Jesus." Declaring salvation, then, is declaring Jesus.

3 Nephi 20:41

The command here is to flee from the wicked world. Live in the world but be not of the world. Avoid the world's contaminating influences (for example, many of Hollywood's

movies, books and magazines and Internet sites that special-
ize in pornographic materials that degrade and destroy moral
and spiritual character)—"touch not that which is unclean."
"Go ye out of the midst of her; be ye clean that bear the vessels of the Lord."

Handling any of the instruments in a hospital, a nurse
must first wash and sterilize her hands. The tools she handles
are for the vital operations of healing. If a nurse gets washed
just to "bear the vessels" or instruments of a doctor, how
much more sterilizing does one need for handling the things
of the Lord? Our society expects certain standards of physical
cleanliness and spends great sums of energy and money to
achieve them, but the expectation of moral cleanliness and
insistence on it seem to be lacking. Those who bear the vessels of the Lord can and must be a light to the world. That is
the whole point of being a covenant people, chosen to show
others how to be clean in a filthy world.

3 Nephi 20:42

The Lord of Hosts will go before his people and will also
protect them from behind (be their "rearward"), but he expects us to do our part in moving the work forward.

Presiding elders in Missouri issued the following counsel in July 1833: "For the disciples to suppose that they can
come to this land without ought to eat, or to drink, or to
wear, or anything to purchase these necessaries with, is a vain
thought. For them to suppose that the Lord will open the
windows of heaven, and rain down angel's food for them by
the way, when their whole journey lies through a fertile country, stored with the blessings of life from His own hand for
them to subsist upon, is also vain. For them to suppose that
their clothes and shoes will not wear out upon the journey,
when the whole of it lies through a country where there are
thousands of sheep from which wool in abundance can be
procured to make them garments, and cattle upon a thousand hills, to afford leather for shoes, is just as vain. . . . Do

not conclude from these remarks, brethren, that we doubt in the least, that the Lord will provide for His Saints in these last days. . . . We know that the saints have the unchangeable word of God that they shall be provided for; yet we know, if any are imprudent, or lavish, or negligent, or indolent, in taking that proper care, and making that proper use of what the Lord has made them stewards over, they are not counted wise; for a strict account of every one's stewardship is required, not only in time, but will be in eternity. . . . 'Let not your flight be in haste, but let all things be prepared before you' [D&C 133:15]."[65]

3 Nephi 20:43–45

Another prophecy with dual fulfillment: Jesus Christ and Joseph Smith were both marred at the hands of wicked men (3 Nephi 21:8–11; D&C 135:1–3).

The word *sprinkle* in 3 Nephi 20:45 was changed to *gather* by the Prophet Joseph in his translation of the Bible (Isaiah 52:15, footnote *a*, from JST, Isaiah 52:15). The high-minded leaders of men will be astonished, and speechless, when they finally recognize and acknowledge the glorious work of the Savior of the world and the Prophet of the Restoration (see also 3 Nephi 21:8).

3 Nephi 21:1–11

"I give unto you a sign, that ye may know the time when these things shall be about to take place." The great and final gathering of Israel, and the establishment of Zion, will occur when:

1. The Book of Mormon is published and the gospel is restored.
2. The United States of America is established to provide the freedoms needed for the Restoration. Note that it is by the power of the Father that this was done. Elder Mark E. Petersen of the Quorum

of the Twelve stated: "When the Savior was among the Nephites, following His Resurrection in [the land of Israel], He also spoke of [the] modern United States. (This is recorded in the twenty-first chapter of 3 Nephi). The Savior said specifically that a great nation would occupy this area in our time and be set up as a free and independent country by act of our Heavenly Father. He specifically said that. Our Country, our government was set up by act of God. . . . The United States then is God's country. It is His government set up specifically to provide freedom of speech and religion in this country so that our Church could be established here and so that we, as the missionaries of the Church, may travel the world over on American passports and have the protection of this great government as we preach the gospel to the world."[66]

3. The true points of the Savior's doctrine come to the descendants of ancient Nephites and Lamanites.

4. The Prophet Joseph Smith is raised up to bring about the great and marvelous work of God in the last days (the Savior applied Isaiah's words to the latter-day Prophet who would be "marred" or martyred but not "hurt" or harmed in the eternal sense). This is a marvelous prophecy of Joseph Smith given directly by Jesus himself.

3 Nephi 21:12–22

Why would the Lord use the metaphor of a *lion* in describing his Saints in the latter days? Study the references given in footnote 12*a*, plus Mormon 5:24 and 1 Nephi 14:14. See also commentary at 3 Nephi 20:15–21.

Verses 13–21 depict images reminiscent of Old Testament prophets as they envision the last days, and the many sins of a society that will be cut off, and try to describe what they see in terms of their own language.

Could the "horses" and "chariots" be cars and other forms of modern transportation? Could "cities" and "strongholds" be massive buildings, various public high-rise construction projects, and air force, army, and naval bases, along with their sophisticated aircraft, missiles, and other weaponry and armaments?

What could "witchcrafts" and "soothsayers" represent in our day? Do "graven images" and "standing images" represent television sets or computers, with their images or icons, or anything else that we covet that dominates our time, distracting us from the work of the Lord—making them our idols?

And the "works of thy hands" that are worshiped in the last days? Could they be recreational vehicles, or a host of appliances and tools, or numerous handheld gadgets like cellular phones, iPods, videogame players, and so forth?

What about "groves," the hilltop shrines where the ancients set up altars for worshipping false gods and fertility goddesses? Is there a modern parallel?

Verse 19 lists moral and ethical violations and misbehaviors that plague those modern societies that the Lord will cut off as he comes to establish a new, righteous, peaceful world.

Verse 22 extends the invitation, once again, for the Gentiles to soften their hearts, repent, be obedient, become part of the covenant people, and partake of all the attendant covenant blessings.

3 Nephi 21:23–25

For additional details on the New Jerusalem built by the house of Israel, under the direction of the house of Joseph (D&C 133:32–34), see references given at 3 Nephi 20:22. The "power of heaven" coming down among the residents of the New Jerusalem could include the Father and the Savior (Revelation 21:22; 22:1, 3; Moses 7:62–63), Enoch and his city of holiness (JST, Genesis 9:21–23, in Bible appendix; Revelation 21:2–10; Ether 13:3; Moses 7:62–63), Melchizedek and his city of holiness (JST, Genesis 14:32–34, in Bible appendix; Alma 13:14–19), and many dispensation heads, key-holders, patriarchs, prophets, and other noble and great ones from throughout the ages (Daniel 7:9–14; D&C 27:4–14; 116).[67]

3 Nephi 21:26

The Father has a very personal interest in this dispensation, and he has definitely commenced his work among the remnant of the Nephite-Lamanite civilization. In the 1970s and 80s there were as many stakes established in Latin America as there were in the entire Church during the administration of President David O. McKay (1950s and 60s). For example, the first stake in Mexico was establish in 1961; by 1989 the one hundredth stake was organized in that nation. The Father's work in Latin America is phenomenal.

The Father's work has commenced also among the lost tribes of Israel, those led away out of "Jerusalem" in the generic, national sense—the Holy City representing the entire land of Israel.

3 Nephi 21:27–29

All dispersed peoples are invited to repent and return to the Father and be "gathered home to the lands of their inheritance," the Father himself even going before them and behind them, to protect and preserve them (compare 3 Nephi 20:42, where the Son of the Father does the same).

3 Nephi 22:1–8

In many cultures, when a woman marries a man she takes his name and is then legally his heir and represents his name as long as she is married to him. So it is in the relationship between God and his bride, his people. Israel, the wayward and estranged wife, had not borne for years; she is invited to return and resume her proper relationship with the Lord.

"In Isaiah 54:1–3 the Lord addresses his barren bride Israel: 'Sing, O barren, thou that didst not bear.' Marriage as a metaphor for the covenant—the Lord being the groom and Israel the bride—occurs frequently in the Old Testament (e.g., Hosea 1–3; Jer. 2–3; Ezek. 23). Israel, as the unfaithful spouse, is guilty of adultery and is a harlot. Certainly these are grounds for divorce, and the penalty for adultery is death. The Lord punished Israel with death, destruction, and scattering by the Assyrians in 721 B.C., by the Babylonians in 587 B.C., and by the Romans in A.D. 70. Many suffered the penalty of death, but the Lord in his mercy spared Israel's posterity and scattered them throughout the earth. In Isaiah's metaphor, there was no divorce ('where is the bill of your mother's divorcement'; Isa. 50:1) but a separation. The Lord explained, 'For thy Maker is thine husband . . . for a small moment have I forsaken thee . . . in a little wrath I hid my face from thee for a moment; but with everlasting kindness will I have mercy on thee' (Isa. 54:5–8). The Lord in his love and mercy, as dramatized by Hosea when he forgave his unfaithful wife (Hosea 1–3), will take back his bride, and her barrenness will be replaced with productivity as the Lord begins to gather their posterity (Isa. 54:7)."[68]

"Children of the desolate" were apostate Israel, those out of the Church, and "children of the married wife" meant members of the Church. The suggestion is that more are born out of the covenant than those born in it.

The scattering and gathering of Israel is not merely a process of moving people about (or moving "trees"; Jacob 5) but of bringing people to Christ, of establishing Zion. There is such a thing as divine positioning. The Lord puts people where he needs them, to help facilitate the "at-*one*-ment," the gathering in and becoming one with him.

3 Nephi 22:2

The gathering of Israel's posterity will necessitate enlarging the family tent, lengthening the cords, and strengthening the stakes. The tent signifies refuge from storms. Stakes, the origin of our Church unit, must be strong to stabilize the whole tent, which is the Church and kingdom of God on earth. Compare Isaiah 33:20 and Doctrine and Covenants 82:14.

3 Nephi 22:2–3

Zion expands worldwide; see also Doctrine and Covenants 133:7–13; Moroni 10:31. "Break forth on the right hand and on the left" suggests expansion.

To "inherit the Gentiles" suggests Latter-day Saints in all the world.

3 Nephi 22:4

In the early years of the nation, Israel departed from her God and slew her husband, causing the "reproach of thy widowhood"; all of that will be forgotten when she is mercifully gathered into his arms once again.

It is we mortals, in all ages, who have deserted our God and find it incumbent on ourselves to repent and return to him, yet it is he who first makes the conciliatory effort to gather us. He is tireless in his efforts to bring us back into his arms.

"Thou shalt forget the shame of thy youth" is an injunction for ancient Israel but also for us individually. There were two great Josephs whose lives teach us a valuable principle: the foolish, shameful, or simply immature mistakes we make in our youth can be forgiven and forgotten; we can rise above and beyond our past. Joseph, son of Jacob, who was later sold into Egypt, was, while a teenager, rather unwise in broadcasting the dreams of his future greatness to his family members who would someday bow down to him (Genesis 37). And

a Joseph in our day admitted, "I frequently fell into many foolish errors, and displayed the weakness of youth, and the foibles of human nature; which, I am sorry to say, led me into divers temptations, offensive in the sight of God. In making this confession, no one need suppose me guilty of any great or malignant sins. A disposition to commit such was never in my nature. But I was guilty of levity [light-mindedness], and sometimes associated with jovial company, etc., not consistent with that character which ought to be maintained by one who was called of God as I had been" (Joseph Smith–History 1:28). The Lord will help us "forget the shame of [our] youth" as we repent and show penitence through many good works during our mature years on earth.

3 Nephi 22:5–6

There is no mistaking who the husband is. He is plainly identified as the Lord of Hosts, the Redeemer, the Holy One of Israel, the God of the whole earth. Zion, the New Jerusalem, is the bride (Isaiah 61:10; Revelation 21:2).

3 Nephi 22:7

The adversities and afflictions experienced during the time away, when the wayward wife was separated ("scattered") from her husband, shall appear to be—in the eternal perspective—only "a small moment" (also D&C 121:7). Actually, the Lord has never forsaken any of his people; it may just seem that way as he tries and tests us. We understandably feel God-forsaken when we abandon him and his Spirit.

3 Nephi 22:8–10

When Israel, the covenant people, forsook her Maker—her husband—she suffered the consequences of her abandonment and incurred his "little wrath" for a moment, but his kindly, merciful promise to gather Israel is as sure as his promise to send no more flood. Verse 9 confirms the historicity of the Flood. Besides the biblical account, we have an additional three witnesses of the Flood in Alma 10:22; 3 Nephi 22:9; and Ether 6:7; 13:2.

Kindness is a good measure of the greatness of a person, and God is great.

3 Nephi 22:11–12

Compare this description of future Zion, the New Jerusalem, with the even more detailed description in Revelation 21:19–21; compare also the words of our hymn number 44, "Beautiful Zion, Built Above."

3 Nephi 22:13

Elder M. Russell Ballard exclaimed: "Peace. What a marvelous, desirable blessing to bring to the souls of our children. If they are at peace within themselves and secure in their knowledge of Heavenly Father and his eternal plan for them, they will be able to cope better with the unrest in the world around them and be prepared better for reaching their divine potential."[69]

3 Nephi 22:14–17

These verses attest how the Saints of Zion will survive and prosper in the face of the high-tech weaponry of the world and how they will escape oppression and "terror [that] shall not come near thee."

Referring to verse 16, Elder Gerald N. Lund wrote, "Joseph was surely the smith who forged the instrument by which the Lord's people continue to prepare individually and collectively for the Savior's return—and that instrument is The Church of Jesus Christ of Latter-day Saints."[70]

The assurances in verse 17 are repeated by the Lord in our day: "There is no weapon that is formed against you shall prosper; and if any man lift his voice against you he shall be confounded" (D&C 71:9–10). This greatest cause on earth will continue to roll forth until it fills the whole earth, as the Prophet Joseph Smith prophesied:

"The Standard of Truth has been erected; no unhallowed hand can stop the work from progressing, . . . but the truth of God will go forth boldly, nobly, and independent, till it has penetrated every continent, visited every clime, swept every country, and sounded in every ear, till the purposes of God shall be accomplished, and the Great Jehovah shall say the work is done."[71]

3 Nephi 23:1

Jesus is our example in all things, and he taught from the scriptures. Here he particularly commends the words of Isaiah to us; in fact, he commands us to search them. Note the sequence of the wording: He tells us it is our duty to search the words of Isaiah, then he adds that it is a commandment. We are not just to read or even study but to *search* them and not just passively but diligently. Seldom does the Savior single out a certain prophet and use adjectives of praise for his writings, but here he eulogizes the contributions of this one prophet of ancient Israel: "great are the words of Isaiah."

Why we should search the writings of Isaiah and *how* to understand them is explained in "Why Study Isaiah" and "How to Understand Isaiah," found just before the commentary at 1 Nephi 20.

3 Nephi 23:2

Why are Isaiah's words so great? Because "he spake as touching all things concerning my people which are of the house of Israel." He expounded the meaningful events and lessons from his own day, but also from all other dispensations—past and future. His visions are all-encompassing, from premortal council, rebellion, and war to millennial reign and celestialized earth. His discourses are all-inclusive: he treats all significant gospel doctrine, from practical religion and basic principles and ordinances to elevated concepts of temple worship, work for the dead, establishment of Zion, and eternal glory. Isaiah saw God while living in mortality (2 Nephi 11:2).

3 Nephi 23:3

By declaring that all things that Isaiah taught *have been* and *shall be,* the Lord described the phenomenon of dual fulfillment or even multiple fulfillment, in which a prophecy may apply in more than one time or place; that is, the prophetic declaration may have a specific fulfillment in Isaiah's day or in the Savior's day (the meridian of time) and also in modern times, in the final dispensation. See commentary at 2 Nephi 6:4–5; see also commentary at 3 Nephi 20:15–21.

3 Nephi 23:4–13

Jesus edited the Nephite records and chastised his disciples for omitting essentials in prophetic writings. Imagine the Savior himself was the editor of records we are now reading. For example, he pointed out that Samuel the Lamanite had prophesied that upon Jesus' resurrection, many of the Saints of past ages would rise from the dead and appear and minister unto many people. The record keepers had failed to include that important prophecy in their religious history, and Jesus wanted the fact preserved that there were numerous eyewitnesses of the Resurrection—indisputable evidence that he, the Savior, was now immortal, and that many others of his faithful followers over thousands of years were also, for the first time in history, in a glorified, immortal, resurrected state. His apostle Matthew had recorded that sublime truth in the Old World's testament (Matthew 27:52–53), and now with the same testimony engraved in the New World's testament, there would be multiple witnesses of this transcendent verity that many people, in the last days, would question and doubt.

3 Nephi 23:14

Jesus "expounded all the scriptures in one," just as he did immediately after his resurrection in Jerusalem. To the two disciples walking the road to Emmaus, "beginning at Moses and all the prophets, he expounded unto them in all the scriptures the things concerning himself. . . . All things [that] must be fulfilled, which were written in the law of Moses, and in the prophets, and in the psalms, concerning me" (Luke 24:27, 44). In other words, the Master brought together all the age-old messianic prophecies and showed how all things were now fulfilled concerning his mission in mortality. All scripture comes from a common source and centers on a common theme: Jesus Christ is the great Jehovah, the earthly Messiah, the literal Son of God in the flesh, the king of Israel, the Lord of heaven and earth, the Redeemer of all creation.

3 Nephi 24 (Malachi 3)

The prophecies and teachings of Malachi are found in all four standard works. They are vital words of Heavenly Father to his children, and because Malachi lived and ministered nearly two hundred years after Lehi's family carried the brass plates out of Jerusalem, the Father wanted his people in ancient America to also have these essential writings.

3 Nephi 24:1

The prophet's name was also his message: "I will send *my messenger*, and he shall prepare the way before me" (emphasis added). The words *my messenger* are in Hebrew *malachi*. And who would the messenger be? Again we have multiple fulfillments of prophecy. John the Baptist was a messenger who prepared the way before the Lord (for his first coming *and* his Second Coming; see Isaiah 40:3; Matthew 3:3; Joseph Smith–History 1:68–72); Elijah also prepared the way before the Lord, as Malachi himself would so plainly prophesy; Joseph Smith was one of the greatest messengers preparing the way of the Lord; and the gospel itself has been "a messenger before my face to prepare the way before me" (D&C 45:9). Jesus Christ, of course, was the "messenger of the covenant," in whom we certainly delight.

THE BOOK OF MORMON

"The Lord whom ye seek shall suddenly come to his temple." Here is another unequivocal sign of the Lord's coming: He will come to his temple (D&C 36:8; 42:36; 133:2). But which temple? He did come to the Kirtland Temple, but he will come again—to the house of the Lord in the New Jerusalem and in the Old Jerusalem. See details about the fulfillment of this prophecy, especially commentary from Elder Bruce R. McConkie, at 2 Nephi 12:1–2.

3 Nephi 24:2

"Who may abide the day of his coming, and who shall stand when he appeareth?" This parallel couplet contains a significant question. Who will be able to survive that day when the harvest will have been gathered and the field will be burned? In that day all telestial people and things will be removed from this planet, and the earth will shift up to a terrestrial or paradisiacal condition. There will be a great cleansing. The Lord and his tens of thousands of holy ones will be like "a refiner's fire, and like fuller's soap." Fire and soap are two well-known cleansing agents. Those who are clean will abide the day of cleansing.

For explanation of the refiner's fire, see commentary at 1 Nephi 20:10. A fuller, who usually had his workshop near a spring or some other water source, worked with his soap to clean cloth, ridding it of all stains to make it white.

3 Nephi 24:3

For details about the refining and purifying through which we must pass, see commentary at 1 Nephi 20:10.

The sons of Levi will yet offer unto the Lord an offering in righteousness. Does that mean that blood sacrifices of animals will be reinstituted? We do know that the sacrificial shedding of the blood of animals, symbolic of the great sacrifice involving the shedding of the Savior's blood, was part of the proper worship of God since the beginning. The practice will be resumed, but for how long? President Joseph Fielding

Smith wrote: "Blood sacrifices will be performed long enough to complete the fulness of the restoration in this dispensation. Afterwards sacrifice will be of some other character."[72]

3 Nephi 24:5–7

The Lord gave a catalog of sins for which the violators will suffer consequence.

3 Nephi 24:8–11

These four verses constitute perhaps the greatest discourse we have on the law of tithing. If we hold back our tithes and offerings, Malachi taught, we are robbing God. In another sense, we are also robbing ourselves. We are cheating ourselves out of enormous blessings. Tithing is as indispensable to our salvation as is baptism.

During an interview, one young elder told President Ogden about a good man he and his companion were preparing for baptism: "But the man has some doubts about tithing. He says he doesn't think he can pay tithing for a while, because they are poor and he is about to finance a medical operation for his little daughter." President Ogden and the young missionary talked about the usual things that the investigator needed to understand about the law of tithing, but then the elder said something else: his companion had told the investigator not to worry about it, that the Lord would understand, and that he wouldn't have to pay tithing for a while yet.

The president called the companion in, and they talked about refraining from denying the blessings of tithe paying to anyone, because tithes are paid with faith. Here was a beautiful opportunity to teach a prospective member how the Lord blesses us if we'll just demonstrate our faith and keep his commandment; then we may anticipate the blessings of obedience. Then President Ogden asked the elder, "By the way, what is the operation the little girl needs?"

He answered, "To repair her cleft palate."

A few weeks earlier, President Ogden had listened to a medical doctor from Utah describe the work of his worldwide medical humanitarian service foundation, which had recently been organized in Santiago to help those with certain physical abnormalities, especially cleft palates. Surely the operation on the prospective member's daughter could be arranged for. The directness and immediacy of the resolution of a need were overwhelming. What an opportunity to teach two missionaries and their investigator that the Lord can indeed provide for those who are willing and obedient.

Tithing is a law with a promise! The Lord assures us that when we faithfully observe this law of spiritual economics, he will open the windows of heaven and pour out blessings, such that we won't be able to contain them all; and he will "rebuke the devourer for [our] sakes"—or keep the wolf from our door; see the commentary at Jacob 2:17–19.

Opening the windows of heaven means revelation, and great revelation—coming to know the Father and the Son—is available in the temple. But of course we have to show our willingness to sacrifice, our willingness to obey—by paying our tithing—before we can enter the holy temple. It is highly unlikely that persons who refuse to pay their tithing will honor the even more demanding covenants that are administered in the temple.

Sacrifice really does bring forth the blessings of heaven. So while we may think we are giving up something to God, he actually enriches us with more than we have given. The word *sacrifice* derives from the Latin *sacer,* meaning "holy" or "sanctified." When we sacrifice something, it is not so much a deprivation as a sanctification. Is the payment of tithing a *loss* of the 10 percent, or is it a consecration, a sanctification, of the 10 percent?

3 Nephi 24:14–17

Some will complain: "Trying to serve God in this world is all in vain; what good has it done us to keep his ordinances and walk soberly before him? The wicked seem to prosper and the righteous just continue to suffer." But their reward is coming. The Lord remonstrates: A book of remembrance is being kept, and the ones who have "thought upon [my] name" will be included in it, "and they shall be mine . . . in that day when I make up my jewels" (also D&C 60:4). The English word *jewels* is in Hebrew *segulla,* and it is the same term elsewhere translated as "peculiar," as in "peculiar people" (Deuteronomy 14:2). *Segulla* means "valued property" or "peculiar treasure." Indeed, the Saints, or holy ones of God, are his jewels, his valued property or treasure. When he comes to reign, they, his jewels or special property, will be with him.

3 Nephi 25 (Malachi 4)

The Savior then gave Malachi's words that are the final lines of our Old Testament as presently constituted, so the Nephite scriptorians could preserve them. These last teachings from Malachi contain some of the most dramatic of all prophecies regarding the Messiah's second coming and the preparations for it.

3 Nephi 25:1

A day of burning is coming. "This is speaking after the manner of the Lord" (D&C 64:24), for fire is symbolic of God's glory (God dwells in "everlasting burnings"; see commentary at Helaman 5:23–50). When the Lord and all his holy ones come to earth at his coming in glory, those people and things that cannot stand his glory will be burned: "I will burn them up," says the Lord (D&C 64:24).

Following is a series of scriptural passages that shed further light on the burning or fire that will destroy the world at his coming and change it to a loftier sphere:

"*The Lord will come with fire,* and with his chariots like a whirlwind, to render his anger with fury, and his rebuke with flames of fire" (Isaiah 66:15; emphasis added).

"The inhabitants thereof are consumed away and utterly destroyed *by the brightness of my coming*" (D&C 5:19; emphasis added).

"All the proud and they that do wickedly shall be as stubble; and *I will burn them up.* . . . For I will reveal myself from heaven *with power and great glory.* . . . Mine apostles, the Twelve which were with me in my ministry at Jerusalem, shall stand at my right hand at the day of *my coming in a pillar of fire,* . . . *in glory even as I am*" (D&C 29:9, 11–12; emphasis added).

"All flesh shall see me together. And *every corruptible thing . . . shall be consumed;* and also that of element *shall melt with fervent heat*" (D&C 101:23–25; emphasis added).

"The presence of the Lord shall be as the melting fire that burneth" (D&C 133:41).

"The day cometh that shall burn as an oven, and all the proud, yea, and all that do wickedly shall burn as stubble; for *they that come shall burn them,* saith the Lord" (Joseph Smith–History 1:37; emphasis added).

See also Ezekiel 1:27; Zephaniah 3:8; 2 Thessalonians 1:7–8; 2:8; D&C 43:32; 45:57; 63:34; 130:7.

Notice who will be burned at the Second Coming: "all the proud, yea, and all that do wickedly." The Lord singles out one particular sin—pride—and lumps all the rest of the sins of humanity into the generic "all that do wickedly." It is obvious that the Lord hates pride (Proverbs 6:16–17). He knows how that one sin is the basis for, and can lead to, so many other sins. Pride is the great distracter and obstructer to all spiritual progress.

Those who cannot abide the day of burning will be left with "neither root nor branch," meaning that they will have in the eternal worlds neither ancestry nor posterity—no eternal family connections. They were unworthy of the sealing ordinances of the holy priesthood.

3 Nephi 25:2

The righteous in the millennial day will enjoy healing and salvation from the Son of Righteousness (one of the Father's name-titles is Righteousness, therefore the Savior is the Son of Righteousness). Brothers McConkie, Millet, and Top explained that the Son's rising with "healing in his wings" refers to the "power in his extremities, the power that came from his having had nails driven through his hands and feet. In short, the Son of Righteousness came with the power of the Atonement."[73] The children of the righteous, says Doctrine and Covenants 45:58, "shall grow up without sin unto salvation." The phrase "calves of the stall" used earlier (1 Nephi 22:24) means to receive special care.

3 Nephi 25:4–5

It is appropriate that Moses and Elijah, the two who epitomize the law and the prophets, should be mentioned together in the final verses of the Old Testament record. These two outstanding messengers of God operated in three different dispensations: as mortals, as translated beings (in Jesus' day on the Mount of Transfiguration), and as resurrected beings (in Joseph Smith's day in the Kirtland Temple). Moses restored in the meridian of time, and again in the fulness of times, the keys of the gathering of Israel; Elijah restored in both dispensations the keys of the sealing power—Moses' keys for gathering the living to Christ and Elijah's keys for gathering the dead to Christ. That takes care of everyone.

3 Nephi 25:5–6

Joseph Smith taught about these last two verses in Malachi's writings, and the last two verses of our Old Testament, more than any other passage of scripture. There is something of utmost importance contained in them.

THE BOOK OF MORMON

3 Nephi 25:5

It is written in everyone's Bible—whether Jewish or Christian—that Elijah the prophet would return before the coming of the Lord. Though many people, especially observant Jews, still maintain expectant tradition of his coming and even prepare a place setting for him at the annual Passover service, the Latter-day Saints are the only people in the world who believe he has actually come, just as prophesied. But Elijah came not to a Jewish home or synagogue but to the house of the Lord in Kirtland, Ohio, on 3 April 1836, the very occasion of the Passover celebration that year.[74]

3 Nephi 25:6

And what did Elijah return to earth to accomplish? The grand and glorious purpose is stated in a single sentence: He came to "turn the heart of the fathers to the children, and the heart of the children to their fathers." The Prophet Joseph Smith later elaborated on the word *turn,* expanding it to mean also "bind" or "seal."[75] The spirit and purpose of Elijah and the sealing powers are to promote the labor of love we call genealogy (from the Greek, meaning the study of race or family) and family history—researching and preparing the basic and necessary data on every child of Heavenly Father, in order to perform the saving ordinances: baptism, confirmation, priesthood ordination, marriage, and sealing of man and woman to each other and children to their parents. "For we without them cannot be made perfect; neither can they without us be made perfect" (D&C 128:18). We all need the welding links of family units, else the earth would be smitten, cursed, and utterly wasted at the Savior's coming (D&C 110:14–16; Joseph Smith–History 1:36–39).

During Moroni's many hours of instructional interviews with Joseph Smith, "respecting what the Lord was going to do, and how and in what manner his kingdom was to be conducted in the last days" (Joseph Smith–History 1:54), the ancient Nephite prophet quoted the first sentence of Malachi's last verse in this way: "And he shall plant in the hearts of the children the promises made to the fathers, and the hearts of the children shall turn to their fathers" (Joseph Smith–History 1:39). The promises made to the fathers (Adam, Enoch, Noah, Melchizedek, Abraham, Isaac, Jacob, and so on) include the great blessings of the covenant: the gospel of Jesus Christ and its associated principles and ordinances, the receiving of which, and the living of which, seals upon the obedient the blessings of exaltation in celestial glory with the Father, the Son, and the Holy Ghost. All these things are available to men, women, and children—and their ancestors—in the holy temples of the Lord. Our most ardent desire will be to have the great covenant promises and blessings for ourselves and our progenitors and our posterity.

3 Nephi 26:1–3

By expounding all things—including the mission of Elijah and the turning of the hearts of fathers and children to each other—Jesus may have caused intense temple activity among the Nephite-Lamanite civilization. They must have received an endowment, eternal marriage, and other sacred ordinances. What and how much they did in their labors for the dead remains to be revealed.

3 Nephi 26:3

For explanation of elements melting with fervent heat, the earth being wrapped together as a scroll, and the heavens and earth passing away, see commentary at 3 Nephi 25:1; Mormon 5:23–24; and Mormon 9:1–6.

3 Nephi 26:6–11

Not even the hundredth part of what the ancient prophets and historians wrote on the plates of Nephi is available to us at this point (see commentary at Words of Mormon 1:5; see also John's witness in John 21:25). Joseph Smith once remarked, "If the Church knew all the commandments, one half they would condemn through prejudice and ignorance."[76]

Jesus explained that he wants to try our faith; if we receive, believe, and live what we have been given, we will be given yet greater things. This is the established pattern to receive the mysteries of the kingdom (Alma 12:9–10; Ether 12:6; D&C 76:7–11). "There are records which contain much of my gospel, which have been kept back because of the wickedness of the people" (D&C 6:26). If we do not pay the price to search out and live by the teachings we have already been given, we will be condemned for it and the greater things will continue to be withheld. "And they shall remain under this condemnation until they repent and remember the new covenant, even the Book of Mormon and the former commandments which I have given them" (D&C 84:57).

3 Nephi 26:13–14

Mormon, the prophet-historian, noted that Jesus taught the people for three days, and after that "he did show himself unto them oft" and did administer some kind of sacred meal often—meaning, perhaps, the sacrament.

Verse 14 describes what can happen when all of God's people are spiritually prepared, worthy, and receptive—with no wicked distracting. All of this will happen again at the Second Coming, when telestial distractions are removed. The Lord will then reveal "many great and important things pertaining to the Kingdom of God" (Articles of Faith 1:9).

The children's tongues were "loosed," apparently speaking things beyond their mortal years, possibly penetrating the veil, using the language of God, and revealing "great and marvelous things" about the premortal life and even the postmortal life—things even greater than what Jesus had taught these righteous disciples.

3 Nephi 26:15

This verse denotes the end of the second of the three-day personal ministry Jesus carried on among the Nephites. Notice that the last thing he did was perform powerful miracles of healing.

3 Nephi 26:16–18

The most sacred things, when given to those worthy of them, are not to be divulged, broadcast, or published to the world. They are the "unspeakable things, which are not lawful to be written." They are kept from others not because they are mysterious and secret but because they are too sacred to share with the unprepared.

We conclude that this ancient people, who for a longer time than anyone else in all of history (who remained on earth) were able to sustain righteousness and a consecrated lifestyle, enjoyed the fulness of the gospel, with the fulness of the sealing power. The fulness of the everlasting gospel, including the endowment and higher ordinances, cannot be preserved in the written word. The Latter-day Saints are anxious for all people, everywhere, to learn from God's words in four volumes of scripture, but there are some higher things that cannot be published to the world; they can be obtained when righteous, prepared souls enter the holy temple.

3 Nephi 26:19–21

All these obedient members of the Church of Christ lived the law of consecration. For the meaning of "all things common" see commentary at 4 Nephi 1:1–19.

3 Nephi 27:1–2

Profound things happen when the Saints of God unite in genuine prayer, accompanied by fasting. Fasting is a conduit of power; it connects the disciples, ancient and modern, with the powers of heaven. Anciently, the prophet Isaiah described

in exulting language some of the blessings that flow from fasting:

"Then shall thy light rise in obscurity . . . :

"And the Lord shall guide thee continually, and satisfy
thy soul in drought, and make fat thy bones: and thou shalt
be like a watered garden, and like a spring of water, whose
waters fail not" (Isaiah 58:10–11).

3 Nephi 27:3–8

In the spirit of fasting and prayer, the disciples asked an
inspired question: What should be the name of the Church
that Jesus established on the earth? His own answer is simple
and indisputable. If it is his Church, it must be named after him: the Church of Jesus Christ. Although we have often
been called Mormons and the way of life we espouse called
Mormonism, it is not the Church nor the way of life of the ancient prophet Mormon. The same with a host of other name-
titles. Catholics are named after the concept of a catholic or
universal church. Protestants are so named because of their
protesting what Catholics and other orthodox churches believed and breaking off to form other churches—for example,
Methodists because of certain methodology, Baptists because
of a particular doctrine of baptism, Presbyterians because
of doctrine about priests or officers (Greek *presbyterion*),
Episcopalians because of doctrine about bishops or pastors
(Greek *episcopos* means one who oversees: a shepherd, pastor,
or bishop) and Lutherans because of Martin Luther. But the
true Church of Jesus Christ may be characterized specifically
by the use of his holy name.

In these latter days he has given the name of his Church
an addition to indicate joint-ownership. It is called The
Church of Jesus Christ of Latter-day Saints (D&C 115:4) because it belongs to Jesus Christ and it belongs to the Latter-
day Saints, the members or citizens of his kingdom on earth.

Names are more than mere labels; names have power. In
a sense, it is astounding that Jesus Christ allows us to bear

his very name. Indeed, it is humbling to be worthy to represent the greatest, most powerful Person ever to reside on this earth.

3 Nephi 27:13–21

Jesus defined what he means by "the gospel." It is, first and foremost, his coming to earth to do the will of his Father—which includes faith in his atonement, repentance, baptism, the gift of the Holy Ghost, and enduring to the end. For emphasis, he repeated and summarized: The gospel, or the good news or glad tidings, includes faith in the Lord Jesus Christ and his atonement, repentance, faithfulness to the end, baptism, receiving the Holy Ghost, and judgment. No one can enter into "his rest," which is "the fulness of his glory" (D&C 84:24), unless he is cleansed by his atoning blood.

The doctrine of Christ is that we embrace the Atonement through the first principles and ordinances of the gospel. These are the works by which we shall be judged (3 Nephi 11:31–41).

3 Nephi 27:21, 27

How shall we behave in this world? Whom shall we emulate? Among all the models, idols, stars, and heroes in our world, whom should we most want to be like? Our Savior asked and answered that very question: "What manner of men ought ye to be? Verily I say unto you, even as I am." "That which ye have seen me do even that shall ye do."

President Ezra Taft Benson said: "The only measure of true greatness is how close a man can become like Jesus. That man is greatest who is most like Christ, and those who love him most will be most like him."[77]

3 Nephi 27:23–26

We keep our personal records and our family records; the Church keeps records; and the Father in Heaven keeps records. Out of all those records we will be judged. Not only that but all things that have ever transpired—everything we have seen, or heard, or done—are recorded in mortal brains and in immortal brains. Except for thoroughly repented of and forgiven sins, which are eternally erased through the Atonement, all things are recorded and will be revealed. See commentary at 2 Nephi 9:13–16 and Alma 5:18; see also Doctrine and Covenants 128:6–8.

3 Nephi 27:29

On asking, knocking, and receiving, see commentary at 3 Nephi 14:7–12.

3 Nephi 27:30–32

The Savior exclaimed that he is full of joy, the Father is full of joy, and the angels are full of joy, because of the generation of righteous souls then living—"none of them are lost"! But he sorrowed for those of the fourth generation (in this case, a "generation" being a hundred years; see commentary at Helaman 13:5, 9–10) because then people will sell him out, caring more for gold, silver, and other corrupting and transitory things.

3 Nephi 27:33

On the strait and narrow way, in contrast to the wide and broad way, see commentary at 2 Nephi 9:39–41 and 3 Nephi 14:13–14.

3 Nephi 28

This chapter describes the condition of the three Nephite disciples who desired to remain on earth for two thousand more years in the work of bringing souls to Christ, the same desire of John the Beloved.

Considerable detail is given about their physical and spiritual condition:

1. They would never taste of death but live until the Second Coming of the Lord (v. 7).
2. They would never endure the pains of death but at his coming would be changed in "the twinkling of an eye" (v. 8).
3. They would experience no pain over the centuries, nor sorrow, except for the sinful conditions around them (vv. 9, 38).
4. They would, in the end, experience a fulness of joy, and be like Jesus and like the Father (v. 10).
5. They were caught up into heaven and saw and heard unspeakable things; they did not talk about those most sacred things (vv. 13–14, 16; see commentary at Alma 12:9; 3 Nephi 26:16–18).
6. They would be miraculously delivered from the hands of evil men—from prisons, from deep pits, from blazing furnaces, and from dens of wild beasts (vv. 19–22, 39; 4 Nephi 1:30–33).
7. Mormon would meet these three men. He personally saw them, and they ministered to him (v. 26). Moroni also knew them (Mormon 8:11).
8. They would be among the Gentiles, and the Gentiles would not know them (v. 27).
9. They would be among the Jews, and the Jews would not know them (v. 28).
10. They would have "convincing power" to bring many souls to Christ from "the scattered tribes of Israel," and from "all nations, kindreds, tongues and people" (v. 29).
11. They would be able to show themselves to whomever they wanted (v. 30).
12. Satan could have no power over them and could not tempt them (v. 39).
13. A change had to be effected in their bodies so they would not experience death (vv. 37–39; see Moses 1:11).

14. They would remain in that changed state until the great judgment day, when they would experience a greater change (v. 40).

The three Nephites' bodies were changed from the regular mortal or telestial condition to a terrestrial condition, where there is no death, pain, sickness, or temptation. Other words we use to describe this state are *transfigured,* which is short term, and *translated,* which is long term. We also use the words *quickened, renewed,* and *paradisiacal.* All of these words also describe the way the earth will be during the Millennium. During the Millennium or at the end of the Millennium these kinds of bodies, and the earth itself, will shift from the terrestrial state up to a celestial glory.

"Those who were translated before the resurrection of our Lord 'were with Christ in his resurrection' (D&C 133:55.) Those who have been translated since the resurrection of Christ shall continue to live as mortals until the Second Coming when they shall receive their immortal glory."[78]

The Prophet Joseph Smith explained the doctrine of translation: "Many have supposed that the doctrine of translation was a doctrine whereby men were taken immediately into the presence of God, and into an eternal fullness, but this is a mistaken idea. Their place of habitation is that of the terrestrial order, and a place prepared for such characters He held in reserve to be ministering angels unto many planets, and who as yet have not entered into so great a fullness as those who are resurrected from the dead."[79] On another occasion, he confirmed, "Translated bodies are designed for future missions."[80]

3 Nephi 28:11

In the English edition of the Book of Mormon, the words of the recently resurrected Lord are contained in 3 Nephi 11:1 to 28:11, thirty-four pages in all.

3 Nephi 29:1–7

When "these sayings" (the Book of Mormon) are published to the latter-day world, it is a sign that covenant promises God made to the children of Israel are "beginning to be fulfilled." And it would not be a good idea to say that the Lord delays his coming to them, that all is vain, and continue spurning God's doings.

Woes are pronounced on those who deny the Christ and his works, such as revelation, prophecy, gifts of the Spirit, miracles, and so on. See commentary at 2 Nephi 28:1–8; Mormon 9:7–20; Moroni 7:35–37.

3 Nephi 29:8

A warning to those who would make fun of the Jews or any Israelites. Elder Bruce R. McConkie asked: "If the hearts of the Christians of the world were truly centered on the Bible, as they profess, would they not have an entirely different feeling toward the Jews? Did not Jesus say that 'salvation is of the Jews'? (John 4:22.) Was not Jesus a Jew, and did not the Bible come to us through Jewish hands? Can anyone truly believe and reverence the Bible without honoring and thanking the Jews?"[81]

3 Nephi 30

The prophet Mormon recorded the words of Jesus Christ commanding latter-day societies to abandon all their sins (he gave a graphic and comprehensive list) and come unto Christ—in order to be numbered among the house of Israel, God's covenant people.

FOURTH NEPHI
THE BOOK OF NEPHI

The small, one-chapter book of 4 Nephi covers approximately 285 years (from A.D. 35 to A.D. 320), nearly one-third of the time covered by the Book of Mormon, from Lehi to Moroni. It very briefly describes the most glorious, happy, progressive, and enlightened time in all the combined Jaredite, Nephite, and Lamanite civilizations. Is it so brief a history because there are more lessons to learn in periods of wickedness? Is righteousness dull reading? Or did the historian Mormon withhold additional details of their lifestyle because of the sacredness of their endowments of knowledge?

4 Nephi 1:1–19

The salient reason given for the lengthy period of peace and happiness among the Nephites after Jesus' ministry was the absence of contention. The phrase "no contention" is repeated in verses 2, 13, 15, and 18. And the reason there was no contention among this blessed people is gratefully preserved in two verses: "There were no contentions and disputations among them . . . [because] every man did deal justly one with another," and "there was no contention in the land, because of the love of God which did dwell in the hearts of the people."

Other reasons for the peaceful, friction-free life include the following: "They had all things common among them; therefore there were not rich and poor, bond and free, but they were all made free, and partakers of the heavenly gift."

"All things common" did not mean that everyone pooled

all their resources and shared everything in common, all having equal amounts. It means that every person and family had an equality according to their needs and wants—if their wants were just (Acts 2:45; 4:32, 35; D&C 51:3; 82:17). They were living the law of consecration. "Every man [was] seeking the interest of his neighbor, and doing all things with an eye single to the glory of God" (D&C 82:19).

Verse 11 seems to suggest, without stating it, that these righteous, consecrated Saints were enjoying the blessings of celestial marriage, which is part of the new and everlasting covenant, or the fulness of the gospel (D&C 66:2; 131:1–4; 132:19–20). They also had been promised all the blessings of the covenant along with Abraham, Isaac, and Jacob. The prophet Nephi whose story we read in Helaman 10 had been given the sealing power (see "Sealing on Earth and in Heaven," in commentary at Helaman 10:1–11). We infer from this that the twelve apostles selected by the resurrected Lord also had the keys of the holy sealing power, allowing for performance of all the exalting ordinances of the temple.

With "no envyings, nor strifes, nor tumults, nor whoredoms, nor lyings, nor murders . . . there could not be a happier people among all the people who had been created by the hand of God. . . . And how blessed were they!" Mormon is the writer here, and he would certainly notice the happiness and the blessedness of these people compared to what he saw in the society of his own time.

The prophets of all dispensations have tried to establish Zion. Some were unsuccessful; for example, Noah (Moses 8:19–24) and Moses (D&C 84:23–24). Others were successful; for example, Enoch and Melchizedek (JST, Genesis 14:25–40; Moses 7:16–19) and the Nephites after Christ (4 Nephi 1:1–3). These successful experiences with the consecrated life are types of the Millennium, when the New Jerusalem, or Zion, will be permanently established in a paradisiacal world (Moses 7:60–65).

The Lord's ultimate objective in every dispensation has

been to establish Zion—to prepare a people ready to receive his presence and literally walk with him. The charge given to Joseph Smith and his successors in this dispensation is to "seek to bring forth and establish the cause of Zion" (D&C 6:6; 11:6; 12:6; 14:6). President Spencer W. Kimball said: "Creating Zion 'commences in the heart of each person.' (*Journal of Discourses,* 9:283) . . . Zion can be built up only among those who are the pure in heart—not a people torn by covetousness or greed, but a pure and selfless people, not a people who are pure in appearance, rather a people who are pure in heart. Zion is to be in the world and not of the world, not dulled by a sense of carnal security, nor paralyzed by materialism."[1]

President Ezra Taft Benson taught: "We must prepare to redeem Zion. It was essentially the sin of pride that kept us from establishing Zion in the days of the Prophet Joseph Smith. It was the same sin of pride that brought consecration to an end among the Nephites. (See 4 Ne. 1:24–25.)

"Pride is the great stumbling block to Zion."[2]

Enoch's dispensation laid out a pattern for every other one to follow, especially our own, when it comes to establishing Zion. Note, for example, the commands given to both Enoch and Joseph Smith:

1. Preach the gospel of Jesus Christ (Moses 6:37; 7:19; D&C 19:21, 31; 38:41).
2. Gather the Saints to places of safety (Moses 7:17–19; D&C 33:6; 45:69, 71; 115:6).
3. Attain unity and righteousness (Moses 7:18; D&C 21:4–7; 38:27).
4. Become "pure in heart" (D&C 97:21; Moses 7:18).
5. Care for the poor and needy (Moses 7:18; D&C 38:35; 42:30–38).
6. Build a city of holiness (Moses 7:19; D&C 45:66–70).

As the Lord declared for every time period: "When men

should keep all my commandments, Zion should again come on the earth" (JST, Genesis 9:21).

4 Nephi 1:20–49

Is spiritual death an event or a process? At what point did this righteous generation begin to turn toward worldliness and wickedness? Verse 20 notes that there was a "small part of the people who had revolted from the church." Later, verse 38 indicates that things had worsened: "They did not dwindle in unbelief, but they did wilfully rebel." Two words in those two verses, *revolt* and *rebel,* show the gradual and then dramatic process of apostasy among the once-favored people. The Greek term *apostasia,* which we often think of as a "falling away" (2 Thessalonians 2:3), means a revolt or conscious breaking away; it is an active defection or desertion.

What were the prime indicators of this breaking away in their society? The very first problem mentioned, once the people had become "exceedingly rich, because of their prosperity in Christ," was *pride,* manifested, as often specified in the Book of Mormon record, by "the wearing of costly apparel" and pursuing the "fine things of the world."

"And from that time forth they did have their goods and their substance no more common among them. And they began to be divided into classes; and they began to build up churches unto themselves." Note that they built up churches "unto themselves," not to Christ. Thus began in A.D. 201 the great apostasy, rooted in pride, and promoting priestcraft.

It is not just good but critical to be reminded of the nature of pride. President Ezra Taft Benson taught: "Pride is a very misunderstood sin, and many are sinning in ignorance. (See Mosiah 3:11; 3 Ne. 6:18.) In the scriptures there is no such thing as righteous pride—it is always considered a sin. Therefore, no matter how the world uses the term, we must understand how God uses the term so we can understand the language of holy writ and profit thereby. (See 2 Ne. 4:15; Mosiah 1:3–7; Alma 5:61.)

"Most of us think of pride as self-centeredness, conceit, boastfulness, arrogance, or haughtiness. All of these are elements of the sin, but the heart, or core, is still missing.

"The central feature of pride is enmity—enmity toward God and enmity toward our fellowmen. *Enmity* means 'hatred toward, hostility to, or a state of opposition.' It is the power by which Satan wishes to reign over us."[3]

Many churches, with more convenient doctrine, dotted the land. They were led by priests and false prophets. They "professed to know the Christ, and yet they did deny the more parts of his gospel." In addition, apostates were possibly revealing and administering sacred temple ordinances to unworthy people (v. 27), the same kind of thing that has been done in our era.

Verse 30 contains a significant insight. The same emotions and feelings that killed Jesus in Jerusalem were those that now existed in the New World. In other words, these people would have tried to kill Jesus if they had had the chance. This is a sobering lesson.

The latter part of 4 Nephi details the destructive nature of the materialism and pride that caused that civilization to decay and self-destruct. Again, President Ezra Taft Benson gave a somber assessment of the causes and the results as they relate to us today:

"In 1787 Edward Gibbon completed his noble work *The Decline and Fall of the Roman Empire*. Here is the way he accounted for the fall.

"1. The undermining of the dignity and sanctity of the home, which is the basis of human society.

"2. Higher and higher taxes and the spending of public monies for free bread and circuses for the populace.

"3. The mad craze for pleasure, sports becoming every year more and more exciting and brutal.

"4. The building of gigantic armaments when the real enemy was within the decadence of the people.

"5. The decay of religion—faith fading into mere form,

losing touch with life, and becoming impotent to warn and guide the people.

"Is there a parallel for us in America today? Could the same reasons that destroyed Rome destroy America and possibly other countries of the free world? . . .

"The lessons of history, many of them very sobering, ought to be turned to during this hour of our great achievements, because during the hour of our success is our greatest danger. Even during the hour of our great prosperity, a nation may sow the seeds of its own destruction. History reveals that rarely is a great civilization conquered from without unless it has weakened or destroyed itself within."[4]

THE BOOK OF MORMON

Mormon 1

Mormon was a sober child and "quick to observe" what was happening around him. *Sober* usually means possessing an earnestly thoughtful character, temperance, moderation, and showing no extreme qualities of fancy, emotion, or prejudice. While still very young, like Joseph Smith he was visited of the Lord. President Spencer W. Kimball reminded us that young people can do great things.[1] Adolescence does not preclude righteousness. In addition to Joseph Smith, look at Nephi (1 Nephi 2:16) and Timothy (1 Timothy 4:12).

How was Mormon able to rise above his environment and not be overwhelmed by the crass wickedness surrounding him? He had apparently learned from an early age to respond to his spiritual sensitivities, and he developed a love for the things of God. He kept the commandments, so he had peace. He lived the higher standards, so he developed deep spirituality. And how did he know the commandments and standards of God? He learned much from his scripture study—from all the plates, the histories, the sacred writings of nearly a thousand years before him. And he learned from visitors from the presence of God and the world of spirits.

In addition, Mormon was a pure descendant of Father Lehi (compare 3 Nephi 5:20) and large in stature even as a young man (Mormon 2:1). But such a brief biographical sketch hardly does justice to the man. The whole is greater than the sum of the parts. He witnessed wicked, horrible events yet kept his sensitivity, and he saw the degeneration of

Mormon Abridging the Plates, *by Tom Lovell.*

his people but did not become embittered. Verse 8 notes how badly fractured that society was.

Mormon 1:3

After his first visit with the angel Moroni, Joseph Smith had to wait four years before he secured the plates (Joseph Smith–History 1:59). After his first visit with the record-keeper Ammaron, Mormon had to wait fourteen years before he secured the plates.

Mormon 1:13–14, 16–19

Wickedness inhibits the work of miracles, such as healing, and the gifts of the Spirit. The Holy Ghost withdraws when people willfully sin. Because of such an environment the Lord took away the three Nephite disciples, who could have been a tremendous boon to the people. Worst of all, Mormon was forbidden to preach to his people because of their willful rebellion.

Mormon 2:2

Mormon became a general in his sixteenth year and served over half a century in that military capacity.

Mormon 2:8–12

Wickedness led to the loss of courage and to an increase in carnage and chaos. The size of the opposing armies doing battle replicates the size of opposing forces engaged in the United States Civil War on the North American continent (1861–1865). Such chaos and the breakdown of society led the Nephites to begin to repent. Mormon rejoiced over his people's suffering because he thought at first this was a sign of true humility and contrition. He was wrong.

Mormon 2:13–15

Mormon's tragic description of his people is epitomized in the phrase "the sorrowing of the damned." The terms *damned* and *dammed* do not have the same meaning. *Dammed* means "blocked, stopped in progress," as in what a beaver does in building a dam in a river, but the scriptural term *damned* means "condemned."

His people were now "past feeling" (1 Nephi 17:45) and had deteriorated to a "fulness of iniquity" (Ether 2:10). Their "day of grace was passed." When they found themselves beyond the point of repenting and returning to God, it was indeed "everlastingly too late" (Helaman 13:38).

President Spencer W. Kimball labeled this passing of the day of grace as "the tragic point of no return": "It is true that the great principle of repentance is always available, but for the wicked and rebellious there are serious reservations to this statement. For instance, sin is intensely habit-forming and sometimes moves men to the tragic point of no return. Without repentance there can be no forgiveness, and without forgiveness all the blessings of eternity hang in jeopardy. As the transgressor moves deeper and deeper in his sin, and the error is entrenched more deeply and the will to change is weakened, it becomes increasingly near-hopeless, and he skids down and down until either he does not want to climb back or he has lost the power to do so."[2]

The Lord, at this point, would not even "suffer them to take happiness in sin." The wicked are always agitated deep inside; for them there is no peace. Compare Isaiah 57:20–21, where a simile shows that the wicked—the proud, the critical, the apostate—are like the troubled sea, always agitated, casting up mire and dirt. Peace is not freedom from conflict but a calm assurance of our good standing before God. The wicked cannot feel such assurance.

Mormon 2:18–19

Even though he had to live in such a sick society, Mormon was assured of exaltation. The Lord gave him promises and spiritual strength to endure the tragic conditions of his countrymen. He had received the more sure word of prophecy and had been visited by the Savior himself (Mormon 1:15), the Second Comforter. See also commentary at Alma 36:28.

Mormon 2:23–27

Though Mormon attempted to rally his people, as Captain Moroni had done centuries earlier, to fight for their wives, children, houses, and homes (Alma 46:12; 58:12), Nephite society was then so enervated or depleted that they had little physical strength and no spiritual power to stand up for good and withstand evil. Without the Lord's Spirit as a constant source of rejuvenation, all things wind down, all things are overtaken by entropy—from people, to planets, to universes. The Nephites were left to themselves in a state of complete weakness and vulnerability.

Mormon 3:3, 12

The general-prophet cried repentance to his people and showed love toward them because he had the love of God in his own heart. He poured out his soul in prayer for them but without faith because of their hardness. He could feel hope and charity for his people, but apparently he had no faith in them because they "had rejected every word of God, and they were ripe in iniquity; and the fulness of the wrath of God was upon them" (1 Nephi 17:35). They had arrived at the point that it was "everlastingly too late, and [their] destruction [was] made sure" (Helaman 13:38).

Mormon 3:4–16

Two victories over the Lamanites in the land of Desolation gave the Nephites a false sense of power and security. Again, they failed to recognize that it was the Lord who was the real source of both. Mormon refused to add to their self-deception by continuing to be their leader. Without a prophet-commander, the people violated the Lord's principle of defensive warfare (D&C 98:33–48) and sought to avenge the blood of their brethren and comrades by initiating an attack on their enemy. Furthermore, the Nephites swore oaths by heaven, the very thing the Lord had forbidden during his sermon at the temple in Bountiful (3 Nephi 12:34) and in the Sermon on the Mount in the Old World (Matthew 5:34).

Mormon 3:18–20

In the midst of Mormon's lamentable tale, he taught the doctrine of judgment. There seems to be a hierarchy of judges at the great and final judgment. Besides the great Judge himself, the Son of God, under the direction of the Father, there is a series of other judges by whom we must pass in order to enter the presence of God. The twelve apostles Jesus chose in the Holy Land will judge all the twelve tribes of Israel, and the twelve apostles Jesus chose in ancient America will judge this remnant of Israel under the direction of that Old World quorum. In our day another dimension in the hierarchy of judgment is added: No one will be saved in glory but under the direction and judgment of the head of this last dispensation, the great Prophet Joseph Smith. Brigham Young said, "No man or woman in this dispensation will ever enter into the celestial kingdom of God without the consent of Joseph Smith."[3]

Many passages of scripture unequivocally confirm that every soul who has ever lived on earth will be judged. The criteria for judgment are these:

1. Degree of knowledge and opportunities available during mortal probation (2 Nephi 2:10; 9:25–26; Moroni 8:22).
2. Works, desires, and intents of the heart (1 Nephi 15:33; Alma 41:13–14; D&C 33:1).
3. Information on records kept both on earth and in heaven (Revelation 20:12; 2 Nephi 29:11; D&C 128:7).
4. A personal knowledge that an individual's reward is just (2 Nephi 9:46; Mosiah 27:31) and that the judgment constitutes a proper decision (Mosiah 16:1; 29:12).

Mormon 3:21

Gentiles and Jews shall have the gospel of Jesus Christ available to them in the last days; they shall also have "other witness" that Jesus is the very Christ and the very God (2 Nephi 25:18). The Book of Mormon is not just another witness of the living Christ. It is the *best* witness.

Mormon 3:22

Mormon told us why he expended such effort in relating this sad tale: to persuade all to prepare to meet God and to help all readers understand how they can be happy and safe.

Mormon 4:1

The land Desolation is rendered in Hebrew *Eretz Horbah,* the latter word having the same root word as *Horeb* (another name for Mount Sinai), which means "destroyed, dry parched land; ruins, deserted or depopulated wasteland." Compare "waste cities" in Isaiah 61:4; see also Jeremiah 49:13.

Mormon 4:5

History attests the truth contained in this verse: It is by the wicked that the wicked are punished. For example, God anciently used the Egyptians, Assyrians, Babylonians, Persians, Greeks, Romans, Lamanites, and others to afflict and punish his wayward children, as instruments in his hands to inflict the wrath decreed for rebellion and wickedness (compare Isaiah 10:5–19).

Mormon 4:11–21

These verses describe sickening scenes of violence, horror, and human sacrifice. Every heart was hardened and delighted in the shedding of blood continually. The incomprehensible practice of human sacrifice recalls scenes from Old Testament history. One example was Molech, who was a fire god, "the abomination of the children of Ammon" (1 Kings 11:7); he was worshipped by the sacrifice and burning of children (see also Deuteronomy 18:10; 2 Chronicles 28:3).

The Aztecs who inhabited Teotihuacan during the later centuries also had some of these abominable habits. The first mention of human sacrifice in the Book of Mormon is A.D. 366. When the Spaniards arrived in the Mexico City valley in A.D. 1519, they observed the diabolical practices of human sacrifice by the Aztecs. Bernal Diaz, a soldier in the army of Cortez, wrote: "When they sacrifice a wretched Indian they saw open the chest with stone knives and hasten to tear out the palpitating heart and blood, and offer it to their idols, in whose name the sacrifice is made. They then cut off the thighs, arms and head and eat the former at feasts and banquets, and the head they hang up on some beams, and the body of the man sacrificed is not eaten but given to . . . fierce animals."[4] And John Sorenson noted: "The scale of the human sacrifices is hard to grasp. During one week shortly before the Spaniards arrived, 70,000 victims were reportedly slain on the altars!"[5]

Mormon 5:1–13

Because the Nephites looked with longing for Mormon to lead them, he did. But he mentioned once again that he was without hope. What a heartsickening feeling! Mormon described a condition known among military commanders as "total war" or war on a "strategic level," where everything in the army's wake is destroyed. General William T. Sherman's march to the sea through Georgia during the American Civil War was such a campaign. In November 1864, with four corps of soldiers, arranged in two wide columns, Sherman cut a huge swath during his infamous march. When leaving Atlanta, he set fire to factories, clothing mills, houses—anything that could be a resource to his enemy.

In like manner, total war was unleashed in the same New World some fifteen hundred years before Sherman. Mormon explicitly mentioned that his reason for recounting the "blood and carnage" is *not* to sicken or sorrow his readers but to teach important lessons in a powerful way to the remnant of the house of Jacob. That is, the wicked will not tell us what wickedness brings, but the results of wickedness are unmistakable.

Mormon 5:14–15

Great purposes of the Book of Mormon: to bring all members of the family of Israel to know that Jesus is the Christ, the Son of the living God, and to fulfill the covenant to restore them to their lands of inheritance and to believe his gospel.

Mormon 5:16–18

Mormon's contemporaries were living "without Christ and God in the world." In times past, they had Christ and God, the Father, as their leaders; now Satan was leading them. They were as vessels on water, without sail or anchor—no stability—and without steerage—no guidance.

Mormon 5:23–24

As part of the physical changes occurring at the Second Coming, several scriptures symbolically note that the heavens or the earth will be changed or transfigured (D&C 63:21); they will be wrapped or "rolled together as a scroll"; see, for example, Isaiah 34:4; Revelation 6:14; 3 Nephi 26:3; Mormon 9:2; Doctrine and Covenants 88:95.

President Brigham Young elaborated: "If anybody wants to know what the Priesthood of the Son of God is, it is the law by which the worlds are, were, and will continue for ever and ever. It is that system which brings worlds into existence and peoples them, gives them their revolutions—their days, weeks, months, years, their seasons and times and by which they are rolled up as a scroll, as it were, and go into a higher state of existence."[6]

Commenting on Isaiah 34:4, gospel scholar Daniel H. Ludlow wrote: "At least three possible interpretations might explain the phrase 'the heavens shall be rolled together as a scroll': 1. The weather phenomena of the last days (D&C 43:25; 133:69) or the manifestations in the skies. (Rev. 6:14; D&C 29:14.) 2. The sealing of the heavens after the completion of one phase or glory of the earth; or the opening of the veil of heaven, indicating a new age. (D&C 77:8; 133:69.) 3. The completion of the work of the telestial world in anticipation of the Millennium and the Second Coming. (D&C 88:95; 101:23.)"[7]

On the symbolic use of the lion, compare 3 Nephi 20:16 and 21:12.

Mormon 6:1–8

The destruction of the Nephites was close at hand, and Mormon knew it. He called his people to fight the final battle at the Hill Cumorah, located in a land with unusual terrain: "many waters, rivers, and fountains." One gets the sense that Mormon was not just older chronologically but feeling old. He had battled the Lamanites his whole life, but more to the point, he had battled the wickedness of his people. Who would not be weary? When his people saw the vast enemy army approaching, they waited with fearful resignation for the battle to begin. Fear is the absence of faith (Mark 4:40). The righteous need not take counsel from their fears. The wicked it seems have no choice but to do so. Thus, Mormon's comment about his old age against the backdrop of knowing this battle "to be the last struggle of my people" is very telling. Mormon hid all the plates for which he had been custodian, except for the few that he passed on to his son Moroni.

Mormon 6:9–22

These verses describe the view from the top of Cumorah, the final scenes, and Mormon's epitaph to his dead civilization (compare Moroni 9). The Nephite nation was destroyed, although some individuals and a mixture continued on, as prophesied in 1 Nephi 13:30 and 2 Nephi 3:3.

Mormon's description is utterly chilling: men, women, and children being "hewn down." United States history teaches that the greatest land battles fought in North America since the founding of the American republic happened during the United States Civil War—the battle of Antietam, with 23,000 casualties in a single day, and the battle of Gettysburg, with some 50,000 casualties in three days. Even combined they pale in comparison to the carnage at Cumorah, which witnessed 230,000 dead and only relatively few survivors among the Nephites. No wonder Mormon's soul was ripped apart with anguish as he cried: "O ye fair ones . . . ! O ye fair ones. . . . I mourn your loss." He concluded his lament with a wish for things that might have been and ultimately with his knowledge of the Resurrection.

Perhaps we can better appreciate why the Lord and his prophets weep for God's children. Enoch poignantly described the scene: "Wherefore, for this shall the heavens weep, yea, and all the workmanship of mine hands. And it came to pass that the Lord spake unto Enoch, and told Enoch all the doings of the children of men; wherefore Enoch knew, and looked upon their wickedness, and their misery, and wept and stretched forth his arms, and his heart swelled wide as eternity; and his bowels yearned; and all eternity shook" (Moses 7:40–41).

Mormon 7:1–7

Chapter 7 contains the last words that Mormon engraved on the plates, and they are words of testimony concerning Jesus Christ, that he is the Son of God, that he rose again and conquered death, and that he will meet us all at his judgment-seat. He invited the survivors, the Lamanites and their posterity, to lay down their weapons of war, to seek peace and the Prince of Peace. He provides redemption for the world and the opportunity to "sing ceaseless praises with the choirs above, unto the Father, and unto the Son, and unto the Holy Ghost . . . in a state of happiness which hath no end."

Mormon 7:8–9

The Bible and the Book of Mormon testify of each other. Whoever believes the Bible should believe the Book of

Mormon. President Brigham Young testified: "No man can say that this book (laying his hands on the Bible) is true . . . and at the same time say that the Book of Mormon is untrue. . . . There is not that person on the face of the earth who has had the privilege of learning the Gospel of Jesus Christ from these two books, that can say that one is true, and the other is false. No Latter-day Saint, no man or woman, can say the Book of Mormon is true, and at the same time say that the Bible is untrue. If one be true, both are."[8]

Mormon 8:1–5

Moroni is now the writer, finishing the plates for his father. He remained alone for thirty-five years after the last battle in A.D. 385.

Mormon 8:10–11

Moroni reminded us that the Lord finally removed the righteous from Nephite society, including the Three Nephites (3 Nephi 28:7; 4 Nephi 1:37). But these three translated beings ministered to Moroni and his father. It is hard to imagine how they could have survived so long without divine assistance, given all the horrors they had seen and experienced.

Mormon 8:12, 17

Does the Book of Mormon claim to be a perfect, flawless record? No. It is a sacred compilation prepared under the direction of the Lord Jesus Christ himself, but he used mortal men in all their weakness to accomplish it. Those who do not belittle and discredit this holy record but instead accept it and try to live by it have the promise of meriting even "greater things than these." See also Mormon 9:31–33.

Mormon 8:14–17

Moroni's feelings about the Book of Mormon record: the plates have no monetary value; their great worth lies in glorifying God and testifying of the Redeemer, especially to benefit the "ancient and long dispersed covenant people of the Lord." He pronounced a blessing upon Joseph Smith, who would bring the record out of the earth, out of darkness into light.

For the meaning of "hell fire," see commentary at 3 Nephi 12:21–22.

Mormon 8:22, 26

"The eternal purposes of the Lord shall roll on, until all his promises shall be fulfilled. . . . [They shall be accomplished] by the hand of the Lord, and none can stay it." Note again Joseph Smith's famous declaration (quoted in commentary at 3 Nephi 22:14–17) that nothing will stop the work of the Lord from progressing.[9]

Mormon 8:23

Moroni gave his own endorsement of Isaiah's writings, just as other Book of Mormon prophets had. This endorsement was intended for those of us who live in the latter days. He also testified that those Saints who have lived in the New World but passed on continue to pray and exercise faith that God will remember his covenant with those still living. Righteous people on the other side of the veil act in faith just as we do. Various individuals have been shown the activities of Saints in the spirit world and have seen that the departed offer prayers for the living and exercise faith in their behalf. The journal of Sister Janet Skinner's grandmother recorded her struggle over the death of a teenage daughter many years before. On one occasion, stricken with grief, the grandmother opened her eyes to a vision of the spirit world. She wrote: "I saw three personages clothed in white, two kneeling and one standing [in] back of them. They had their hands folded in the attitude of prayer. I knew they were praying for me. This was the first time I knew that loved ones on the other side could pray for us here."

Compare the statement from President Joseph F. Smith in "Angels Are Coming to Visit the Earth," in the commentary at 1 Nephi 3:29–30.

Mormon 8:26–41

Moroni wrote specifically to us in the last days. He saw our time, and he described it with perfect accuracy. "Jesus Christ hath shown you unto me, and *I know your doing*" (emphasis added). He made a list of conditions—the sicknesses of society—in the final dispensation when the Book of Mormon would come forth and the gospel would be restored. Nephi saw all this, too (compare 2 Nephi 28).

1. People will say that "miracles are done away."

2. Secret combinations, such as gangs, drug cartels, mafia, terrorist groups, etc., and works of darkness will prevail.

3. "The power of God shall be denied" (compare 2 Nephi 26:20).

4. Churches will be defiled and lifted up in pride.

5. Leaders and teachers of churches will envy even their own church members.

6. Fires, tempests, and vapors of smoke will be reported in foreign lands.

7. Wars, rumors of wars, and earthquakes will be reported in various places.

8. Great pollutions will abound; for example: pollutions of the lungs (contaminated air of large cities, smoking); pollutions of the stomach (poor diet, many unhealthy foods); pollutions of the nerves (hard rock music, drugs); and pollutions of the heart and mind (pornography, immoral and violent movies and television shows).

9. Murders, robbing, lying, and sexual sins will be rampant.

10. Lax attitudes about God's commandments and permissiveness—for example, "don't worry about it; God will go along with it" will be pervasive.

11. Churches will offer forgiveness of sins for money.

12. Churches will be built up for personal aggrandizement and gain.

13. Holy words of God, the scriptures, will be changed and corrupted.

14. Excesses in fine apparel, envy, strife, malice, persecution, and pride will be evident everywhere.

15. People will manifest greater love of money, worldly things, and adorning of churches than love for the poor and needy.

16. Some will be ashamed to take upon them the name of Christ, preferring the praise of the world.

17. The hungry, needy, naked, and sick will be ignored and neglected.

Mormon 9:1–6

Moroni issued some startling questions to those who say they do not believe in God or Christ. "The day of your visitation" is the day of his coming in glory, when the earth shall be "rolled together as a scroll" and "the elements shall melt with fervent heat." This is exactly what will happen when the Creator of the elements returns in fire or glory, with tens of thousands of holy ones accompanying him, to consume and then re-create, re-form, and re-fashion those elements into a new, transfigured, terrestrial world. For more details about this fire and melting with fervent heat, see 2 Peter 3:10–13; see also commentary at Helaman 5:23–50 and 3 Nephi 25:1.

The second phase of "the day of your visitation" is our day to appear before the Savior for judgment. Moroni boldly interrogates, "Then will ye say that there is no God?" "Then will ye longer deny the Christ?" "Do ye suppose that ye could be happy to dwell with that holy Being, when your souls are racked with a consciousness of guilt that ye have ever abused his laws?" Thought-provoking questions, indeed!

The wicked and unbelieving shall be "brought to see [their] nakedness before God" and stand exposed, having refused to be "clothed upon with robes of righteousness"

(D&C 109:76). They will not want to dwell in the presence of righteousness, even if they could. They would be glad to have the rocks fall on them (Alma 12:14). For the stark contrast in the day of judgment between having one's nakedness exposed or being clothed upon with righteousness, see commentary at 2 Nephi 9:13–16.

Ultimately, in the eternities, we will report to the kingdom where we deserve to live, given our behavior on earth, and where we feel most comfortable.

Mormon 9:7–20

Moroni wrote a powerful treatise in defense of a perfect and just God, a God of miracles (see also Moroni 7:35–37). God is unchanging; he is constant. Impartiality and fairness are possible because he is consistent. God's constancy is also what makes justice possible. In fact, justice is one of his attributes.[10] The plan of salvation, the gospel itself, is based on his constancy. Miracles are based on his unchanging nature and his omniscience, his knowledge of all things, all laws and their results, from beginning to end (2 Nephi 9:20). All things are present before him—past as well as future (Moses 1:6; D&C 130:7). What are miracles to us are to him simply a manifestation of the supremacy of higher law, which issues from him (D&C 88:41–42).

God always has been and always will be a God of miracles. Revelations, prophecies, healings, speaking in tongues, and interpretation of tongues are all miracles, and they are always part of the gospel of Jesus Christ. Note Moroni's most compelling arguments in verses 17–20.

Mormon 9:11–13

Throughout the Book of Mormon we see the prophets laying down the basic principles of the plan of salvation: the Creation, the Fall, the Redemption by Jesus Christ, the Resurrection, and the return to God's presence for the Judgment.

Compare the teachings of Lehi (2 Nephi 2), Jacob (2 Nephi 9), Abinadi (Mosiah 16), Alma I (Alma 12–13), Ammon (Alma 18), Aaron (Alma 22), Alma II (Alma 42), and Samuel the Lamanite (Helaman 14).

Once again the Book of Mormon emphasizes that *all* humankind will be taken back into the presence of God, to stand before him in judgment. See "Two Inseparable Parts of the Plan" in the commentary at 2 Nephi 2:8–10; see also commentary at Helaman 14:17.

Mormon 9:14

A word of warning to anyone who surmises that at the future day of judgment our attitudes and behaviors will, all of a sudden, improve and brighten. Moroni's words are quite pointed: "He that is filthy shall be filthy still; and he that is righteous shall be righteous still; he that is happy shall be happy still; and he that is unhappy shall be unhappy still." If we don't like the way we are at present, right here and now is the time to change!

Mormon 9:20

If someone never sees the miraculous hand of God in his life, it is because of unbelief. Moroni taught this three different times: also Ether 12:12 and Moroni 7:37.

Mormon 9:24

In all dispensations of the gospel, the promise of certain confirmatory proofs has been given, evidence that the name and true power of Jesus Christ are being used: casting out devils, speaking with new tongues, meaning miraculous ability to speak otherwise unknown languages, taking up serpents, being unaffected by the poisons of venomous snakes or serpents, drinking lethal liquids but not being harmed, and laying hands on, and administering to, the sick and healing them.

A GOD OF MIRACLES STILL TODAY

Evidences of Christ's miraculous power are still found among his believing disciples. One among many examples is that of Elder Jacob Roberts, who suffered a near-fatal fall from a moving bus in Santiago, Chile, in 1998, and spent a month in intensive care in the hospital, with all the missionaries praying fervently day and night for his recovery. Upon his release from the hospital, Elder Roberts and his mother attended the fast and testimony meeting of his previous ward in Santiago, where tender expressions of love and gratitude were freely given in person and in testimonies. The ward leaders asked Elder Roberts and President Ogden to begin the testimony portion of the meeting. The elder bore a sweet, humble witness in Spanish. President Ogden then took the congregation through a few lines that Moroni wrote for our day:

"I speak unto you who deny the revelations of God, and . . . healing. . . .

"But behold, I will show unto you a God of miracles. . . .

"O all ye that have imagined up unto yourselves a god who can do no miracles, I would ask of you, have all these things passed . . . ? Behold I say unto you, Nay; and God has not ceased to be a God of miracles. . . .

"And who shall say that Jesus Christ did not do many mighty miracles? And there were many mighty miracles wrought by the hands of the apostles.

"And if there were miracles wrought then, why has God ceased to be a God of miracles and yet be an unchangeable Being? . . .

" . . . Whoso believeth in Christ, doubting nothing, whatsoever he shall ask the Father in the name of Christ it shall be granted him. . . .

[Then Moroni cites the instructions of Jesus to his disciples:] "Go ye into all the world, and preach the gospel to every creature; . . .

"And these signs shall follow them that believe—in my name shall they cast out devils; they shall speak with new tongues; they shall take up serpents; and if they drink any deadly thing it shall not hurt them; *they shall lay hands on the sick and they shall recover*" (Mormon 9:7, 11, 15, 18–19, 21, 22, 24; emphasis added).

That final line of Moroni's teachings was once again fulfilled in January 1998 in Santiago, Chile, in the person of Elder Jacob Roberts. God answers prayers. He sees our faith in fasting. He is still a God of miracles.

Given his practical and cautious view of things as a medical doctor, Dr. Richardson, the mission medical adviser, must have wondered about such bold words when he heard a priesthood blessing at Elder Roberts's most serious and dangerous moment that he would be miraculously healed. Admittedly, the person giving the blessing may have wondered also about such spiritual boldness, to declare such a remarkable promise, yet that was the will of God, and it was sealed upon Elder Roberts through God's power. Elder Roberts was an instrument in helping many witness the strength and power of the Master Healer.

Mormon 9:28

"Ask not, that ye may consume it on your lusts." We need to be careful what we desire. We need to be sure our motives are true and pure, not asking for things just to satisfy our curiosity; nor to gratify the illicit cravings of the flesh; nor to yield to the natural man by wasting the days of our probation on meaningless, lustful, worldly things; nor even to desire righteous, heavenly manifestations so we can impress others with our superior religiosity.

Mormon 9:31–33

Moroni was concerned, again (see Mormon 8:12, 17, and the final sentence of the title page to the Book of Mormon), that people in the last days would find imperfections in this sacred record and therefore belittle it. In his humble apology for mistakes that may be found, he gave some sage advice to critics: "Condemn me not because of mine imperfection, . . .

but rather give thanks unto God that he hath made manifest unto you our imperfections, that ye may learn to be more wise than we have been."

Nephites used a modified form of Egyptian in their written records.[11] Moroni made an unusual claim: Had they used Hebrew, he felt, there would have been no imperfections in the record. Could that suggest that Hebrew is a remnant of the pure language of God or at least related to it in some way?

Mormon 9:34

Moroni made another important point: No other people know the reformed Egyptian language that the Lehite civilization created. Therefore, God prepared "means for the interpretation thereof," an instrument that in the Hebrew is called *Urim and Thummim* and that operated through the power of the Holy Ghost.

THE BOOK OF ETHER

The Book of Ether is, as its subtitle indicates, "the record of the Jaredites, taken from the twenty-four plates found by the people of Limhi in the days of King Mosiah" (see also Ether 1:2). King Mosiah made a translation of the record in the Nephite language. A promise was made back in the book of Mosiah that this record would be included in the compilation to come forth (Mosiah 28:19). The book of Ether is a greatly abridged history (it contains only a hundredth part of all that happened; Ether 15:33) of a people that came from the Tower of Babel in the Old World and occupied part of the ancient Americas from approximately 2200 to at least the 500s B.C.

The summary by Elder James E. Talmage is helpful: "Of the two nations whose histories constitute the Book of Mormon, the first in order of time consisted of the people of Jared, who followed their leader from the Tower of Babel at the time of the confusion of tongues [Genesis 11:6–9]. Their history was written on twenty-four plates of gold by Ether, the last of their prophets, who, foreseeing the destruction of his people because of their wickedness, hid away the historic plates. They were afterward found, about B.C. 122, by an expedition sent out by King Limhi, a Nephite ruler. The record engraved on these plates was subsequently abridged by Moroni, and the condensed account was attached by him to the Book of Mormon record; it appears in the modern translation under the name of the Book of Ether."[1]

Ether 1:3–5

Moroni explained that since the historical report of Creation, Eden, and Adam down to Babel (approximately Genesis 1 through 10) is available in the biblical record and on the plates of brass, he omitted all that and commenced his abridgment at the time of the great tower. When we have access to the plates of brass, we will "get the full account" of those early events. We also know that Abraham possessed "records of the fathers" from the beginning (Abraham 1:28, 31).

Ether 1:6–32

This genealogy is that of the prophet Ether, a direct descendant of Jared; the brother of Jared and his sons are not mentioned here. Also, we cannot become too dogmatic about the precision of chronologies since some are "sons" and some are "descendants."

Ether 1:33

The historicity of the biblical account of the confounding of language and scattering of the people at the great tower in the land of Babel is hereby confirmed by another scriptural record.

Ether 1:34

There is no suggestion by Moroni as to why the chief character in the narrative is known as "the brother of Jared." Daniel H. Ludlow offered three possible reasons why the actual name is not used: the brother of Jared himself, out of modesty, may have intentionally omitted his name, just as the apostle John did as he prepared his Gospel; the final writer of the plates of Ether was a direct descendant of Jared (Ether 1:6, 32) and wanted to emphasize the name of his progenitor; or Moroni may have felt the name was too difficult to adequately translate into the Nephite language.[2]

In 1892 George Reynolds wrote that Joseph Smith revealed the name of the brother of Jared: "While residing in Kirtland Elder Reynolds Cahoon had a son born to him. One day when President Joseph Smith was passing his door he called the Prophet in and asked him to bless and name the baby. Joseph did so and gave the boy the name of Mahonri Moriancumer. When he had finished the blessing he laid the child on the bed, and turning to Elder Cahoon he said, the name I have given your son is the name of the Brother of Jared; the Lord has just shown (or revealed) it to me. Elder William F. Cahoon, who was standing near, heard the Prophet make this statement to his father; and this was the first time the name of the brother of Jared was known in the Church in this dispensation."[3]

Ether 1:35

Because the language of Jared, his brother, and their families and friends (vv. 33, 36–37, 41; 2:1) was not confounded, we may infer that they had used and continued to use the Adamic language, which is the pure language of God (Moses 6:5–6).[4]

Ether 1:36–38

That Jared requested his brother to importune the Lord for all of them implies his brother's favored status, but it also may mean that Jared recognized his brother had the birthright, that it was his brother's right and obligation to go before the Lord on behalf of the family. Jared himself appears to be a righteous man, receiving a premonition that the Lord might be intending to take them away and carry them forth "into a land which is choice above all the earth." If that is the case, Jared exclaimed, "Let us be faithful unto the Lord, that we may receive it for our inheritance." Notice that Jared's concern also extended to their friends, as other righteous men have demonstrated (for example, Enos 1:9).

Ether 1:42–43

The Lord said, "I will go before thee into a land which is choice above all the lands of the earth" and raise up "a great nation" and "there shall be none greater." President Joseph Fielding Smith clarified that all of North, Central, and South America constitutes a "choice land":

"The Book of Mormon informs us that the whole of America, both North and South, is *a choice land above all other lands, in other words—Zion.* The Lord told the Jaredites that he would lead them to a land 'which is choice above all the lands of the earth.'"[5] See also Joseph Smith's statement quoted in the commentary at 2 Nephi 12:3.

Notice that one of the reasons the brother of Jared was promised this blessing from the Lord was because he had prayed fervently for a "long time."

The Lord's statement "I will go before thee" provides a paradigm for all disciples of every age. This same promise was repeated in this dispensation: "For I will go before your face. I will be on your right hand and on your left, and my Spirit shall be in your hearts, and mine angels round about you, to bear you up" (D&C 84:88). Every missionary in our day, for example, is sent forth with this promise.

Ether 2:1, 4

The Jaredites left what we call Mesopotamia, today's Iraq, for a promised land approximately two centuries before Abraham did the same. The Lord also guided Moses and the Israelites, the Nephites, and the Latter-day Saints to promised lands.

Nimrod was a renowned character who had established Babylon, Erech, Accad, and Nineveh in ancient Mesopotamia, according to tradition.

Ether 2:2

As the Jaredites contemplated and prepared for their journey, they remarkably created an aquarium and small aviaries.

Ether 2:3

The Jaredite word *deseret* means "honey bee."[6]

Ether 2:4–5, 14

For further explanation about the "cloud" in which the Lord appeared, see commentary at Helaman 5:23–50.[7]

Ether 2:7–12

The Americas, "the land of promise," "choice above all other lands," has been specifically preserved by the Lord for those people he brings (see commentary at 2 Nephi 1:5–6), "for a righteous people." And if they abandon him after establishing themselves here, and become "ripened in iniquity," to the "fulness of iniquity," he will remove them from the land. The Book of Mormon is a witness of that truth: two civilizations, the Jaredite and Nephite, were "swept off" and destroyed when they abandoned their God.

The Book of Mormon is given to the inhabitants of the Americas to lead them to repentance and to help them avoid the calamities that would otherwise come upon them. Serving America's God, Jesus Christ, precludes the possibility of bondage and captivity.

THE PROMISED LAND—ALL OF THE AMERICAS

The scriptures and the modern prophets clearly identify all of the Americas as the land of promise and the inheritance of Zion for God's righteous people:

Alma 46:17: "[Moroni] named all the land which was south of the land Desolation, yea, and in fine, *all the land, both on the north and on the south—A chosen land,* and the land of liberty" (emphasis added).

Joseph Smith: "You know there has been great discussion in relation to Zion—where it is, and where the gathering of the dispensation is, and which I am now going to tell you. The prophets have spoken and written upon it; but I will make a proclamation that will cover a broader ground. *The whole of America is Zion itself from north to south,* and is described by the Prophets, who declare that it is the Zion where the mountain of the Lord should be, and that it should be in the center of the land. When Elders shall take up and examine the old prophecies in the Bible, they will see it."[8]

President Spencer W. Kimball, then a member of the Quorum of the Twelve, at a meeting held in Guatemala City 16 November 1952 offered a prayer in Spanish to dedicate the lands of Central America for the preaching of the gospel. Following are excerpts from the English translation of the dedicatory prayer.[9]

"*We stand this day on the land of Zion, the promised land* made sacred by the works, the movements and the activities of the righteous saints and prophets of earlier times and especially sanctified by the repeated visits of Thy Beloved Son, the Lord Jesus Christ. . . .

" . . . These children of Lehi, . . . *this part of Zion,* even to *Central America,* . . . [and] the great truths of Thy everlasting Gospel have been established on this land through Thy Son Jesus Christ in person . . . [and all this happened on] *our American Zion.* . . .

"Thy spirit has touched these Central American countries . . . and [we] ask that the seed of Lehi in these Central American countries and the gentiles among them may see and hear and understand and have the courage and fortitude to accept and live the exalting program of Thy divine gospel . . . that this great people may be converted and be healed."

Elder Bruce R. McConkie: "The Book of Mormon . . . contains a record of God's dealings with the ancient inhabitants of *the Americas.*"[10]

Elder Joseph B. Wirthlin: "[Joseph] became the birthright son in the house of Israel and received an inheritance in *the lands of the Americas.* (See Ether 13:8.)"[11]

Elder Mark E. Petersen: "If the modern *nations of the Americas* will repent and serve the Lord, great blessings will be theirs, for the prophet has said: '. . . *this is a choice land,* and whatsoever nation shall possess it shall be free from bondage, and from captivity, and from all other nations under heaven, if they will but serve the God of the land, who is Jesus Christ. . . .' (Eth. 2:12.)"[12]

President Ezra Taft Benson, then a member of the Quorum of the Twelve Apostles: "To the peoples who should inhabit this blessed land of *the Americas, the Western Hemisphere,* an ancient prophet uttered this significant promise and solemn warning: 'Behold, this is a choice land, and whatsoever nation shall possess it shall be free from bondage, and from captivity, and from all other nations under heaven, if they will but serve the God of the land, who is Jesus Christ.'"[13]

President Spencer W. Kimball: "About twenty-five centuries ago, a hardy group left the comforts of a great city, crossed a desert, braved an ocean, and came to the shores of this, their promised land. There were two large families, those of Lehi and Ishmael, who in not many centuries numbered hundreds of millions of people on *these two American continents.* . . . They were given, by the creator of this land, a clear title to the Americas—a certificate of title, free and clear of all encumbrance."[14]

President J. Reuben Clark Jr.: "The Constitution of the United States is the basic law for *all of the Americas, or Zion,* as it has been defined by the Lord."[15]

"Clearly, if the people of *this land, this whole land of America, all of it,* must serve Jesus Christ, 'the God of the land,' or be swept off, and this is the very gist of all and every blessing promised for, and every judgment uttered against this land, then God must so provide that men in all the Americas could serve Him."[16]

Book of Mormon Reference Companion: "The story of the

Jaredite civilization gives perspective to the history and destiny of *the Americas* as *'a choice land above all other lands, a chosen land* of the Lord; wherefore the Lord would have that all men should serve him who dwell upon the face thereof' (Ether 13:2)."[17]

Encyclopedia of Mormonism: "Several doctrines taught within the book of Ether are greatly valued among Latter-day Saints, namely, that prosperity in *the Promised Land (the Americas)* is conditioned on serving 'the God of the land who is Jesus Christ' (Ether 2:12)."[18] "The Book of Mormon Peoples, including the family of Lehi and the Jaredites, were given a *promised land in the hemisphere now called the Americas,* on condition of keeping God's commandments (1 Ne. 2:20; Ether 1:42–43)."[19]

Ether 2:13

The Jaredites camped on the seashore for four years at Moriancumer, apparently denominated after the brother of Jared. For examples of the cultural phenomenon of naming places after the original or most famous settler, see commentary at Alma 8:7.

Ether 2:14–15

Imagine being chastised by the Lord *for three hours.* The brother of Jared had failed to call upon the Lord to prepare for a manifestation. Doctrine and Covenants 93:1 notes that "every soul who forsaketh his sins and cometh unto me, and *calleth on my name,* and obeyeth my voice, and keepeth my commandments, *shall see my face and know that I am*" (emphasis added). That was about to happen to the brother of Jared, and he had seriously neglected his preparation for it. Neglecting that spiritual preparation, according to the Lord, was a sin. As President Spencer W. Kimball once urged the Saints, "We have paused on some plateaus long enough. Let us resume our journey forward."[20]

Humility and meekness are surely hallmarks of the brother

of Jared. To accept chastening requires both, and chastening itself is required by the Lord: "For all those who will not endure chastening, but deny me, cannot be sanctified" (D&C 101:5). The Lord's chastening is done out of profound love for us, to help us be better, to raise us to celestial heights, to make us worthy heirs of our Heavenly Parents. As the apostle Paul wrote, "For whom the Lord loveth he chasteneth, and scourgeth every [child] whom he receiveth. If ye endure chastening, God dealeth with you as with [children]; for what [child] is he whom the father chasteneth not?" (Hebrews 12:6–7).

Ether 2:16–17

The brother of Jared followed the Lord's instructions for building ships, just as Noah did earlier (Genesis 6:14–16) and as Nephi did later (1 Nephi 17:51; 18:1).

Verse 17 notes, five times, that the "barges" were "tight like unto a dish"; that is, they were watertight, or waterproof.

Ether 2:19–20, 23–25

The brother of Jared was perplexed about what to do; he recognized three major problems. The group needed lighting, steering, and breathing mechanisms for their vessels. Each craft would be, in some sense, a submarine, "as a whale in the midst of the sea," at times "swallowed up in the depths" or submerged, at other times brought back "up again out of the depths of the sea" (see also Ether 6:7, 10).

How were the three challenges or problems resolved? In three ways, which suggest to us how the Lord trains us and how we in turn can teach and train others, such as children, family members, and those associated with our callings. First, the Lord commanded a course of action be taken, "you do this . . ." Second, the Lord, by implication, asks for the brother of Jared's best thinking, and then he tells him to request a course of action from the Lord. "What will ye that I should do . . . ?" the Lord asked his prophet. Though all-powerful, God doesn't just step in and do everything for us. It is our responsibility to suggest a remedy or solution. There is no waste of divine energy. What man can do, man must do; then God steps in to help. Finally, the Lord says in effect, "Trust me, I will do such and such . . ."

As the Lord knew, boats were not the only kind of vessels to be concerned about in this situation. People are vessels as well, as we know. Mary, the mother of Jesus, for example, was "a precious and chosen vessel" (Alma 7:10), and so are Heavenly Father's other children. Leaders and teachers are charged with helping to fill those vessels with light.

Ether 3:1–5

The brother of Jared prepared two stones for each of the Jaredites' eight seagoing vessels and took them to the Lord with the request that he touch them and make them shine. It is interesting that our modern scientific advances have taught us that some types of stone, as silicon, have chemical properties that can provide luminescence, but God, the Master Creator, who knows the physical properties of stones, can energize them with his light. See also commentary at Ether 6:2–3, 7–8.

Ether 3:2–3

The brother of Jared, as a natural man—carnal, fallen, and sinful—was admitting his "own nothingness" (recall Mosiah 3:19; 4:5, 11), but at the same time he was confident that God is approachable—merciful and condescending to hear our mortal cries and respond to our righteous desires.

The fact remains, however, that the Fall is so powerful and pervasive that without the regenerating power of the Atonement, our very natures are "evil continually," even though we were born as spirit children of God the Father. The Fall is so powerful that it changed not only our *condition* but also our *location* in relation to God's presence.

President Boyd K. Packer taught: "It is easier for me to

understand that word *Fall* in the scriptures if I think both in terms of *location* and of *condition*. The word *fall* means to descend to a lower place.

"The fall of man was a move from the presence of God to mortal life on earth. That move down to a lower place came as a consequence of a broken law.

"*Fall* may also describe a change in *condition*."[21]

President Brigham Young declared: "When the earth was framed and brought into existence and man was placed upon it, it was near the throne of our Father in heaven. . . . But when man fell, the earth fell into space, and took up its abode in this planetary system, and the sun became our light. When the Lord said—'Let there be light,' there was light, for the earth was brought near the sun that it might reflect upon it so as to give us light by day, and the moon to give us light by night. This is the glory the earth came from, and when it is glorified it will return again unto the presence of the Father, and it will dwell there, and these intelligent beings that I am looking at, if they live worthy of it, will dwell upon this earth."[22]

The atonement of Jesus Christ changes both our fallen condition and our location. The Prophet Joseph Smith taught that by the power of the Atonement, "this earth will be rolled back into the presence of God and crowned with celestial glory."[23]

"These many years we have been in the wilderness." Moses and Lehi and their peoples later spent many years in the wilderness also, as a testing ground of their faith and obedience. We, too, are "trav'ling thru this wilderness" of life to test our faith and obedience.[24]

Ether 3:4–5

The two exclamations, "I know, O Lord, that thou hast all power" and "we know that thou art able to show forth great power," pointedly show the prophet's great faith and, as he presented himself at the veil, would be rewarded with an extraordinary manifestation and endowment of knowledge.

Ether 3:6–13

The immense faith of the brother of Jared gave him the privilege of parting the veil and seeing the spirit body of the Savior. "Because of thy faith thou hast seen that I *shall take* upon me flesh and blood" (emphasis added). The brother of Jared was seeing what Jehovah would look like when he came into the world as Jesus Christ. The Savior's spirit body resembled the body he would inhabit centuries later in mortality (see also D&C 77:2).

The prophet's faith was so perfect that his redemption was secured—that is, his calling and election was made sure—and, even as a mortal, he was "brought back into my presence; therefore I show myself unto you" (see also commentary at Alma 36:28).

Ether 3:14

Jesus Christ became "the Father and the Son" by providing all mankind—at least those who believe on his name— with eternal life, "and they shall become my sons and my daughters." See further commentary at Mosiah 5:7–8.

Ether 3:15–20

A possible explanation of the otherwise puzzling first sentence of this verse is as follows: Jehovah appeared to the brother of Jared as he would during his life on earth; he appeared *as* Jesus Christ, just as he announced and entitled himself. President Joseph Fielding Smith wrote: "The Savior showed to the Brother of Jared His entire body just as it would appear when he dwelt among men in the flesh. It is a reasonable conclusion for us to reach, and fully in accordance with the facts, that the Lord had never before revealed Himself so completely and in such a manner. We may truly believe that very few of the ancient prophets at any time actually beheld the full person of the Lord."²⁵

Elder Jeffrey R. Holland provided a unique perspective on this verse: "We would assume all . . . of the major prophets living prior to the brother of Jared had seen God. . . . Adam's face-to-face conversations with God in the Garden of Eden can be exempted because of the paradisiacal, prefallen state of that setting and relationship. Furthermore, other prophets' visions of God, such as Moses and Isaiah in the Bible, or Nephi and Jacob in the Book of Mormon, came after this 'never before' experience of the brother of Jared. But before the era of the Tower of Babel, the Lord did appear unto Adam and 'the residue of his posterity who were righteous' in the valley of Adam-ondi-Ahman three years before Adam's death (see D&C 107:53–55). And we are left with Enoch, who said very explicitly, 'I saw the Lord; and he stood before my face, and he talked with me, even as a man talketh one with another, face to face' (Moses 7:4). We assume there would have been other prophets living in the period between Adam's leaving the Garden of Eden and the building of the Tower of Babel who also saw God in a similar manner, including Noah who 'found grace in the eyes of the Lord' and 'walked with God' (Genesis 6:8–9), the same scriptural phrase used to describe Enoch's relationship with the Lord (see Genesis 5:24). . . .

"Surely the most persuasive . . . explanation for me is that Christ is saying to the brother of Jared, 'Never have I showed myself unto man *in this manner, without my volition, driven solely by the faith of the beholder.*' As a rule, prophets are *invited* into the presence of the Lord, are bidden to enter his presence by him and only with his sanction. The brother of Jared, on the other hand, stands alone then (and we assume now) in having thrust himself through the veil, not as an unwelcome guest but perhaps technically an uninvited one. . . . (Ether 3:9, 15, emphasis added). . . .

"Indeed it would appear that this is Moroni's own understanding of the circumstance, for he later writes, 'Because of the knowledge [which has come as a result of faith] of this man *he could not be kept from beholding within the veil. . . .* Wherefore, having this perfect knowledge of God, he could not be kept from within the veil; therefore he saw Jesus' (Ether 3:19–20; emphasis added). . . .

"This may be an absolutely unprecedented case of a prophet's will and faith and purity so closely approaching that of heaven's that the man moves from understanding God to being actually like him, with his same thrust of will and faith, at least in this one instance."[26]

Ether 3:21–28

The brother of Jared was commanded to write down all the glorious things revealed to him and then seal them up until after the Lord's coming (see also 4:1–2, 5). Others, including Adam, Enoch, Abraham, Moses, Isaiah, Daniel, and Nephi, received the same instruction following divine tutelage: Write it down and seal it up. The only one instructed to write it and reveal it was John. His Revelation, the Apocalypse, was intended to be published to the world (1 Nephi 14:18–30, especially v. 26). We have at least part of what he wrote.

Ether 3:23

The two stones, or the interpreters (see 4:5), were a Urim and Thummim (Hebrew, meaning "lights and perfections"; see footnote references), the very same instrument that Joseph Smith would later use (D&C 17:1). See "History of the Urim and Thummim" in commentary at Mosiah 28:11–14, 20.

Ether 3:25

The brother of Jared saw, as Enoch before had seen (Moses 7:4, 21) and as Moses would later see (Moses 1:8, 27–28), a panoramic vision of the entire history of the world and every person who ever did or ever would live on this earth. We do not know how many souls that would be, of

THE BOOK OF MORMON

course, because our earth is not finished being populated, but a conservative estimate might be 125 billion inhabitants. If the brother of Jared saw each person for only one second, the vision would have been 125 billion seconds in duration. But 125 billion seconds is over 3,963 years! Therefore, he saw them all in a whole different time reference than we mortals can understand.

Moses 1:28 indicates that Moses, when he saw every soul created for this earth, "discerned them by the Spirit of God." In other words, he was overshadowed by the power of the Holy Ghost; that is, he was transfigured (Moses 1:11). So was Joseph Smith, when the grand vision of the degrees of glory (D&C 76) was opened up to him. "By the power of the Spirit our eyes were opened and our understandings were enlightened, so as to see and understand the things of God" (D&C 76:12; see also vv. 116–118).

Ether 3:26

Moroni, the abridger of this record, reemphasized that in all the history of this world, the brother of Jared is one of our greatest examples of faith: "The Lord could not withhold anything from him."

Ether 4:1–4

The brother of Jared had his vision upon a mountain, like others have had, including Moses (Moses 1:1, 27–28), Nephi (1 Nephi 18:3), and Peter, James, and John (Matthew 17:1, 9; D&C 63:21), to name a few. The brother of Jared was commanded to write down and hide up the description of his vision. It was prohibited for this record to be made known until after the Atonement was completed. Moroni inserted this editorial comment: "I have written upon these plates the very things which the brother of Jared saw." They are written on the sealed portion of the plates. Greater things were never shown to anyone.

Ether 4:6–7, 13

When will we have access to "the greater things," to all of the brother of Jared's vision? When we repent and become clean and sanctified and show the same kind of faith in the Savior that the brother of Jared did. At least some of the greater things are known in the house of the Lord. Articles of Faith 1:9 also tells us that the Lord "will yet reveal many great and important things pertaining to the Kingdom of God."

Ether 4:9

The Lord testified of his own great power: the ability to control all things that he created, to command and have all things obey him.

Ether 4:8, 10–11, 15

Whoever fights against and denies the word of God will be shown none of the "greater things." On the other hand, whoever will break through his veil of unbelief and hardness of heart and pray with a broken heart and contrite spirit, to him great and marvelous things will be revealed. The Lord will visit him with manifestations of his Spirit, and he will know of their truth and so testify. When it comes to seeing and knowing sacred things, it all boils down to trust. Whom does the Lord know he can trust?

Ether 4:12

Whatever persuades people to do good originates from God; he is the source of all good. He is the Most High God, and he is the most high good. Moroni continued this theme in his own concluding writings (see commentary at Moroni 7:5–18; 7:15–17).

Ether 5:1

Chapter 5 is an interlude, a personal message directed to the future translator of the sacred record, Joseph Smith. He was warned not to touch the sealed portion of the plates (see also 2 Nephi 27:21).

Ether 5:2–4

The gold plates will be shown to those called to assist in bringing forth the record, including eleven witnesses, and to three witnesses (compare 2 Nephi 11:3) specifically by the miraculous power of God, and their testimony will be a sure, irrefutable one. In addition to those witnesses, two other witnesses will stand in the latter days to affirm the truth of the Book of Mormon record: the book itself and Moroni himself, whom Joseph Smith would see face-to-face.

Witnesses often come in multiples of three: the Three Witnesses of the ancient American records; the Bible, the Book of Mormon, and the Doctrine and Covenants; and the Father, the Son, and the Holy Ghost.

Ether 6:2–3, 7–8

After the stones had been prepared, "the Lord caused stones to shine in darkness, to give light unto men, women, and children." This passage refers to the real, physical stones he prepared for providing light in the barges for the Jaredite colony, but we also note the symbolic message here. The Savior is the Stone of Israel, the Rock of our salvation, and he gives light to the world. Stone and rock represent in the scriptures something firm, solid, immovable (see commentary at 3 Nephi 14:24–27). All who follow the Savior also become, in a sense, "stones" for Israel and all the earth and "rocks" of salvation to earth's inhabitants.

On the historicity of the "ark of Noah" and the Flood, see also commentary at 3 Nephi 22:8–10. Genesis 6:16 mentions a "window" in the ark, but read the curious footnote 16a. Some translations have an alternate rendering of the Hebrew *tsohar*, meaning "light." According to one Jewish source, this "window" could refer to "a precious stone, which illuminated the whole interior of the Ark."[27] Compare Ether 3:1–5.

Like Noah's ark, the Jaredite vessels contained food and animals and plenty of faith. Some of these kinds of animals were likely found later by Lehi's family (1 Nephi 18:25). Moroni's abridgment gives us some small idea of the truly miraculous and spectacular nature of the Jaredite adventure, wherein the eight barges were propelled toward their destination by a furious wind, created by the Lord, which "did never cease to blow towards the promised land" (Ether 6:8). While some may question the veracity of such a story, it should be remembered that God is Lord over all the elements of the earth. As he himself told Moroni, "At my command the heavens are opened and are shut; and at my word the earth shall shake" (Ether 4:9).

Even those modern-day skeptics who most disbelieve maritime theories concerning the ancient peopling of the Americas from the Near and Middle East admit that some early transoceanic voyages are probable, due to the oceanic currents and prevailing winds. In fact, historical sources attest to such transoceanic crossings as experienced by the Jaredites. In the 18th century A.D., about twenty Japanese craft in the north Pacific were caught in currents and carried against their will across the ocean to the west coast of America.[28]

For additional information on transoceanic crossings, see Skinner, "Promises Fulfilled," in Jackson, *Alma 30 to Moroni,* 264; and Sorenson, *Ancient American Setting,* 111.

Ether 6:11

The colony members were in their ships, traveling through the ocean waters for a total of 344 days, only 26 days less than Noah in his ark.

Ether 6:12–21

Exactly where the Jaredites landed is not known. Some say they landed in what would later be known as Central America.[29] Others have suggested the western shores of North

America.[30] Yet others have suggested the southwestern shores of the Gulf of Mexico.[31]

Once the travelers landed, they were filled with the Spirit of the Lord. We know this because they bowed down before God, shedding "tears of joy" before him, and spiritual promptings sometimes move us to shed tears of joy. The Holy Ghost causes our feelings to be more tender; we feel more charitable and compassionate, calmer, with more capacity to love.

The original Jaredites were "taught from on high." The Lord's people are always to be "taught from on high" (D&C 43:16). A census was taken and a family council convened before their spiritual leaders passed on.

Ether 6:22–30

The people desired a king, but the brother of Jared warned, "Surely this thing leadeth into captivity." Ultimately, one of Jared's sons, Orihah, became king. He was the exception that proves the rule, because he did execute judgment in righteousness all his days (Ether 7:1). See further commentary about the disadvantages and negative consequences of having a king at 2 Nephi 10:10–17 and Mosiah 29.

Ether 7–8

These chapters tell of battles between fathers and sons, lands full of prisons, and prophets decrying the sins of the people.

Corihor's behavior fits the long-observed pattern of a wicked son rebelling against his righteous father, as seen from the beginning when Lucifer rebelled against our Heavenly Father (Moses 4:1–4; D&C 76:25). Not much later the shoe was on the other foot, so to speak, as "Noah rebelled against Shule, the king, and also his father Corihor" even though Corihor had repented (Ether 7:15). And then one Jared rebelled against his father, Omer (Ether 8:1–2).

Jaredite civilization foreshadowed the Nephites as they

divided into two kingdoms (compare Ether 7:20 and 2 Nephi 5:5–9). Prophets condemned the wickedness of the people, who then repented but fell into apostasy again. This is also an important pattern because we constantly see the merciful and forgiving nature of the Lord. He never turns away the truly penitent, and sometimes the vilest of sinners so reverse their behavior that they become the most righteous of mortals. This was seen, for example, with the people of Melchizedek (Alma 13:17–18), who were the vilest of sinners but ultimately became so righteous that they were translated (JST, Genesis 14:33–34).

Ether 8:9, 15, 22–23

Unrighteous, binding oaths were a corrupt imitation of a true, sacred principle of righteous, binding oaths and covenants (see commentary at Helaman 6:21–25). Whatever nation or people countenances secret oaths and combinations will be destroyed by them.

Perhaps the prominent hallmark of secret combinations is the perpetuation of the Mahanic principle—murder to get gain and then conceal it with oaths inspired and administered by Satan (compare Moses 5:29–31 with Ether 8:7, 9, 15–16). One of the greatest lessons of scripture is found in Ether 8. We must put our trust in God and not in the things of the world. Jared's exceeding sorrow over the loss of the kingdom shows that obsession with the kingdoms and glory of the world can lead those who are unbalanced to seek allegiance with anyone guaranteeing what they want, even Satan. It might also be noted that promises of kingdoms and the glory of the world were some of the temptations Satan threw at Jesus early in his ministry (Matthew 4:8–10). Moroni explained why he discussed these things—to warn us, so that we who live in the latter days might repent and refuse to allow these murderous combinations to infiltrate and destroy us.

Ether 8:24

This is a stark warning to the United States of America and other freedom-loving nations: "*When ye shall see these things come* among you . . . awake to a sense of your awful situation, because of this secret combination which *shall be among you*" (emphasis added).

Ether 8:25

Again, note what President Ezra Taft Benson said in 1988: "I testify that wickedness is rapidly expanding in every segment of our society. (See D&C 1:14–16; 84:49–53.) It is more highly organized, more cleverly disguised, and more powerfully promoted than ever before. Secret combinations lusting for power, gain, and glory are flourishing. A secret combination that seeks to overthrow the freedom of all lands, nations, and countries is increasing its evil influence and control over America and the entire world. (See Ether 8:18–25.)"[32] Make no mistake, the overthrow of freedom was Satan's plan from the beginning (Moses 4:1–4). Totalitarianism—whether labeled communism, fascism, or any other kind of dictatorship—is a prime example of combinations that seek to overthrow the freedom of all lands and bring destruction upon all people. The devil is behind them.

Ether 8:26

So what shall we do when we see these evils in our society? Teach the gospel of Jesus Christ! Bring people to the Redeemer. It is the best and only remedy. Helaman 6:37 records a classic illustration of how the preaching of the word can reverse a tragic and destructive course: "The Lamanites did hunt the band of robbers of Gadianton; and they did preach the word of God among the more wicked part of them, insomuch that this band of robbers was utterly destroyed from among the Lamanites." Our utmost effort as a people must be to work "that evil may be done away" and "do good continually, [to] come unto the fountain of all righteousness and be saved."

Ether 9–11

These chapters record further accounts of corrupt societies, conspiracies, assassinations, lands full of prisons, and appearance and rejection of more prophets. Now and then we read about a ray of hope and light; for example, Emer "saw the Son of Righteousness, and did rejoice and glory in his day" (9:22). He stands in bold contrast to individuals like

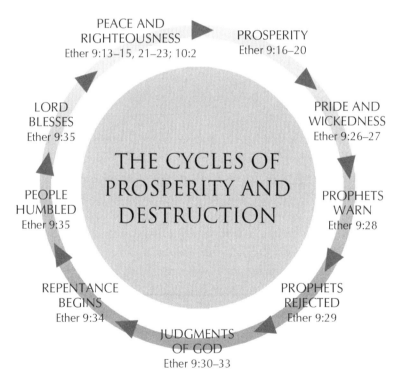

PEACE AND
RIGHTEOUSNESS
Ether 9:13–15, 21–23; 10:2

PROSPERITY
Ether 9:16–20

LORD
BLESSES
Ether 9:35

PRIDE AND
WICKEDNESS
Ether 9:26–27

THE CYCLES OF PROSPERITY AND DESTRUCTION

PEOPLE
HUMBLED
Ether 9:35

PROPHETS
WARN
Ether 9:28

REPENTANCE
BEGINS
Ether 9:34

PROPHETS
REJECTED
Ether 9:29

JUDGMENTS
OF GOD
Ether 9:30–33

Compare the same cycle later in history as recorded
in Helaman 3–4; 7; 11 and 3 Nephi 5–6; 9.

Akish, who sought the life of his father-in-law, Jared, his partner in crime (9:4–5). The pattern was perpetuated.

Ether 11 describes the final stages of the Jaredite cycle of apostasy. The people had earlier rejected, mocked, and reviled the prophets. Though King Shule had passed a law protecting prophets and punishing persecutors (Ether 7:23–26), we see how a later king, Shiblom's brother, made it state policy to execute prophets (11:5). So the prophets withdrew from among the people but returned in the days of Coriantor to warn them that they would be destroyed if they did not repent and that others would be brought by the Lord to this chosen land. Yet, they rejected all the words of the prophets. Their fate was sealed! Thus, in Ether 11 we see what we have seen before: wars and contentions in the land, rejection of the prophets, "and also many famines and pestilences, insomuch that there was a great destruction, such an one as never had been known upon the face of the earth." And still, there was no repentance, no spiritual soundness among the people.

Ether 12:1–2

Coriantumr was the last king and Ether the last of the Jaredite prophets. The Spirit was so strong in Ether that he could not hold back; he had to open his mouth and teach and correct the people. So also testified the prophet Jeremiah: the reception he was getting out in the streets of Jerusalem was too painful, so he wanted to quit proclaiming the word. "But his word was in mine heart as a burning fire shut up in my bones, and I was weary with forbearing, and I could not stay" (Jeremiah 20:9).

Ether 12:4

In this chapter Moroni highlighted the teachings of Ether. What do Ether and Moroni have in common? They were the last prophets of their civilizations, and interestingly, in their final instructions and warnings they both focused on faith, hope, and charity in Jesus Christ—the only way they

THE BOOK OF ETHER

could have a positive attitude in their lives (see also Moroni 7). Faith leads to hope, and hope is an anchor that makes people sure and steadfast, always doing good, and giving God the glory.

Hope engenders a positive outlook and an upbeat attitude, even in times of personal adversity and social perversity. Hope is much more than wishing. It is a twin sister of faith, an anticipation of the all-powerful redemption of Christ, which is manifested by a person's commitment to and demonstration of good works. Moroni speaks of hope "with surety." Ether, Mormon, and Moroni are impressive models of hope even in the face of the gross corruption and despair that surrounded them.

Ether 12:5

Ether's people did not believe the great and marvelous things he taught "because they saw them not." They were blinded to spiritual things, not having an "eye of faith" (Alma 5:15) to view and comprehend matters of eternal consequence (see commentary at Alma 5:15).

Ether 12:6

Moroni commented further on Ether's teachings about faith, hope, and charity. "Faith is things which are hoped for and not seen." We may not see God and his heavenly hand moving in the events of mortality, but we nevertheless trust that he is there, and we have confidence that he is guiding our lives. Just because we cannot see him with our physical eyes does not mean he is not alive and involved. We know our mortal vision is extremely limited; there is a wide spectrum of waves and rays all around us that our eyes, incredible instruments as they are, do not see. In spiritual matters we see not with our eyes but with our spirits. Our spirit, enhanced and quickened or accelerated by the Spirit of God, can see and understand far beyond any mortal capacity. Read carefully and learn in the following verses how the "eyes of understanding" or "spiritual eyes" are opened and greater things can be seen: Doctrine and Covenants 76:12, 19, 116–118, and 138:11.

There is a spiritual realm, attempting to understand the things of God, where our "seeing" comes not through the two little orbs in the top front of our heads but through the spirit within us. The Holy Ghost can show us—Spirit revealing to spirit—things that can be engraved into every fiber of our being, a spiritual witness that is far greater than the physical sight registered in a small portion of our cerebrum.

"By my Spirit will I enlighten them, and by my power will I make known unto them . . . those things which eye has not seen. . . .

". . . For they are only to be seen and understood by the power of the Holy Spirit, which God bestows on those who love him, and purify themselves before him;

"To whom he grants this privilege of seeing and knowing for themselves" (D&C 76:10, 116–117).

Exercising our faith comes first; then comes the ability to see through the veil. In the world generally the saying is "seeing is believing," but in spiritual matters the reverse is true—*believing is seeing.*

So, Moroni continued, don't ever complain against God, or shake a fist at heaven, or argue against spiritual things just because the empirical method doesn't work to prove them, "for ye receive no witness until after the trial of your faith." The testimony, the sure witness of the Spirit, comes only after we are tested, tried, and proved, not through the scientist's empirical method but through the Father's laboratory of testing called mortal probation. This life is a test. "They must needs be chastened and tried" (D&C 101:4). "My people," says the Lord, "must be tried in all things" (D&C 136:31). "God hath said that He would have a tried people."[33] (See commentary at Alma 7:5.)

His greatest blessings, the ultimate privileges of being sealed up to eternal life and enjoying the Divine Presence, come to a man "when the Lord has thoroughly proved him, and finds that the man is determined to serve Him at all hazards."[34]

Ether 12:10–12

Faith precedes the priesthood, the power. Faith precedes the saving grace. Faith precedes the miracle (compare Moroni 7:37).

Ether 12:13–22

Moroni made a list of some of the best examples of faith from the ancient Americas, similar to Paul's list of best examples from the ancient biblical world recorded in Hebrews 11. Moroni said there were *many* who had the "eye of faith" and could not be kept from within the veil; they saw glorious things.

Ether 12:23–26

Moroni was worried about the reaction of later peoples to his weak writing skills. He felt that he was ineffective at verbalizing or expressing in proper grammatical syntax the powerful words and teachings the Lord gave him, and he succumbed to the common mortal inclination to compare his abilities with others. Comparison is the root of all inferiority. Moroni lamented that he could not even come near the ability of the brother of Jared to create "mighty" writings, "unto the overpowering of man to read them."

The Lord reassured Moroni, confirming that fools will indeed mock but the humble followers of Christ will not be concerned with any weakness in writing. Through the Holy Spirit they will be accepting of the life-changing messages.

Ether 12:27

This is one of the most magnificent single-verse sermons in all of scripture! We learn the origin and purpose of weaknesses and how to overcome them. Weaknesses make us stronger because they bring our pride down to a level where we must look up.

Paul wrote: "Lest I should be exalted above measure through the abundance of the revelations, there was given to me a thorn in the flesh, the messenger of Satan to buffet me, lest I should be exalted above measure. For this thing I besought the Lord thrice, that it might depart from me. And he said unto me, My grace is sufficient for thee: for my strength is made perfect in weakness. Most gladly therefore will I rather glory in my infirmities, that the power of Christ may rest upon me. Therefore I take pleasure in infirmities . . . [and] in distresses for Christ's sake: for when I am weak [in the things of the world], then am I strong [in the things of the Spirit]" (2 Corinthians 12:7–10).

All of us have weaknesses in our fallen condition. We are each given a "thorn in the flesh" to make us humble, and if we allow the humility to work in us properly, we can make the weaknesses our strengths. We can actually become strong, even powerful; but the power does not originate in us. Paul wrote, "I rather glory in my infirmities, *that the power of Christ may rest upon me*" (2 Corinthians 12:9; emphasis added). In and of ourselves, we are nothing; we are totally dependent upon the Lord. He is our strength. The Lord has said, "The weak things of the world shall come forth and break down the mighty and strong ones . . . that the fulness of my gospel might be proclaimed by the weak and the simple" (D&C 1:19, 23). "He that is weak among you hereafter shall be made strong" (D&C 50:16). "By the weak things of the earth the Lord shall thrash the nations" (D&C 133:59).

As we learn patience, long-suffering, and self-mastery, we will overcome the weaknesses that God granted us and be "made perfect in weakness" (2 Corinthians 12:9) and have the power of Christ rest upon us.

Besides the apostle Paul, other great prophet-teachers

have taught the purpose and potential good that may come from our weaknesses:

Jacob: "The Lord God showeth us our weakness that we may know that it is by his grace . . . that we have power to do these things" (Jacob 4:7).

Ammon: "I know that I am nothing; as to my strength I am weak; therefore I will not boast of myself, but I will boast of my God, for in his strength I can do all things" (Alma 26:12).

Moroni: "If ye shall deny yourselves of all ungodliness, and love God with all your might, mind and strength, then is his grace sufficient for you, that by his grace ye may be perfect in Christ" (Moroni 10:32).

Thus, the atonement of Christ redeems the faithful from two kinds of weakness. The first is the natural result of the Fall—the overarching, pervasive weakness of the natural, fallen, unregenerate man. The second kind comprises individual frailties and challenges.

Ether 12:29–30

Our spiritual attainments in this life are directly proportional to our faith or our lack thereof. Moroni attested, "I know that thou workest unto the children of men according to their faith; . . . wherefore thou workest *after* men have faith" (emphasis added).

Ether 12:33–34

God himself was willing to lay down his life for us. That is the epitome of love. And that love is charity. And we also must be *willing* to pay the price to gain that love or charity, or we will not reside in the mansions of the Father.

Ether 12:36–38

These verses were read by Hyrum Smith just before his martyrdom and that of his brother Joseph (D&C 135:4–5). And how appropriate were these words to that occasion: the

Lord's assurance that Joseph and Hyrum were full of charity and were faithful, that they would be cleansed, made strong, and exalted. They bid farewell, as did Moroni, to the Gentiles and to their brethren whom they loved (compare 2 Nephi 33:14; Jacob 6:13; Moroni 10:34).

Ether 12:39

Moroni gained knowledge and testimony by personal, face-to-face experience with the Lord Jesus. This is the opportunity extended to all individuals who measure up to the standard set by Moroni, Nephi, Jacob, Isaiah (2 Nephi 11:2–3), and many others. The Lord said to the Prophet Joseph Smith: "Verily, thus saith the Lord: It shall come to pass that every soul who forsaketh his sins and cometh unto me, and calleth on my name, and obeyeth my voice, and keepeth my commandments, shall see my face and know that I am" (D&C 93:1). Note what Moroni himself said in verse 41.

Ether 12:41

"And now, I would commend you to seek this Jesus." Indeed, we should actively *seek* the Lord, pursue rigorously to become acquainted with him by study, by faith, and by service. When we want to know him more than anything else in the world, when we seek him first, above all things, then we will have the privilege of seeing and knowing for ourselves (D&C 76:117; 93:1).

Ether 13

This chapter contains one of the most significant discussions in scripture of the three Jerusalems that are to be restored on earth in preparation for and as part of the Millennium. These are first, the New Jerusalem, the city of Zion or city of Enoch, which was taken from the earth when Enoch was translated and which will come down out of heaven; second, the Jerusalem of Lehi's residence, rebuilt after its several destructions according to the prophecy by

Ezekiel; and, third, the New Jerusalem in America, Jackson County, Missouri, built by the seed of Joseph.

Enoch foresaw the day of his city's return: "And righteousness will I send down out of heaven . . . and righteousness and truth will I cause to sweep the earth as with a flood, to gather out mine elect from the four quarters of the earth, unto a place which I shall prepare, an Holy City, that my people may gird up their loins, and be looking forth for the time of my coming; for there shall be my tabernacle, and it shall be called Zion, a New Jerusalem.

"And the Lord said unto Enoch: Then shalt thou and all thy city meet them there, and we will receive them into our bosom, and they shall see us, and we will fall upon their necks, and they shall fall upon our necks, and we will kiss each other; and there shall be mine abode, and it shall be Zion, which shall come forth out of all the creations which I have made; and for the space of a thousand years the earth shall rest" (Moses 7:62–64).

Ether 13:2

Ether taught about all things from the beginning; but even the greatest vision means nothing to the wicked.

The waters of the Flood had to recede off the face of these lands that would later be called the Americas, which is evidence of the great Flood as a worldwide disaster; the Flood covered the whole earth and was its baptism by water (see also 3 Nephi 22:8–9).

The Lord set the Western Hemisphere apart for his special purposes. He brought groups of people here to these chosen lands to serve him (see commentary at 2 Nephi 1:5–6 and 2 Nephi 1:7–11).

Ether 13:3

As Articles of Faith 1:10 also indicates, "Zion (the New Jerusalem) will be built upon the American continent; that Christ will reign personally upon the earth; and that the earth will be renewed and receive its paradisiacal glory." Other terms to describe that paradisiacal condition are "translated" or "transfigured," all referring to a terrestrial condition (see commentary at 3 Nephi 28).

The New Jerusalem that comes down out of heaven is the city of Enoch and of Melchizedek (compare JST, Genesis 14:32–34; see also Moses 7:18–19; 7:62; Revelation 21:2, 10–27). Those translated and then resurrected people will bring also the holy sanctuary of the Lord. Enoch's city, and Zion, and the temple are inseparably connected. "I expect that in the city of Enoch there are temples; and when Enoch and his people come back, they will come back with their city, their temples, blessings and powers."[35]

Ether 13:4

"Ether saw the days of Christ, and he spake concerning a New Jerusalem upon this land." The phrase "the days of Christ" refers to his glorious Second Coming and his millennial reign.

Ether 13:5

Old Jerusalem would be built up again, unto the house of Israel, and become a holy city unto the Lord. Remember what the resurrected Lord said to the yet future Nephites: "Verily, verily, I say unto you, all these things shall surely come, even as the Father hath commanded me. Then shall this covenant which the Father hath covenanted with his people be fulfilled; and then shall Jerusalem be inhabited again with my people, and it shall be the land of their inheritance" (3 Nephi 20:46).

Jerusalem is already entitled by many "the Holy City," but the true meaning of the title is revealed in the Hebrew terms: "the holy city" in Hebrew is *HaIr HaQdosha*, but the scriptural phrase is *Ir HaQodesh*, which is translated "the city of holiness." The phrases "the holy city" and "the city of holiness" have profoundly different connotations.

Enoch's city was also called "the City of Holiness" (Moses 7:19). The two cities, on the two sides of the world, will become cities of holiness unto the Lord, and the uniting of continents will bring them closer together. "And the land of Jerusalem [in the Holy Land] and the land of Zion [in Missouri, USA] shall be turned back into their own place, and the earth shall be like as it was in the days before it was divided" (D&C 133:24).

Ether 13:6

So Old Jerusalem will be built up unto the house of Israel, and the New Jerusalem will be built up specifically unto the remnant of Joseph (and it will be built up only on "the principles of the law of the celestial kingdom"; D&C 105:5). Two of the most important signs of the times are the building of temples in Old Jerusalem and New Jerusalem, or Jackson County (Isaiah 2:2–3; Ether 13:8–12; D&C 84:2–4; 133:12–13). Speaking of Old Jerusalem, Joseph Smith said: "Judah must return, Jerusalem must be rebuilt, and the temple, and water come out from under the temple, and the waters of the Dead Sea be healed [see Ezekiel 47:1–9]. It will take some time to rebuild the walls of the city and the temple, etc.; and all this must be done before the Son of Man will make His appearance."[36]

Ether 13:7–8

A type or symbolic parallel is explained: Joseph of old invited his aging father, Jacob or Israel, and his family into Egypt to save them, just as the Lord took a remnant of Joseph's descendants out of Jerusalem to save them. Now the descendants of the remnant of Joseph will build up the New Jerusalem as a beacon of salvation until this present earth passes away and is renewed.

Ether 13:9–11

"There shall be a new heaven and a new earth." All things are renewed; the old earth and its atmosphere, its "heaven," are elevated to terrestrial condition (see commentary at Alma 40:11). A New Jerusalem will be physically built up at the same place where earth's history began, the Garden of Eden, and a New Jerusalem will come down out of heaven (the peoples of Enoch and Melchizedek and others who joined them; see Moses 7:27), and the united cities called New Jerusalem will join the Old Jerusalem to serve as world capitals for the Savior's millennial reign.

These Jerusalems, cities of holiness, full of people of holiness, will, after the millennial era, become one grand celestialized New Jerusalem.

Regarding this New Jerusalem, President Joseph Fielding Smith said: "After the close of the millennial reign we are informed that Satan, who was bound during the millennium, shall be loosed and go forth to deceive the nations. Then will come the end. The earth will die and be purified and receive its resurrection. During this cleansing period the City Zion, or New Jerusalem, will be taken from the earth; and when the earth is prepared for the celestial glory, the city will come down according to the prediction in the Book of Revelation."[37]

For more details on the various stages of the Old and the New Jerusalems, see commentary at 3 Nephi 20:29–33, 46.[38]

Ether 13:10–11

For garments made "white through the blood of the Lamb" and "washed in the blood of the Lamb," see commentary at 1 Nephi 12:10–11.

Many passages in modern scripture refer to the great gathering from "the four quarters of the earth" (see also Revelation 20:8; 1 Nephi 19:16; 22:25; 3 Nephi 5:24, 26; 16:5; D&C 33:6; 45:46; 135:3; Moses 7:62; Joseph Smith–Matthew

1:27), representing the four cardinal directions, or the four regions of the great circle or globe of the earth.

"The north countries" (see also D&C 133:23, 26) represent the northern regions of the globe; that is, northward from the Holy Land.

A related image used in scripture signals the gathering "from the four winds, from one end of heaven to the other" (D&C 133:7; Joseph Smith–Matthew 1:37). The expression "four winds" also represents the universal extent of God's gathering of his faithful children (see also Jeremiah 49:36; Ezekiel 37:9; Zechariah 2:6; Revelation 7:1).

Ether 13:13–15:34

Ether, hiding by day in a "cavity of a rock" (a cave), continued to record the destruction and eventual extinction of his people. Near the end of what may amount to the greatest civil war ever fought in the Western Hemisphere, Coriantumr saw that nearly two million men, besides women and children, had been slain, and Ether pathetically recorded that Coriantumr "began to sorrow in his heart" and "he began to repent of the evil which he had done." That reprehensible leader of men had indeed lost any vestige of the Spirit of the Lord, and "Satan had full power over the hearts of the people." When all except Coriantumr were dead, Ether concluded his record on gold plates and hid them so that the people of Limhi could find them (compare Omni 1:20–22; Mosiah 8:5–18; 28:17–19).

Ether 14:15–17 gives us a glimpse of the horrors of this last great battle of annihilation in which even women and children were armed with weapons and fought for their very existence. The brutality of this culture is almost unimaginable. Brothers McConkie, Millet, and Top stated: "When we understand that even little children and nursing mothers along with all others were engaged in bloody hand-to-hand combat, we do not wonder why Ether recorded that at the end of each day's warring 'their howlings and lamentations . . . did rend the air exceedingly.' This poignant, graphic image shows not only mourning for the death of young, strong soldiers but also anguished cries of pain and suffering for the inhumane destruction of entire families."[39]

The unusual and graphic tale of Shiz's death (Ether 15:29–32) has been discussed by modern medical authorities. "People have long wondered how Shiz could raise himself up, fall, and gasp for breath if his head had been cut off. Dr. M. Gary Hadfield, M.D., professor of pathology (neuropathology) at the Medical College of Virginia, [stated]: 'Shiz's death struggle illustrates the classic reflex posture that occurs in both humans and animals when the upper brain stem . . . is disconnected from the brain. The extensor muscles of the arms and legs contract, and this reflex action could cause Shiz to raise up on his hands. . . . The brain stem is located inside the base of the skull and is relatively small. It connects the brain proper, or cerebrum, with the spinal cord in the neck. Coriantumr was obviously too exhausted to do a clean job. His stroke evidently strayed a little too high. He must have cut off Shiz's head through the base of the skull. . . . Significantly, this nervous system phenomenon (decerebrate rigidity) was first reported in 1898, long after the Book of Mormon was published.' Thus, the account of the staggering death of Shiz is not a figment of dramatic imagination, but the Book of Mormon account is plausibly consistent with medical science. Moreover, linguistic analysis sustains the foregoing clinical analysis by confirming that the words *smote off* need not mean that Shiz's head was completely severed by Coriantumr. In Judges 5, an equally gruesome account is given of Sisera's death at the hands of Jael, the wife of Heber. The English translation of the relevant verses reads: 'She put her hand to the nail, and her right hand to the workmen's hammer; and with the hammer she smote Sisera, she *smote off* his head, when she had pierced and stricken through his temples. At her feet he bowed, he fell, he lay down: at her feet he bowed, he fell: where he bowed, there he fell down dead. (Judges 5:26–27; emphasis added).'"[40]

THE BOOK OF MORONI

Moroni 1

After one thousand years of prophetic writings, what could Moroni possibly add to his father's abridgment? He had already added some valuable teachings at the end of Mormon's writings (Mormon 8–9), and he had attached his abridgment of the Jaredite history, the book of Ether, inserting his own extraordinary commentary and insights into the life and teachings of the brother of Jared and of Ether.

Here Moroni became very personal, and we notice stylistic differences between his abridgment (Ether) and his own writing. The book of Ether is narrative almost throughout, while the book of Moroni contains almost no narrative, chapter 9 being a possible exception. Moroni used the phrase "and it came to pass" at least 117 times in forty pages of his abridgement of Jaredite civilization but not once in his own book.

Moroni began with a frank confession and perhaps a bit of a personal surprise—he didn't think he would write more, probably because he didn't know he would still be alive. He is the perfect picture of a hunted man; every Nephite found who would not deny the Christ would be killed. But he said boldly and nobly, "I, Moroni, will not deny the Christ." Therefore, he wandered wherever he could to keep from being killed.

Moroni 2–5

After so much was already written, and with so little space left on the plates, why would Moroni write about ordinances? What is so important about ordinances? Few of his own people remained, so he was writing to us, in the last days. Moroni knew that there would be a host of churches at the end of time that placed little or no value on ordinances. But as God has clearly taught, "in the ordinances [of the gospel], the power of godliness is manifest. And without the ordinances thereof, and the authority of the priesthood, the power of godliness is not manifest unto men in the flesh" (D&C 84:20–21). At the heart of our quest to obtain the power of godliness are the ordinances. The holy ordinances received only in the holy place can make us a holy people, even like God, as we keep them.

We all need more spirituality in our lives. The prayers spoken to bless the sacrament constitute an essential covenant-renewal, and they specifically tell us how we can have the Holy Ghost as a constant companion: take upon us the name of Jesus Christ, always remember him, and keep his commandments. Then comes the promise that "they may always have his Spirit to be with them."

In chapter 2 we learn that the Nephite Twelve were apostles, which is sometimes not understood by students of the scriptures. In chapter 3 the importance of the Holy Ghost in relation to the priesthood and priesthood ordinations is emphasized. The Prophet Joseph Smith stated, "We believe that it [the gift of the Holy Ghost] is necessary to make and to organize the Priesthood, that no man can be called to fill any office in the ministry without it."[1] In fact, the Holy Ghost is that same Holy Spirit of Promise the Lord promised to the Saints, which approves, ratifies, and seals the acts of righteous people, including ordinances, and makes them binding on earth and in heaven. The Lord revealed: "And verily I say unto you, that the conditions of this law are these: All covenants, contracts, bonds, obligations, oaths, vows, performances, connections, associations, or expectations, that are not made and entered into and sealed by the Holy Spirit of promise, of him who is anointed, both as well for time and for all eternity, . . . are of no efficacy, virtue, or force in and after the resurrection from the dead; for all contracts that are not made unto this end have an end when men are dead" (D&C 132:7).

Chapters 4 and 5 give us the sacrament prayers. That Moroni chose to repeat them, knowing he had only so much space left, is truly significant.

Moroni 6:1–3

Moroni listed the conditions and requirements for baptism into the kingdom of God on earth:

1. Bring forth fruit worthy of it—for example, pray, study the scriptures, and attend Church.

2. Come forth with a broken heart and a contrite spirit—that is, we have rid ourselves of pride and are humble.

3. Witness unto the Church that we have truly repented of all our sins.

4. Be willing to take upon ourselves the name of Christ.

5. Be determined to serve him to the end—not just for a few weeks or months but to the end; and someday we will realize there is no end. Here we see that the principle of enduring to the end is part of the baptismal covenant.

Moroni 6:4

How much time and effort do we spend on bringing individuals into the Church? How much time and effort do we spend on *keeping* each person in the Church?

For missionaries and members, this verse talks about *retention*. The verse also contains specific guidelines and instructions for priesthood home teachers. What happens after baptism?

1. We receive the gift of the Holy Ghost, are cleansed by his power, and become one with the Saints.

2. Our names are placed on ward or branch membership lists and on lists for receiving the priesthood (males), for callings, for interviews, and for home and visiting teachers.

3. We are nourished by the good word of God through our own scripture study and through visits with our priesthood leaders, class teachers, and home and visiting teachers to keep us in the right way—continually watchful to prayer and relying upon the merits of Christ, recognizing him as the only source of forgiveness for our sins. President Gordon B. Hinckley gave clear instruction involving verse 4: "Every [new member of the Church] needs three things: a friend, a responsibility, and nurturing with 'the good word of God.'"[2] On nourishing the members, see also Alma 32:37.

Once baptized, disciples of Christ must rely alone on the merits of Christ and nothing else! What are the *merits of Christ?* Besides this verse there are five other occurrences of this concept in the scriptures (2 Nephi 2:8; 31:19; Alma 24:10; Helaman 14:13; D&C 3:20). These passages teach of Christ's praiseworthy and everlasting qualities, virtues, and accomplishments: his justice, his mercy, his grace, his forgiveness, his compassion, his love, and his infinite sacrifice. These are the merits of Christ. Only he can save. We cannot do enough good works to save ourselves without him.

Moroni 6:5–6

It has been suggested that an appropriate epitaph for a Latter-day Saint would be: "Gone to another meeting." Indeed, we do attend many meetings. But there is one meeting in particular that we should attend often. We need to gather together often to fast, to pray, to talk about the doctrines of the kingdom, to partake of the sacramental emblems to remember our Savior, to renew covenants made at baptism, and to cleanse ourselves on a weekly basis and become totally free from sin—if we have exercised faith in him and repented of our sins before attending the meeting and partaking of the sacrament.

We sometimes hear people say from the pulpit after the

sacrament has been administered, "Well, we've fulfilled our purpose in being here today." Not according to Moroni. We also attend sacrament meeting to fast, to pray, and to speak to one another concerning the welfare of our souls.

Moroni 6:7–9

The people of God in the ancient Americas were strict to keep the Church free from contaminating sin. Members who were accused of serious transgression before a disciplinary council, and who refused to confess and repent so that their sins could be blotted out, had their names blotted out instead, and they were not numbered among the people of Christ. The same option is available to latter-day members of Christ's Church: we can have our sins blotted out or our names blotted out; it is our choice.

Then and now, when we sincerely repent and seek forgiveness, our sins are forgiven. Moroni 6:8 ought to be one of our favorite verses. We can be forgiven of *every* wrongdoing except one. Both the Savior and the Prophet Joseph Smith affirm that the *only* sin for which any of us cannot be forgiven is denying the Holy Ghost; it is the only *unpardonable* sin. The Savior said, "All manner of sin and blasphemy shall be forgiven unto men: but the blasphemy against the Holy Ghost shall not be forgiven unto men" (Matthew 12:31). And the Prophet reiterated the promise that there is only one sin beyond the redeeming power of the Atonement; essentially, it is the only sin that involves refusing to accept the efficacy of the Atonement. He said: "All sins shall be forgiven, except the sin against the Holy Ghost; for Jesus will save all except the sons of perdition. What must a man do to commit the unpardonable sin? He must receive the Holy Ghost, have the heavens opened unto him, and know God, and then sin against him. After a man has sinned against the Holy Ghost, there is no repentance for him. He has got to say that the sun does not shine while he sees it; he has got to deny Jesus Christ when the heavens have been opened unto him, and to deny the plan of salvation with his eyes open to the truth of it; and from that time he begins to be an enemy."[3]

Then and now, the Spirit guides meetings and the individuals who pray, sing hymns, and prepare and deliver talks—and those who hear them.

Moroni 7:1–4

Moroni cited the words of his father, Mormon. Mormon delivered one of the great discourses recorded in the scriptures to members of the Church, "the peaceable followers of Christ." Some members had obtained sufficient hope to be able to enter into the rest of the Lord. "The rest here referred to is not physical rest, for there is no such thing as physical rest in the Church of Jesus Christ."[4] The rest of the Lord is "the fulness of his glory" (D&C 84:24).

Moroni 7:5–18

Wouldn't we love for someone to tell us plainly and perfectly how to judge if something is good for us or bad for us? Here it is. There is probably no simpler, clearer explanation in all the world's literature than these lines from Mormon.

Verse 5. We can know people by their works. If their works are good, they are good.

Verses 6–10. An evil man cannot do good, or at least anything that will do him any good because, if the motives of his heart are not right before the Lord, "it is not counted unto him for righteousness." But we should also remember that we must be careful not to presume that we know another person's thoughts or the intents of his or her heart. For "there is none else save God that knowest [our] thoughts and the intents of [the] heart" (D&C 6:16).

Verse 11. One of the most effective and favorite forms of teaching used by the ancient prophets was to illustrate something in human conduct with something in nature. On avoiding hypocrisy and living with integrity, James, the New

Testament writer, metaphorically inquired: "Doth a fountain send forth at the same place sweet water and bitter? . . . So can no fountain both yield salt water and fresh" (James 3:11–12). Mormon later used this same image: "A bitter fountain cannot bring forth good water; neither can a good fountain bring forth bitter water."

Jesus taught the same idea with the image of a tree: "Every good tree bringeth forth good fruit; but a corrupt tree bringeth forth evil fruit" (Matthew 7:17).

The meaning of all these images is given in plain terms by Mormon: "Wherefore, a man being a servant of the devil cannot follow Christ; and if he follow Christ he cannot be a servant of the devil."

Verses 12–13. There were never plainer words written than these. Here is how we can discern good from evil:

1. All good things come from God.

2. All evil things come from the devil.

3. Whatever is from the devil invites and entices to sin and to do evil continually. If something invites and entices us to love God and to serve him, if it draws us closer to the fulness of the gospel, it is inspired of God.

Moroni 7:14

Warning! Do not misjudge and mislabel evil things to be of God and good things to be of the devil. This is the same message Isaiah gave centuries earlier, and Nephi reiterated, "Woe unto them that call evil good, and good evil; that put darkness for light, and light for darkness" (Isaiah 5:20; 2 Nephi 15:20). See commentary at 2 Nephi 15:20 for examples of this very thing in our day.

Moroni 7:15–17

Mormon has told us how to judge, that we may know good from evil. He said: "The way to judge is as plain, that ye may know with a perfect knowledge, as the daylight is from the dark night. For behold, the Spirit of Christ is given to every man [we often call it the light of Christ, or conscience], that he may know good from evil; wherefore, I show unto you the way to judge; for *every thing which inviteth to do good, and to persuade to believe in Christ, is sent forth by the power and gift of Christ; wherefore ye may know with a perfect knowledge it is of God"* (emphasis added).

In judging what we wear, what we listen to, what we read, and what we watch, we can know perfectly well whether or not it is good for us—if it is uplifting, if it is inspiring, if it will bring us to Christ, or if we would feel comfortable wearing it, listening to it, reading it, or watching it *with him present.* When exposed to immorality, violence, profanity, vulgarity, or the promotion of deviant behavior, our spirits start squirming. A lot of what the world is trying to feed us will make us sick. It is junk food. See also Doctrine and Covenants 50:23–24.

The criteria, then, for discerning good from evil—how we can judge what is good for us and what is bad for us—may be summarized as follows:

1. We may know with a perfect knowledge that every-thing that invites us to do good, that persuades us to believe in Christ, is from God.

2. We may know with a perfect knowledge that everything that persuades us to do evil and believe not in Christ but deny him and serve him not, is from the devil. Neither the devil nor his angels nor anyone who subjects himself to the devil will persuade us to do good.

3. We should listen carefully to our conscience. Elder Richard G. Scott reminded us that what we call conscience, God calls the Spirit of Christ.[5] President Joseph F. Smith said: "It is by the spirit which lighteth every man that cometh into the world that our minds are quickened and our spir-its enlightened with understanding and intelligence. And all men are entitled to this. It is not reserved for the obedient alone; but it is given unto all the children of men that are born into the world."[6] For baptized members of Christ's Church,

conscience is a powerful guide. President Spencer W. Kimball once said that he would challenge any normal baptized persons who said they did not know they were doing wrong (see commentary at 2 Nephi 15:20).[7]

Moroni 7:18

The New Testament text reads, "Judge not, that ye be not judged" (Matthew 7:1), but Joseph Smith changed it to read, "Judge not unrighteously" (Matthew 7:1, footnote *a*, from JST, Matthew 7:1). In these verses Mormon instructed how to judge righteously. He warns not to misjudge or judge wrongfully or harshly. Whatever criteria we use to judge other people, we will be judged by those same criteria (see also commentary at 3 Nephi 14:1–5).

Moroni 7:22–23

"God [knoweth] all things"; see commentary at 2 Nephi 9:20.

"He sent angels to minister"; see "Angels Are Coming to Visit the Earth" in commentary at 1 Nephi 3:29–30.

"God also declared unto prophets . . . that Christ should come"; see "All the Prophets Prophesied of Christ," in commentary at Mosiah 13:33.

Moroni 7:26–28

Christ taught that whatever we want that is good, showing faith in him, we may receive it (see also 3 Nephi 18:20).

Have miracles ceased just because Christ has left the earth? Of course not; his power remains with his disciples. See commentary at Mormon 9:7–20 and "A God of Miracles Still Today," in commentary at Mormon 9:24.

The phrase "Christ hath ascended into heaven . . . to claim of the Father his rights of mercy" refers to the Savior's right and ability to decide who receives the full benefits of the Atonement, including forgiveness of sin, and who does not.

This is illustrated by the Savior's description to Joseph Smith of His advocacy on our behalf:

"Listen to him who is the advocate with the Father, who is pleading your cause before him—

"Saying: Father, behold the sufferings and death of him who did no sin, in whom thou wast well pleased; behold the blood of thy Son which was shed, the blood of him whom thou gavest that thyself might be glorified;

"Wherefore, Father, spare these my brethren that believe on my name, that they may come unto me and have everlasting life" (D&C 45:3–5).

In other words, the fulness of Christ's mercy will be applied only to those who exercise faith in him, as Mormon taught later on in his sermon. They who have faith in Christ will cleave unto every good thing. See commentary at Moroni 7:15–17.

Christ "advocateth the cause of the children of men." Christ will be our Advocate and Defender before the Father; see also commentary at 2 Nephi 19:6–7, under "Counselor."

Moroni 7:29–30

For those who have "strong faith and a firm mind in every form of godliness," miracles still happen, and angels still minister to them. See commentary at Moroni 7:22–23 and 7:26–28.

Moroni 7:31

The role of angels is to call men to repentance, to help fulfill the covenants of the Father, and to prepare the way for the Savior by declaring his words to the chosen vessels of the Lord so they can bear sure testimony of him. See "Angels Are Coming to Visit the Earth" in commentary at 1 Nephi 3:29–30.

Moroni 7:33

Christ repeats: If you have faith in me, you will have power to accomplish anything that is necessary for the work. President Heber J. Grant indicated that we can pray for greater faith: "Faith is a gift of God, and faith comes to each and all of us who serve God and supplicate him for the guidance of his Spirit. There is no danger of any man or woman losing his or her faith in this Church if he or she is humble and prayerful and obedient to duty. I have never known of such an individual losing his faith. By doing our duty faith increases until it becomes perfect knowledge."[8]

Moroni 7:35–37

Has the day of miracles ceased? Have angels ceased to appear? Has the power of the Holy Ghost been withheld? The answer to all three questions is a resounding No! With faith, all these things still occur; and if they have ceased, it is because of lack of faith. See commentary on miracles at Mormon 9:7–20 and "A God of Miracles Still Today" in commentary at Mormon 9:24.

Moroni 7:40–43

Hope breeds faith, and faith breeds hope. They work hand in hand to promote an optimistic view of the future, and they both center in Christ and his atonement. Faith and hope come from meekness and lowliness of heart, which are divine qualities of the Savior.

Hope comes from the Holy Ghost (8:26). The opposite of faith and hope is despair. None of the Lord's people need to despair, even though they might live in environments of despair.

Moroni 7:44–48

What is the best thing we could possess when we leave this life? Is it knowledge, even the spiritual kind? Is it titles?

Awards? Money? Friendships? Spirituality? Moroni 7:47 answers the question unequivocally: The best and most important possession is charity, the pure love of Christ. Luke 7:47 is an example of just how valuable it is: "Her sins, which are many, are forgiven; for she loved much."

The greatest objective of the true followers of Christ in the dream of Lehi and Nephi was to get to the tree of life, which represents the love of God. The loftiest goal of this mortal existence is to acquire the love of God. Elder C. Max Caldwell said: "If we must have charity, then we must know what it is. The phrase 'love of Christ' might have meaning in three dimensions:

"1. Love *for* Christ;

"2. Love *from* Christ;

"3. Love *like* Christ."[9]

And how do we acquire it? "Pray unto the Father with all the energy of heart, that ye may be filled with this love."

THE LOVE OF GOD

We know that faith is the first principle of the gospel. Repentance is the number one doctrine of the kingdom. Obedience is the first law of heaven. And happiness is the object of our existence. But of all things in the gospel, in the scriptures, and in the plan of salvation, that which is *the most important* of all is the *love of God!*

Circumstances and people come into our lives to teach us important lessons. A woman entered the office of the Santiago Chile East Mission to speak for a moment with the mission president. She wanted to talk to him about getting her name removed from membership records of this "incorrect" Church. "I've learned," she announced, "that this is not the true way back to God, and I want to go back to my other church and just live by my Bible. I don't believe that the Book of Mormon is God's word, and I don't believe Joseph Smith was a prophet. I don't want anything to do with this church anymore." She carried on and on. President Ogden felt irritation mounting and tried to interject some counterarguments here and there, especially some testimony, but it all fell on deaf ears. She was sincere, but her heart was closed.

Near the end of her tirade, a thought entered the mission president's mind: "What would Jesus do in this situation?" The thought calmed him, and he began feeling compassion for her pain. She had said, accusingly, "Your missionaries only want to baptize people, and then they leave them and don't care for them." It came to the president's mind, as clearly as if he had defrosted the windshield of his soul, that her problem was that no one had shown her the love she needed. She just needed some honest-to-goodness *love*. She might be hard for others to love, but she needed it anyway.

Following is a summary of what love is, why we want it, how we get it, what to be careful of, the blessings that come from having it, and its visible influence in our lives. If we ponder carefully and prayerfully what the Lord teaches, we may be inspired to desire and work toward the love of God above all else. We have a right, as we consider these teachings, to receive specific inspiration about how to improve and strengthen our own lives right now.

Love—What It Is

Love is powerfully defined in the Book of Mormon. We can know exactly what it is. "All men should have charity, which charity is love. And except they should have charity they were nothing" (2 Nephi 26:30).

"Charity is the pure love of Christ . . . ; and whoso is found possessed of it at the last day, it shall be well with him" (Moroni 7:47).

"Charity suffereth long, and is kind, and envieth not [there is no resentment or discontent over the good fortune of others], and is not puffed up [there is no contention for superiority; those converted to Christ are not threatened by others' abilities and successes; there is no pride], seeketh not her own [there is no selfishness], is not easily provoked, thinketh no evil, and rejoiceth not in iniquity" (Moroni 7:45).

"I am filled with charity," exclaimed Moroni, "which is everlasting love" (Moroni 8:17).

Love is one of God's perfect attributes. Knowing of this attribute allows us to exercise faith in him. "And lastly, but not less important to the exercise of faith in God, is the idea that he is love; for with all the other excellencies in his character, without this one to influence them, they could not have such powerful dominion over the minds of men; but when the idea is planted in the mind that he is love, who cannot see the just ground that men of every nation, kindred, and tongue, have to exercise faith in God so as to obtain eternal life?"[10] The attribute of divine love is the one that influences, shapes, energizes, and mediates all the other qualities and characteristics of Deity. This is true for the Father, the Son, and the Holy Ghost.

Love—Why We Want It

We want the love of God because it is a commandment to love him and others. "Love the Lord thy God," Moses wrote (Deuteronomy 6:5), and "love thy neighbour as thyself" (Leviticus 19:18). The grand secret is selflessness! The Lord revealed in modern times: "Thou shalt live together in love" (D&C 42:45) and "let thy love abound unto all men" (D&C 112:11). "Let thy bowels . . . be full of charity towards all men" (D&C 121:45).

Seeking and receiving the love of God is not just a commandment; it is the commandment, the number one of all commandments: "Above all these things put on charity" (Colossians 3:14); "above all things have fervent charity among yourselves: for charity shall cover the multitude of sins" (1 Peter 4:8); "above all things, clothe yourselves with the bond of charity" (D&C 88:125).

Getting the love of God in our hearts is a test: "The Lord your God proveth you, to know whether ye love the Lord your God with all your heart" (Deuteronomy 13:3). It is to prove our discipleship: "By this shall all men know that ye are my disciples, if ye have love one to another" (John 13:35).

We want the love of God because it brings joy into our lives. "The love of God . . . is the most desirable above all things . . . and the most joyous to the soul" (1 Nephi 11:22–23). After the Savior's visit to the inhabitants of the ancient Americas, Mormon was able to report that "there was no contention in the land, because of the love of God . . . in the hearts of the people [they did not have a mind to injure one another; see Mosiah 4:13] . . . ; and surely there could not be a happier people" (4 Nephi 1:15–16).

We want the love of God because we must have it to be able to successfully serve in his work and to get where we eventually want to be. "No one can assist in this work except he shall be humble and full of love" (D&C 12:8). "Wherefore, except men shall have charity they cannot inherit that place . . . prepared in the mansions of thy Father" (Ether 12:34).

Love—How We Get It

We can get God's love by being obedient to him. "If ye keep my commandments, ye shall abide in my love" (John 15:10). "Keep the commandments of God, that [you] might . . . be filled with love towards God and all men" (Mosiah 2:4).

We must also be willing to give up some things; in fact, we must be willing to sacrifice all things for the cause of Christ. Said he, "Greater love hath no man than this, that a man lay down his life for his friends" (John 15:13). Jesus admonished his presiding leader in the meridian of time with this pointed challenge: "Simon Peter, . . . lovest thou me more than these? . . . Feed my lambs. . . . Feed my sheep. . . . Feed my sheep" (John 21:15–17). We get God's love by dedicated service to others. "Teach them to love one another," King Benjamin declared, meaning that they must "serve one another" (Mosiah 4:15). "Succor those that stand in need" (Mosiah 4:16).

One specific thing we can do to have godly love in our lives is to keep ourselves clean; quickly expel immoral, lustful thoughts and feelings when they come; and maintain control of our physical desires. Alma counseled his son, "Bridle all your passions, that ye may be filled with love" (Alma 38:12).

Sincere prayer from our hearts is a key to obtaining the love of God. "Pray continually, that ye may . . . [be] full of love" (Alma 13:28). The prophet Mormon explained step-by-step how love comes: "Fulfilling the commandments bringeth remission of sins; and the remission of sins bringeth meekness, and lowliness of heart; and because of meekness and lowliness of heart cometh the visitation of the Holy Ghost, which Comforter filleth with hope and perfect love, which love endureth by diligence unto prayer" (Moroni 8:25–26). "Pray . . . with all the energy of heart, that ye may be filled with this love" (Moroni 7:48).

Even doing all of that is not sufficient. Love isn't something we can just work on, checking off each qualification on our checklists, and then receive it because we earned it. It is a gift. It is *the* gift of the Holy Ghost.

Love—Stumbling Blocks to Watch Out For

There are a few warnings in the scriptures about what to be careful of while working toward the gift of love. Along with his encouragement for us to pursue that greatest quality of godliness, Moroni advised: Do not "love money, and your substance, and your fine apparel . . . more than ye love the poor and the needy, the sick and the afflicted" (Mormon 8:37).

Paul cautioned us not to allow intellectual pursuits to displace the quest for the infinitely more satisfying acquisition of love: "To know the love of Christ . . . passeth knowledge" (Ephesians 3:19); "knowledge puffeth up, but charity edifieth" (1 Corinthians 8:1); "though I . . . understand all mysteries, and all knowledge . . . , and have not charity, I am nothing" (1 Corinthians 13:2).

So we need to be careful about money, worldly things, and intellectualism. They can distract us from the best possession of all.

Love—The Blessings of Having It

Paul learned by his own experience to prize the love of God that was granted to him, and he wrote in superlative terms about the mighty changes that can come to those who likewise experience this greatest gift: "Eye hath not seen, nor ear heard, neither have entered into the heart of man, the things which God hath prepared for them that love him" (1 Corinthians 2:9). "All things work together for good to them that love God" (Romans 8:28).

John, the same that we call "the Beloved" because of his possessing the gift of love, wrote, "Every one that loveth is born of God, and knoweth God . . . ; for God is love" (1 John 4:7–8). John also knew the serenity that can come into the life of one who is filled with the love of Christ, for "perfect love casteth out fear" (1 John 4:18; see also Moroni 8:16).

One missionary was concerned about returning home to an inactive family after his mission, and he wrote just before leaving for home: "There is no fear in love. I learned that while studying my scriptures, while trying to answer the question: 'How can I call my mother and my family to the tree of life?' (1 Nephi 8:15)—the answer came to my mind so clearly: 'With love; just as you've always done.' I felt that perfect love and from that time I've not had any fear of returning home, nor will I have."

Moroni described how we can achieve the ultimate reward of becoming like God and dwelling with him: "Deny yourselves of all ungodliness, and love God with all your might, mind and strength, then . . . by his grace ye may be perfect in Christ" (Moroni 10:32).

Spiritual preparedness, the readiness to dwell in God's presence, which involves "sanctification through the grace of our Lord . . . [is given] to all those who love and serve God" (D&C 20:31).

Love—Its Influence in Our Personal Lives

To have the pure love of Christ means that we are praying fervently every day. We are studying the scriptures and writing new impressions, the revelation that comes while we are in the Spirit (see commentary at Mosiah 26:33). We are testifying of the Savior and of his work with everyone that we can. We are learning to love every person who comes into our lives.

When we have the pure love of Christ, we do more than just

try to get along with others. In early 1967 young Elder Ogden used that phrase in one of his weekly reports from Paraná, Argentina, to his mission president, Richard G. Scott. He wrote, "My companion and I are getting along okay; we have some minor companionship problems, as I suppose all missionaries do." That was the subject of the next zone conference. President Scott quoted from Elder Ogden's report, without mentioning his name, and taught the missionaries that good, successful missionaries don't just get along; they learn to love each other.

When we love God, we keep his commandments; we are obedient and happy. We are constant, or as the Book of Mormon says, "firm and steadfast" (1 Nephi 2:10; Helaman 15:8; 3 Nephi 6:14). We can be trusted. We do things for the right reasons.

Moroni 8

Mormon's letter to his son concerns the baptism of little children. Why would this subject be included in a record written for us, in the latter days? Because Mormon and Moroni saw our day, and they knew that there would be a serious problem with this particular "gross error" and "solemn mockery." Baptism of children under the age of eight years is wrong for several reasons: They are whole; they are not capable of committing sin nor accountable for it—not because they lack the ability but because Christ's blood "atoneth for their sins" (Mosiah 3:16); little children need no repentance, and "baptism is unto repentance"; "little children are alive in Christ"; little children should not, and cannot, be denied the "pure mercies of God."

It is interesting to note that at the same time Mormon was inspired to provide the Lord's doctrine on infant baptism in the New World, a debate about infant baptism raged in the Old World. The first creedal statement on the necessity of infant baptism seems to have been issued by Saint Augustine around A.D. 418.

Moroni 8:1–3

There is much counsel given in the Book of Mormon by fathers to their sons (examples are 2 Nephi 1–4; Mosiah 1; Alma 36–42; Moroni 8–9).

Mormon, like Paul, desired to quickly eradicate doctrinal misunderstanding and false practices among the people. So he, like Paul, wrote letters of clarification and correction. For instance, Paul wrote to Timothy, his son in the gospel, to give him guidance and encouragement to rectify apostate conditions. Now, more than three centuries later, Mormon wrote to Moroni, his son, to lay down the very points of the true doctrine of Christ. There is a tender and loving feeling between the father and the son. "I am mindful of you always in my prayers," wrote Mormon (compare what Paul wrote to Timothy, in 2 Timothy 1:3).

Moroni 8:8–20

"Listen to the words of Christ," not to errant church councils and edicts. Little children are not capable of committing sin; that is, that which they do wrong is not accounted to them as sin, for their faults and transgressions are taken from them by Christ; "little children are alive in Christ." In his great sacrifice the Savior paid for, or covered up (the meaning of the word *kippur* in Hebrew), all their transgressions, until they arrive at the age of accountability. "Children are not accountable before me until they are eight years old" (JST, Genesis 17:11; see also D&C 20:71; 68:25), and at that age they become responsible for their own conduct. "He that supposeth that little children need baptism is in the gall of bitterness and in the bonds of iniquity," and "he that saith that little children need baptism denieth the mercies of Christ, and setteth at naught the atonement of him and the power of his redemption" (see also Moses 6:53–55).

The Prophet Joseph Smith declared: "The doctrine of baptizing children, or sprinkling them, or they must welter in hell, is a doctrine not true, not supported in Holy Writ, and is not consistent with the character of God. All children are redeemed by the blood of Jesus Christ, and the moment that children leave this world, they are taken to the bosom of Abraham."[11]

Another argument attached to the preachment against infant baptism was the issue of circumcision, a rite or ceremony performed at eight days, foreshadowing the rite of baptism at eight years (JST, Genesis 17:11). The great covenant between God and his people had been on the earth from the beginning (see "Why Does God Have a Covenant People?" in commentary at 3 Nephi 5:21–26); it had been renewed in the days of Abraham, and because of his extraordinary faithfulness in adherence to the conditions of the covenant, it has often been named in his honor: the Abrahamic covenant. A sign or token of the covenant for two thousand years, from Abraham to Christ, was the practice of circumcision. Each male would receive a sacred and symbolic cutting around (literally, *circumcision*) of his male organ, the portal of the seeds (the "continuation of the seeds" being an eternal part of the covenant; see D&C 132:19). With the coming of Jesus Christ, the covenant would of course continue, but that sign of the covenant was no longer needed and was discontinued (Genesis 17:13, footnote *a*); as Mormon quoted Christ's words, "the law of circumcision is done away in me." See also Doctrine and Covenants 74:2–7, where the Lord explains that the ancient Jewish tradition, perpetuated by some modern Christians, that little children are congenital sinners and unholy and therefore need immediate circumcision or baptism, is false.

Moroni 8:16, 21

Mormon spoke boldly because he was not afraid of the opinions of men and he had authority from God, as well as a direct command from God to so speak.

Moroni 8:22

Not only are little children alive in Christ, needing no baptism, but so are those who do not know God's commandments. Where no law is in force, no punishment is exacted. The Atonement satisfies the demands of justice in their case (2 Nephi 9:25–26). This is also true of individuals with diminished mental capacity. President Joseph Fielding Smith taught: "We have good reason to believe that all spirits while in the pre-existence were perfect in form, having all their faculties and mental powers unimpaired. . . .

"The Lord has made it known by revelation that children born with retarded minds shall receive blessings just like little children who die in infancy. They are free from sin, because their minds are not capable of a correct understanding of right and wrong. Mormon, when writing to his son Moroni on the subject of baptism places deficient children in the same category with little children who are under the age of accountability, they do not require baptism, for the atonement of Jesus Christ takes care of them equally with little children who die before the age of accountability, as follows: [Moroni 8:22 is quoted]. . . .

"Again the Lord has stated:

"'And again, I say unto you, that whoso having knowledge, have I not commanded to repent?

"'And he that hath no understanding, it remaineth in me to do according as it is written. . . . [D&C 29:49–50].'

"Therefore The Church of Jesus Christ of Latter-day Saints considers all deficient children with retarded capacity to understand, just the same as little children under the age of accountability. They are redeemed without baptism and will go to the celestial kingdom of God, there, we believe, to have their faculties or other deficiencies restored according to the Father's mercy and justice."[12]

Regarding the deaths of little children, we also add here the following historical note: "Sister M. Isabella Horne said: 'In conversation with the Prophet Joseph Smith once in Nauvoo, the subject of children in the resurrection was broached. I believe it was in Sister Leonora Cannon Taylor's house. She had just lost one of her children, and I had also lost one previously. The Prophet wanted to comfort us, and he told us that we should receive those children in the morning of the resurrection just as we laid them down, in purity and innocence, and we should nourish and care for them as their mothers. He said that children would be raised in the resurrection just as they were laid down, and that they would obtain all the intelligence necessary to occupy thrones, principalities and powers. The idea that I got from what he said was that the children would grow and develop in the Millennium, and that the mothers would have the pleasure of training and caring for them, which they had been deprived of in this life.'"[13]

Moroni 8:25–26

Note in verse 26 that real meekness and lowliness of heart not only bring love into our lives but also the visitation of the Holy Ghost. Charity and spirituality are two of the greatest gifts of God. See also "The Love of God," section entitled "Love—How We Get It," near the commentary at Moroni 7:44–48.

Moroni 9

Chapter 9 stands in stark contrast to the themes of the previous chapters: faith, hope, charity, and other supernal gifts of the Spirit. Mormon here described the most depraved conditions and abominable acts of his people, their brutal atrocities and perversions: "they have lost their love, one towards another" and they lust for blood and revenge; "they are without principle, and past feeling." Yet in the midst of these depressing scenes Mormon encouraged his son, "Notwithstanding their hardness, *let us labor diligently;* . . . for we have a labor to perform" (emphasis added). What an attitude: Never give up!

Verses 11 through 20 might justly be called Mormon's final lament. His people had gone from being "a civil and a delightsome people" to "a people . . . that are without civilization" in "only a few years." No wonder his heart cried out, "Wo unto this people. . . . O the depravity of my people!" Modern readers who reel from contemporary instances of incivility, brutality, and depravity truly empathize with Mormon's injured and depressed psyche: "I [can] dwell no longer upon this horrible scene."

Mormon's final words to his son, as engraved in this present record, show his faith and hope in Christ, reveal an eternal optimism, and are filled with heavenly comfort: "May Christ lift thee up, and may his sufferings and death, and . . . his mercy and long-suffering, and the hope of his glory and of eternal life, rest in your mind forever."

Moroni 10

Moroni, one of the greatest prophets who ever lived, concluded this inspired record from God with matters "as seemeth me good." What suited him and the Lord was a series of powerful exhortations: "I would exhort you . . ."

- to remember and ponder the mercies of God toward the human family (v. 3)
- to pray to the Father in the name of Christ about the truthfulness of the Book of Mormon (v. 4)
- to "deny not the [very real] power of God" (v. 7)
- to "deny not the gifts of God" or gifts of the Spirit to human beings (v. 8)
- to "remember that every good gift come[s] of Christ" (v. 18)
- to remember the Lord's consistency and the constancy of spiritual gifts (v. 19)
- to "come unto Christ, and be perfected in him" (v. 32)

Moroni 10:3–7

When examining the Book of Mormon, try Moroni's test: God is the Author of its teachings; ask him if they are true. If we ask sincerely, with real desire and faith, we will receive a witness through the power of the Holy Ghost. That is the way we can know the truth about God and all things.

Moroni 10:8–19, 24

Moroni counseled all of us to actively seek the gifts of the Spirit. It is our duty to plead for gifts that will overcome our specific weaknesses. The best two are the gift of the Holy Ghost and the gift of charity. If the good gifts of God are not present and active in our lives, it is because of unbelief (see also 7:37). (On spiritual gifts, see 1 Corinthians 12:1–11 and D&C 46:8–30.)

Elder Marvin J. Ashton, a great apostle of the twentieth century, noted some possible additions to the wonderful lists of spiritual gifts: "the gift of asking; the gift of listening; the gift of hearing and using a still, small voice; the gift of being able to weep; the gift of avoiding contention; the gift of being agreeable; the gift of avoiding vain repetition; the gift of seeking that which is righteous; the gift of not passing judgment; the gift of looking to God for guidance; the gift of being a disciple; the gift of caring for others; the gift of being able to ponder; the gift of offering prayer; the gift of bearing a mighty testimony; and the gift of receiving the Holy Ghost."[14]

The gifts mentioned in scripture, along with many other gifts, are, in the righteous sense of the word, to be coveted. "If there is anything virtuous, lovely, or of good report or praiseworthy, we seek after these things" (Articles of Faith 1:13). We may rigorously pursue these noble gifts. Brigham Young lamented that "we live far beneath our privileges."[15]

Moroni 10:20–21

Only those who have and use faith, hope, and charity will be able to enter and be saved in the kingdom of heaven.

Moroni 10:22

"No hope" means that we are in despair. The word *despair* in the Spanish translation of the Book of Mormon is *desesperación* (English, *desperation*).

President Gilbert Sandberg of the Guatemala City Temple observed once that we should never feel true desperation; in fact, he concluded that the word *desperate* shows a lack of faith. Perhaps we should never feel *desperate* about any event or condition in our life if we really trust Heavenly Father and the Savior that our life is in their hands, and they know what they are doing with us. We should have confidence in them. Desperation, like doubt, is the antithesis of faith.

If sometime we find ourselves without hope, we will experience despair; and despair, as Moroni said, comes because of sin. When we get rid of the sin and are rid of the effects or consequences of that sin, we will discover hope once again.

Moroni 10:27, 29

Moroni's final testimony. Compare Nephi's final testimony and see the commentary at 2 Nephi 33:4–15. We will all stand before God one day. Each of us will be there. Moroni will also be there (see also Ether 5:6). But it will not be Moroni who accuses us. God himself will question us: "Did I not declare my words unto you, which were written by this man?" and if we have not paid attention before, we will pay attention then. God will show us the truth of Moroni's writings.

Moroni 10:30, 32

Moroni's final exhortation: "Come unto Christ." John the Beloved repeatedly gave the same invitation at the conclusion of his great Apocalypse; see Revelation 22:17.

Everyone likes gifts. But there are evil gifts out there, too. Moroni encouraged us to seek every good gift but not to touch—not to even get near—"the evil gift, nor the unclean thing." "Deny yourselves of all ungodliness." Examples of the "unclean things" or "ungodliness" are identified in commentary at Alma 5:57–60.

Moroni 10:31

Moroni called up an image from the prophet Isaiah, who described the future holy city of God using the metaphor of an immovable tent, whose stakes will never be pulled up, nor any of its cords be broken (Isaiah 33:20). The expansion of God's kingdom, which serves as a refuge from gathering storms, will indeed necessitate enlarging the tent of the family of God, lengthening its cords, and strengthening its stakes (this is the origin of the term "stakes" of the Church). Stakes must be strong to stabilize the whole tent, or the house of God (Isaiah 54:2).

Zion, the New Jerusalem, will be not the "center *stake*" but the "center *place*," as the scriptures call it (D&C 57:3; emphasis added). The stakes are round about it, throughout the world, to strengthen the center place. Within the strengthened stakes and enlarged borders, the Saints will no more be confounded, and the Father's covenants will all be fulfilled.

Moroni 10:32–33

The invitation is extended to become perfected in Christ. How is that accomplished? By denying ourselves all ungodliness and acquiring the love of God. By keeping all ungodliness or uncleanness out of our lives, and filling our hearts and lives with the love of God, we become sanctified by his grace, made holy or perfect, with no worldly stains at all.

Moroni 10:34

Moroni's body and spirit were reunited, and he was brought forth triumphant through the air in 1823 to meet with Joseph Smith on numerous occasions in that year and the succeeding four years, but he will yet meet all of us at the "pleasing bar of the great Jehovah." Hopefully we will be among the spiritually "quick" (meaning "alive," in Christ) and not among the spiritually dead at that decisive meeting.

If we are privileged to see Moroni after we finish our mortal probation, perhaps we will truly begin to understand something of his greatness and exceptional ministry. Moroni was raised in a righteous home and nurtured in gospel practices (Moroni 8:2–3). He witnessed the degradation and destruction of his society, yet kept the faith (Moroni 9). In mortality, Moroni saw and spoke with Jesus face-to-face (Ether 12:39). Moroni spoke with assurance about conditions that would exist on earth in the last days because Jesus Christ showed all things to him, he saw us, and he knew of our activities (Mormon 8:35). Between 1823 and 1829 Moroni appeared to Joseph Smith and others at least twenty times. Moroni was the custodian of the plates and sacred records of American Israelites, showing them to different individuals and groups but always taking them back (see Joseph Smith–History 1:60; Testimony of the Eight Witnesses). He "holds the keys of the stick or Record of Ephraim."[16] He is the guardian angel of America.

Elder Orson Hyde declared: "This same angel presides over the destinies of America, and feels a lively interest in all our doings. He was in the camp of Washington; and, by an invisible hand, led on our fathers to conquest and victory; and all this to open and prepare the way for the Church and kingdom of God to be established on the western hemisphere, for the redemption of Israel and the salvation of the world.

"This same angel was with Columbus, and gave him deep impressions, by dreams and by visions, respecting this New World. Trammeled by poverty and by an unpopular cause, yet his persevering and unyielding heart would not allow an obstacle in his way too great for him to overcome; and the angel of God helped him—was with him on the stormy deep, calmed the troubled elements, and guided his frail vessel to the desired haven. Under the guardianship of this same angel, or Prince of America, have the United States grown, increased and flourished, like the sturdy oak by the rivers of water."[17]

President Brigham Young said that Moroni dedicated the site of the Manti Utah Temple. "At a conference held in Ephraim, Sanpete County, June 25th, 1875, nearly all the speakers expressed their feelings to have a temple built in Sanpete County. . . . At 4 P.M. that day President Brigham Young said, 'The Temple should be built on Manti stone quarry.' Early on the morning of April 25th, 1877, President Brigham Young asked Brother Warren S. Snow to go with him to the Temple hill. Brother Snow says: 'We two were alone: President Young took me to the spot where the Temple was to stand; we went to the southeast corner, and President Young said: "Here is the spot where the prophet Moroni stood and dedicated this piece of land for a Temple site, and that is the reason why the location is made here, and we can't move it from this spot; and if you and I are the only persons that come here at high noon today, we will dedicate this ground.""[18]

Truly, the more we learn about the prophet-angel named Moroni, the more amazing he becomes in our eyes. Someday, if we are worthy, we will comprehend the full and towering stature of the last of the great Book of Mormon figures.

NOTES

THE BOOK OF ALMA (CONTINUED)

1. Benson, "Book of Mormon Is the Word of God," 63–64.
2. *Joseph Smith* [manual], 318.
3. Smith, *History of the Church,* 3:385; 5:268.
4. Brigham Young, cited in Roberts, *Comprehensive History of the Church,* 2:417.
5. Benson, "Born of God," 6.
6. Benson, "Beware of Pride," 6.
7. Uchtdorf, "Pride and the Priesthood," 56–58.
8. McConkie, *Lord, Increase Our Faith,* 9, 11.
9. Widtsoe, *Evidences and Reconciliations,* 26–27.
10. "If You Could Hie to Kolob," *Hymns,* 1985, no. 284.
11. Skinner, "Serpent Symbols and Salvation," 42–55.
12. *Joseph Smith* [manual], 48.
13. "Improve the Shining Moments," *Hymns,* 1985, no. 226.
14. Compare Herford, *Pirke Avoth,* 55–56.
15. Rodney Turner, "Infinite Atonement of God," cited in Jackson, *Alma 30 to Moroni,* 34–35.
16. See Ogden, *Before You Get to Heaven,* 102–18.
17. Romney, in Conference Report, Oct. 1965, 22.
18. Packer, *Follow the Brethren,* 4.
19. Ashton, "'Neither Boast of Faith Nor of Mighty Works,'" 65.
20. Hafen and Hafen, *Belonging Heart,* 302.
21. Durant and Durant, *Lessons of History,* 35–36.
22. Packer, "Little Children," 17.
23. Maxwell, *One More Strain of Praise,* x.
24. *For the Strength of Youth,* 26–27.
25. Monson, "Priesthood Power," 68.
26. "Things They're Saying," 18.

27. Smith, *Sharing the Gospel with Others,* 42–43.
28. Monson, "True to the Faith," 18.
29. Monson, "Until We Meet Again," 113.
30. McConkie and Millet, *Doctrinal Commentary on the Book of Mormon,* 3:295.
31. Cannon, *Gospel Truth,* 58.
32. Smith, *Answers to Gospel Questions,* 2:85.
33. Young, *Discourses of Brigham Young,* 376; see also Smith, *Doctrines of Salvation,* 2:230.
34. Smith, *Doctrines of Salvation,* 2:230.
35. McConkie and Millet, *Doctrinal Commentary on the Book of Mormon,* 3:299.
36. *Joseph Smith* [manual], 51.
37. Smith, *History of the Church,* 4:555.
38. Smith, *Gospel Doctrine,* 449.
39. Ibid., 24.
40. Smith, *Doctrines of Salvation,* 2:293–94.
41. Ibid., 2:292.
42. Oaks, "Resurrection," 15.
43. Personal correspondence with Andrew C. Skinner.
44. Talmage, *Jesus the Christ,* 575.
45. McConkie, *New Witness for the Articles of Faith,* 119–20.
46. Benson, *Witness and a Warning,* 20–21; emphasis added.
47. McKay, in Conference Report, Apr. 1942, 71–74.
48. Widtsoe, in Conference Report, Oct. 1940, 61–62.
49. Benson, *Title of Liberty,* 214.
50. Hinckley, "Times in Which We Live," 72–74.
51. Hinckley, "War and Peace," 80.
52. Packer, "Mantle Is Far, Far Greater Than the Intellect," 267.
53. Eyring, "'Man Down!'" 63.
54. Kimball, "False Gods We Worship," 6.
55. "Let Us All Press On," *Hymns,* 1985, no. 243.
56. "Onward, Christian Soldiers," *Hymns,* 1985, no. 246.
57. "We Are All Enlisted," *Hymns,* 1985, no. 250.
58. "Behold! A Royal Army," *Hymns,* 1985, no. 251.
59. "Hope of Israel," *Hymns,* 1985, no. 259.
60. Uchtdorf, "Two Principles for Any Economy," 55.
61. Smith, *History of the Church,* 4:425.
62. "The Star-Spangled Banner," *Hymns,* 1985, no. 340.

63. Nibley, *Since Cumorah*, 274–75.
64. Maxwell, *Men and Women of Christ*, 4.
65. Bytheway, *Righteous Warriors*, 30.
66. Hinckley, "Times in Which We Live," 72.
67. Personal notes of Andrew C. Skinner.
68. Webster, *American Dictionary of the English Language*, "curious, curiousness."

THE BOOK OF HELAMAN

1. Benson, *Witness and a Warning*, 21, 38.
2. Brigham Young, in *Journal of Discourses*, 19:38; see also Largey, *Book of Mormon Reference Companion*, 223.
3. Brinley, *Strengthening Your Marriage and Family*, 143.
4. Ballard, "Keeping Covenants," 7.
5. Hafen, *Disciple's Life*, 268.
6. Wirthlin, "Seeds of Renewal," 9.
7. Monson, "Preparation Brings Blessings," 65–66.
8. Spencer W. Kimball, cited in Parsons, "Practices of the Church," in Jackson, *Alma 30 to Moroni*, 286; emphasis added.
9. Smith, "Your Good Name," 139.
10. See also Ogden and Skinner, *Acts through Revelation*, 383–86.
11. *Joseph Smith* [manual], 224.
12. *Book of Mormon* [student manual, 1979], 271.
13. *Words of Joseph Smith*, 74.
14. "Put Your Shoulder to the Wheel," *Hymns*, 1985, no. 252.
15. Smith, *History of the Church*, 3:380.
16. Ibid., 3:381.
17. McConkie and Millet, *Doctrinal Commentary on the Book of Mormon*, 3:390.
18. Kimball, "The Lord Expects His Saints to Follow the Commandments," 4.
19. Hunter, *Teachings of Howard W. Hunter*, 66–67.
20. Ezra Taft Benson, cited in Dahl, "Fit for the Kingdom," in Jackson and Millet, *Gospels*, 369.
21. Brigham Young, cited in Nibley, *Brigham Young*, 128.
22. Harold B. Lee, cited in Dahl, "Abrahamic Test," in Draper, *Witness of Jesus Christ*, 60.
23. Oaks, "Focus and Priorities," 84.

24. McConkie and Millet, *Doctrinal Commentary on the Book of Mormon,* 3:397.
25. Lee, in Conference Report, Oct. 1970, 152.
26. Smith, *Doctrines of Salvation,* 2:224.
27. William Lane Craig, cited in Strobel, *Case for Christ,* 217; see also Kloner, "Did a Rolling Stone Close Jesus' Tomb?" 29, referring to the phrase "on the third day": "The counting of the days . . . follows Jewish custom, which included both the first and the last day in the count."
28. Evans, "On Being a Prophet," 672.

THIRD NEPHI

1. McConkie, Millet, and Top, *Doctrinal Commentary on the Book of Mormon,* 4:5.
2. Smith, *Doctrines of Salvation,* 1:27.
3. McConkie, Millet, and Top, *Doctrinal Commentary on the Book of Mormon,* 4:12.
4. Oaks, "Preparation for the Second Coming," 8.
5. Uchtdorf, "Christlike Attributes—The Wind beneath Our Wings," 102.
6. Benson, *Witness and a Warning,* 37–38.
7. Benson, "I Testify," 87.
8. To read more about the great catastrophe, see Sorenson, *Ancient American Setting,* 318–25; note especially the 1835 account of volcanic eruption in Nicaragua, page 321.
9. Benson, "Mighty Change of Heart," 5.
10. Talmage, *Jesus the Christ,* 620–21.
11. *Webster's New World Dictionary.*
12. Packer, "'From Such Turn Away,'" 35.
13. Talmage, *Jesus the Christ,* 673; emphasis added.
14. Faust, "Second Birth," 2.
15. Holland, "Teaching, Preaching, Healing," 42.
16. Ludlow et al., *Encyclopedia of Mormonism,* 2:734.
17. McConkie, "Purifying Power of Gethsemane," 11.
18. Eyring, "That We May Be One," 67.
19. Ludlow, *Companion to Your Study of the Book of Mormon,* 262–63.
20. Talmage, *Jesus the Christ,* 360.
21. Smith, *History of the Church,* 5:368.

22. Melvin J. Ballard, cited in Kimball, *Miracle of Forgiveness,* 168.

23. Lee, *Decisions for Successful Living,* 57, 56.

24. For a detailed discussion of this three-way connection between beatitudes, psalms, and the temple, see Skinner, "Israel's Ancient Psalms," *Sermon on the Mount in Latter-day Scripture,* 59–75.

25. Condie, "Agency," 19.

26. Lee, *Decisions for Successful Living,* 60.

27. Hinckley, *Stand a Little Taller,* 18.

28. *Joseph Smith* [manual], 428.

29. Hinckley, *Teachings of Gordon B. Hinckley,* 338.

30. Derrick, *Temples in the Last Days,* 80.

31. McConkie, *Doctrinal New Testament Commentary,* 1:219–20.

32. *Joseph Smith* [manual], 155.

33. Kelly, "Case against Anger," 10.

34. Christiansen, "Be Slow to Anger," 37.

35. Burton, "'Blessed Are the Peacemakers,'" 56.

36. Ogden and Ogden, *President and the Preacher,* 152–53, 148.

37. Ibid., 177.

38. Robbins, "Agency and Anger," 80.

39. Smith, *Gospel Doctrine,* 257.

40. Dahl, "Higher Law," 8.

41. Kimball, in Conference Report, Oct. 1962, 58.

42. Hinckley, "What God Hath Joined Together," 74.

43. Rector, "Following Christ to Victory," 30.

44. Wernberg-Moller, *The Manual of Discipline,* I:9–11, IX:21–23.

45. *Joseph Smith* [manual], 523.

46. Brown, in Conference Report, Oct. 1966, 102.

47. McConkie, "Probationary Test of Mortality," 8; paragraphing altered.

48. *Joseph Smith* [manual], 393.

49. Sowell, "On Measuring Flour and Forgiveness," 51–52.

50. Benson, "Great Commandment—Love the Lord," 4.

51. "Let Each Man Learn to Know Himself," *Hymns,* 1948, no. 91.

52. Scott, "Trust in the Lord," 17.

53. Ashton, "Tongue Can Be a Sharp Sword," *Ensign,* May 1992, 20.

54. Ludlow et al., *Encyclopedia of Mormonism,* 3:1419.

55. John Taylor, cited in Smith and Sjodahl, *Doctrine and Covenants Commentary*, 462–63.
56. Hunter, in Conference Report, Oct. 1967, 13.
57. Smith, *Teachings of the Prophet Joseph Smith*, 59–60.
58. *Joseph Smith* [manual], 185.
59. Holland, "'For a Wise Purpose,'" 19.
60. "While of These Emblems We Partake," *Hymns*, 1985, no. 173.
61. See also Ogden and Skinner, *Acts through Revelation*, 383–86.
62. Ogden and Skinner, *Four Gospels*, 148–49, 654.
63. *Words of Joseph Smith*, 15.
64. Seixas, *Hebrew Grammar*, page 50, paragraph 53, item 2.
65. Smith, *History of the Church*, 1:382–83.
66. Petersen, *Church and America*, 6–7.
67. See also Galbraith, Ogden, and Skinner, *Jerusalem, the Eternal City*, 538–39, 545–48.
68. David Rolph Seely, "Lord Will Bring Salvation," in Jackson, *1 Kings to Malachi*, 155.
69. Ballard, "'Great Shall Be the Peace of Thy Children,'" 60.
70. Lund, "Prophet for the Fulness of Times," 54.
71. Smith, *History of the Church*, 4:540.
72. Smith, *Doctrines of Salvation*, 3:94.
73. McConkie, Millet, and Top, *Doctrinal Commentary on the Book of Mormon*, 4:165.
74. Smith, *Doctrines of Salvation*, 2:100–101.
75. *Joseph Smith* [manual], 472.
76. Smith, *History of the Church*, 2:477.
77. Benson, "Listen to a Prophet's Voice," 57.
78. McConkie, *Mormon Doctrine*, 807–8.
79. Smith, *History of the Church*, 4:210.
80. Ibid., 4:425.
81. McConkie, *New Witness for the Articles of Faith*, 462–63.

FOURTH NEPHI

1. Kimball, "Becoming the Pure in Heart," 4.
2. Benson, "Beware of Pride," 7.
3. Ibid., 4.
4. Benson, *God, Family, Country*, 363–64.

NOTES

THE BOOK OF MORMON

1. Kimball, "Boys Need Heroes Close By," 47.
2. Kimball, *Miracle of Forgiveness,* 117.
3. Brigham Young, in *Journal of Discourses,* 7:289.
4. Diaz del Castillo, *The Discovery and Conquest of Mexico,* cited in Allen and Allen, *Exploring the Lands of the Book of Mormon,* 29.
5. Sorenson, *Ancient American Setting,* 101.
6. Brigham Young, *Discourses of Brigham Young,* 130.
7. Ludlow, *Companion to Your Study of the Old Testament,* 298.
8. Young, in *Journal of Discourses,* 1:38.
9. Smith, *History of the Church,* 4:540.
10. *Lectures on Faith,* 4:13, 17.
11. Nibley, *Lehi in the Desert,* 13–20; Sorenson, *Ancient American Setting,* 75–76.

THE BOOK OF ETHER

1. Talmage, *Articles of Faith,* 260–61.
2. Ludlow, *Companion to Your Study of the Book of Mormon,* 310.
3. George Reynolds, cited in "Questions and Answers," 705.
4. Smith, *Way to Perfection,* 69.
5. Smith, *Doctrines of Salvation,* 3:73.
6. For elaboration on possible Egyptian linguistic connections, see Hugh Nibley, *Lehi in the Desert,* 184–85.
7. See also Ogden and Skinner, *Acts through Revelation,* 383–86.
8. Smith, *History of the Church,* 6:318–19.
9. O'Donnal, *Pioneer in Guatemala,* 63–65.
10. McConkie, "What Think Ye of the Book of Mormon?" 72; emphasis added.
11. Wirthlin, "Personal Integrity," 31; emphasis added.
12. Petersen, "Warnings from the Past," 49; emphasis added.
13. Benson, in Conference Report, Apr. 1962, 103; emphasis added.
14. Kimball, *Teachings of Spencer W. Kimball,* 601; emphasis added.
15. Clark, in Conference Report, Oct. 1942, 58; emphasis added.
16. J. Reuben Clark Jr., in Clark, *Messages of the First Presidency,* 6:108; emphasis added.
17. Largey, *Book of Mormon Reference Companion,* 436; emphasis added.

18. Ludlow et al., *Encyclopedia of Mormonism*, 1:157; emphasis added.
19. Ibid., 4:1160; emphasis added.
20. Kimball, "Let Us Move Forward and Upward," 82.
21. Packer, "Funerals—A Time for Reverence," 18.
22. Brigham Young, in *Journal of Discourses*, 17:143.
23. *Joseph Smith* [manual], 258.
24. "Lord, Dismiss Us with Thy Blessing," *Hymns*, 1985, no. 163.
25. Smith, *Answers to Gospel Questions*, 2:125.
26. Holland, "Rending the Veil of Unbelief," 15–18.
27. Hertz, *Pentateuch and Haftorahs*, 26–27; see also Skinner, "Promises Fulfilled," in Jackson, *Alma 30 to Moroni*, 265.
28. Highwater, *Native Land*, 16.
29. *Book of Mormon* [student manual, 1979], 478.
30. Ibid. [1989], 137.
31. Allen and Allen, *Exploring the Lands of the Book of Mormon*, 255–57, 261, 276.
32. Benson, "I Testify," 87.
33. Smith, *History of the Church*, 3:294.
34. Ibid., 3:380.
35. Franklin D. Richards, in *Journal of Discourses*, 25:237.
36. *Joseph Smith* [manual], 252.
37. Smith, *Answers to Gospel Questions*, 2:106.
38. See also Galbraith, Ogden, and Skinner, *Jerusalem, the Eternal City*, 349–64, 491–93, 524–36.
39. McConkie, Millet, and Top, *Doctrinal Commentary on the Book of Mormon*, 4:316.
40. "FARMS Update," 2.

THE BOOK OF MORONI

1. *Joseph Smith* [manual], 97.
2. Hinckley, "Converts and Young Men," 47.
3. Smith, *History of the Church*, 6:314.
4. Smith, "Rest for the Peaceable Followers of Christ," 714.
5. Scott, "Happiness Now and Forever," 70.
6. Smith, "'I Know That My Redeemer Lives,'" 380.
7. Kimball, *Love versus Lust*, 7.
8. Grant, in Conference Report, Apr. 1934, 131.
9. Caldwell, "Love of Christ," 29.

10. *Lectures on Faith,* 43.
11. Smith, *History of the Church,* 4:554.
12. Smith, *Answers to Gospel Questions,* 3:19–21.
13. Smith, *History of the Church,* 4:556 note.
14. Ashton, "'There Are Many Gifts,'" 20.
15. Young, *Discourses of Brigham Young,* 32.
16. Peterson, *Moroni,* 94n.
17. Orson Hyde, in *Journal of Discourses,* 6:368.
18. Whitney, *Life of Heber C. Kimball,* 436.

SOURCES

Allen, Joseph Lovell, and Blake Joseph Allen. *Exploring the Lands of the Book of Mormon*. Orem, Utah: SA Publishers, 1989.

Ashton, Marvin J. "'Neither Boast of Faith Nor of Mighty Works.'" *Ensign*, May 1990, 65–67.

———. "'There Are Many Gifts.'" *Ensign*, Nov. 1987, 20–23.

———. "The Tongue Can Be a Sharp Sword." *Ensign*, May 1992, 18–20.

Ballard, M. Russell. "'Great Shall Be the Peace of Thy Children.'" *Ensign*, Apr. 1994, 59–61.

———. "Keeping Covenants." *Ensign*, May 1993, 6–8.

Benson, Ezra Taft. "Beware of Pride." *Ensign*, May 1989, 4–7.

———. "The Book of Mormon Is the Word of God." *Ensign*, May 1975, 63–65.

———. "Born of God." *Ensign*, Nov. 1985, 5–7.

———. *God, Family, Country*. Salt Lake City: Deseret Book, 1974.

———. "The Great Commandment—Love the Lord." *Ensign*, May 1988, 4–6.

———. "I Testify." *Ensign*, Nov. 1988, 86–87.

———. In Conference Report, Apr. 1962, 103–6.

———. "Listen to a Prophet's Voice." *Ensign*, Jan. 1973, 57–59.

———. "A Mighty Change of Heart." *Ensign*, Oct. 1989, 2–5.

———. *Title of Liberty*. Salt Lake City: Deseret Book, 1964.

———. *A Witness and a Warning: A Modern-day Prophet Testifies of the Book of Mormon*. Salt Lake City: Deseret Book, 1988.

Book of Mormon [student manual]. Prepared by the Church Educational System. Salt Lake City: The Church of Jesus Christ of Latter-day Saints, 1979, 1989, 2009.

Brinley, Douglas. *Strengthening Your Marriage and Family*. Salt Lake City: Bookcraft, 1994.

Brown, Hugh B. In Conference Report, Oct. 1966, 101–5.

Burton, Theodore M. "'Blessed Are the Peacemakers.'" *Ensign,* Nov. 1974, 54–56.

Bytheway, John. *Righteous Warriors: Lessons from the War Chapters in the Book of Mormon.* Salt Lake City: Deseret Book, 2004.

Caldwell, C. Max. "Love of Christ." *Ensign,* Nov. 1992, 29–30.

Cannon, George Q. *Gospel Truth: Discourses and Writings of George Q. Cannon.* Edited by Jerreld L. Newquist. 2 vols. in 1. Classics in Mormon Literature series. Salt Lake City: Deseret Book, 1987.

Christiansen, ElRay L. "Be Slow to Anger." *Ensign,* June 1971, 37–38.

Clark, J. Reuben, Jr. In Conference Report, Oct. 1942, 54–59.

Clark, James R., comp. *Messages of the First Presidency of The Church of Jesus Christ of Latter-day Saints.* 6 vols. Salt Lake City: Bookcraft, 1965–75.

Condie, Spencer J. "Agency: The Gift of Choices." *Ensign,* Sept. 1995, 16–22.

Dahl, Larry E. "The Higher Law." *Ensign,* Feb. 1991, 6–11.

Derrick, Royden G. *Temples in the Last Days.* Salt Lake City: Bookcraft, 1987.

Diaz del Castillo, Bernal. *The Discovery and Conquest of Mexico —1517–1521.* Translated by A. P. Maudslay. New York: Farrar, Straus, and Cudahy, 1956. Cited in Allen and Allen, *Exploring the Lands of the Book of Mormon.*

Draper, Richard D., ed. *A Witness of Jesus Christ: The 1989 Sperry Symposium on the Old Testament.* Salt Lake City: Deseret Book, 1990.

Durant, Will, and Ariel Durant. *The Lessons of History.* New York: Simon & Schuster, 1968.

Evans, Richard L. "On Being a Prophet." *Improvement Era,* Nov. 1939, 672.

Eyring, Henry B. "'Man Down!'" *Ensign,* May 2009, 63–66.

———. "That We May Be One." *Ensign,* May 1998, 66–68.

"FARMS Update." *Insights* 14, no. 6 (Nov. 1994): 2.

Faust, James E. "A Second Birth." *Ensign,* June 1998, 2–5.

For the Strength of Youth: Fulfilling Our Duty to God. Salt Lake City: The Church of Jesus Christ of Latter-day Saints, 2001.

Galbraith, David B., D. Kelly Ogden, and Andrew C. Skinner. *Jerusalem, the Eternal City*. Salt Lake City: Deseret Book, 1996.

Grant, Heber J. In Conference Report, Apr. 1934, 130–32.

Hafen, Bruce C. *A Disciple's Life: The Biography of Neal A. Maxwell*. Salt Lake City: Deseret Book, 2002.

Hafen, Bruce C., and Marie K. Hafen. *The Belonging Heart: The Atonement and Relationships with God and Family*. Salt Lake City: Deseret Book, 1994.

Herford, R. Travers. *Pirke Avoth, The Ethics of the Talmud: Sayings of the Fathers*. New York: Schocken Books, 1962.

Hertz, J. H., ed. *The Pentateuch and Haftorahs*. London: Soncino Press, 1961.

Highwater, Jamake. *Native Land: Sagas of the Indian Americas*. Boston: Little Brown & Co, 1986.

Hinckley, Gordon B. "Converts and Young Men." *Ensign*, May 1997, 47–50.

———. *Stand a Little Taller: Counsel and Inspiration for Each Day of the Year*. Salt Lake City: Eagle Gate Publishers, 2001.

———. *Teachings of Gordon B. Hinckley*. Salt Lake City: Deseret Book, 1997.

———. "The Times in Which We Live." *Ensign*, Nov. 2001, 72–74.

———. "War and Peace." *Ensign*, May 2003, 78–81.

———. "What God Hath Joined Together." *Ensign*, May 1991, 71–74.

Holland, Jeffrey R. "'For a Wise Purpose.'" *Ensign*, Jan. 1996, 12–19.

———. "Rending the Veil of Unbelief." In *Nurturing Faith through the Book of Mormon: The 24th Annual Sidney B. Sperry Symposium*, 1–24. Salt Lake City: Deseret Book, 1995.

———. "Teaching, Preaching, Healing." *Ensign*, Jan. 2003, 32–43.

Hunter, Howard W. In Conference Report, Oct. 1967, 11–14.

———. *The Teachings of Howard W. Hunter*. Edited by Clyde J. Williams. Salt Lake City: Bookcraft, 1997.

Hymns: The Church of Jesus Christ of Latter-day Saints. Salt Lake City: The Church of Jesus Christ of Latter-day Saints, 1948.

Hymns of The Church of Jesus Christ of Latter-day Saints. Salt Lake City: The Church of Jesus Christ of Latter-day Saints, 1985.

Jackson, Kent P., ed. *1 Kings to Malachi*. Vol. 4 of Studies in Scripture series. Salt Lake City: Deseret Book, 1993.

———. *Alma 30 to Moroni.* Vol. 8 of Studies in Scripture series. Salt Lake City: Deseret Book, 1988.

Jackson, Kent P., and Robert L. Millet, eds. *The Gospels.* Vol. 5 of Studies in Scripture series. Salt Lake City: Deseret Book, 1986.

Joseph Smith [manual]. Teachings of Presidents of the Church series. Salt Lake City: The Church of Jesus Christ of Latter-day Saints, 2007.

Journal of Discourses. 26 vols. London: Latter-day Saints' Book Depot, 1854–86.

Kelly, Burton C. "The Case against Anger." *Ensign,* Feb. 1980, 9–12.

Kimball, Spencer W. "Becoming the Pure in Heart." *Ensign,* Mar. 1985, 2–5.

———. "Boys Need Heroes Close By." *Ensign,* May 1976, 45–47.

———. "The False Gods We Worship." *Ensign,* June 1976, 2–6.

———. In Conference Report, Oct. 1962, 55–60.

———. "Let Us Move Forward and Upward." *Ensign,* May 1979, 82–84.

———. "The Lord Expects His Saints to Follow the Commandments." *Ensign,* May 1977, 4–7.

———. *Love versus Lust.* Brigham Young University Speeches of the Year. Provo, Utah, 5 Jan. 1965.

———. *The Miracle of Forgiveness.* Salt Lake City: Bookcraft, 1969.

———. *The Teachings of Spencer W. Kimball.* Edited by Edward L. Kimball. Salt Lake City: Deseret Book, 1982.

Kloner, Amos. "Did a Rolling Stone Close Jesus' Tomb?" *Biblical Archaeology Review* 25, no. 5 (Sept./Oct. 1999): 23–29, 76.

Largey, Dennis L., ed. *Book of Mormon Reference Companion.* Salt Lake City: Deseret Book, 2003.

Lectures on Faith. Salt Lake City: Deseret Book, 1985.

Lee, Harold B. *Decisions for Successful Living.* Salt Lake City: Deseret Book, 1973.

———. In Conference Report, Oct. 1970, 152–53.

Ludlow, Daniel H. *A Companion to Your Study of The Book of Mormon.* Salt Lake City: Deseret Book, 1976.

———. *A Companion to Your Study of the Old Testament.* Salt Lake City: Deseret Book, 1981.

——— et al. *Encyclopedia of Mormonism.* 4 vols. New York: Macmillan, 1992.

Lund, Gerald N. "A Prophet for the Fulness of Times." *Ensign,* Jan. 1997, 50–54.

Maxwell, Neal A. *Men and Women of Christ.* Salt Lake City: Bookcraft, 1991.

———. *One More Strain of Praise.* Salt Lake City: Bookcraft, 1999.

McConkie, Bruce R. *Doctrinal New Testament Commentary.* 3 vols. Salt Lake City: Bookcraft, 1966–73.

———. *Lord, Increase Our Faith.* Brigham Young University Speeches of the Year. Provo, Utah, 31 Oct. 1967.

———. *Mormon Doctrine.* 2d ed. Salt Lake City: Bookcraft, 1966.

———. *A New Witness for the Articles of Faith.* Salt Lake City: Deseret Book, 1985.

———. "Probationary Test of Mortality." Address at LDS Institute, University of Utah, 10 Jan. 1982.

———. "The Purifying Power of Gethsemane." *Ensign,* May 1985, 9–11.

———. "What Think Ye of the Book of Mormon?" *Ensign,* Nov. 1983, 72–74.

McConkie, Joseph Fielding, and Robert Millet. *Doctrinal Commentary on the Book of Mormon.* 3 vols. Salt Lake City: Bookcraft, 1987–91.

McConkie, Joseph Fielding, Robert L. Millet, and Brent L. Top. *Doctrinal Commentary on the Book of Mormon.* Volume 4. Salt Lake City: Bookcraft, 1992.

McKay, David O. In Conference Report, Apr. 1942, 70–74.

Monson, Thomas S. "Preparation Brings Blessings." *Ensign,* May 2010, 64–67.

———. "Priesthood Power." *Ensign,* May 2011, 66–69.

———. "True to the Faith." *Ensign,* May 2006, 18–21.

———. "Until We Meet Again." *Ensign,* May 2009, 112–14.

Nibley, Hugh. *Lehi in the Desert; The World of the Jaredites; There Were Jaredites.* Edited by John W. Welch. Vol. 5 of The Collected Works of Hugh Nibley. Salt Lake City: Deseret Book, 1988.

———. *Since Cumorah.* Salt Lake City: Deseret Book, 1967.

Nibley, Preston. *Brigham Young: The Man and His Work.* Salt Lake City: Deseret Book, 1970.

Oaks, Dallin H. "Focus and Priorities." *Ensign,* May 2001, 82–84.

———. "Preparation for the Second Coming." *Ensign*, May 2004, 7–10.

———. "Resurrection." *Ensign*, May 2000, 14–16.

O'Donnal, John Forres. *Pioneer in Guatemala*, 63–65. Cited in *Church News*, 13 Dec. 1952, 5.

Ogden, D. Kelly. *Before You Get to Heaven: 8 Mighty Changes God Wants for You*. Salt Lake City: Deseret Book, 2004.

Ogden, D. Kelly, and Marcia H. Ogden. *The President and the Preacher: Memoirs of a Mission President and Companion*. Privately published, 2000.

Ogden, D. Kelly, and Andrew C. Skinner. *Acts through Revelation*. Verse by Verse series. Salt Lake City: Deseret Book, 1998.

———. *The Four Gospels*. Verse by Verse series. Salt Lake City: Deseret Book, 2006.

Packer, Boyd K. *Follow the Brethren*. Brigham Young University Speeches of the Year. Provo, Utah, 23 Mar. 1965.

———. "'From Such Turn Away.'" *Ensign*, May 1985, 33–35.

———. "Funerals—A Time for Reverence." *Ensign*, Nov. 1988, 18–21.

———. "Little Children." *Ensign*, Nov. 1986, 16–18.

———. "The Mantle Is Far, Far Greater Than the Intellect." *BYU Studies* 21, no. 3 (Summer 1981): 259–78.

Petersen, Mark E. *The Church and America*. Salt Lake City: The Church of Jesus Christ of Latter-day Saints, Military Relations Committee, 1978.

———. "Warnings from the Past." *Ensign*, June 1971, 47–49.

Peterson, H. Donl. *Moroni: Ancient Prophet, Modern Messenger*. Salt Lake City: Deseret Book, 2000.

"Questions and Answers." *Improvement Era*, July 1905, 704–5.

Rector, Hartman, Jr. "Following Christ to Victory." *Ensign*, May 1979, 29–31.

Robbins, Lynn G. "Agency and Anger." *Ensign*, May 1998, 80 81.

Roberts, B. H. *A Comprehensive History of the Church of Jesus Christ of Latter-day Saints Century I in Six Volumes*. 6 vols. Salt Lake City: Deseret Book, 1930.

Romney, Marion G. In Conference Report, Oct. 1965, 20–23.

Scott, Richard G. "Happiness Now and Forever." *Ensign*, Nov. 1979, 70–71.

———. "Trust in the Lord." *Ensign*, Nov. 1995, 16–18.

Seixas, Joshua. *A Manual Hebrew Grammar for the Use of Beginners.* 1832.

Skinner, Andrew C. "Israel's Ancient Psalms: Cornerstone of the Beatitudes." In *The Sermon on the Mount in Latter-day Scripture: The 39th Annual Brigham Young University Sidney B. Sperry Symposium,* 59–75. Provo, Utah: Religious Studies Center; Salt Lake City: Deseret Book, 2010.

———. "Serpent Symbols and Salvation in the Ancient Near East and the Book of Mormon." *Journal of Book of Mormon Studies* 10, no. 2 (2001): 42–55.

Smith, George Albert. *Sharing the Gospel with Others.* Salt Lake City: Deseret Book, 1948.

———. "Your Good Name." *Improvement Era,* Mar. 1947, 139.

Smith, Hyrum M., and Janne M. Sjodahl. *Doctrine and Covenants Commentary.* Rev. ed. Salt Lake City: Deseret Book, 1978.

Smith, Joseph. *History of The Church of Jesus Christ of Latter-day Saints.* Edited by B. H. Roberts. 7 vols. 2d ed. rev. Salt Lake City: The Church of Jesus Christ of Latter-day Saints, 1932–51.

———. *Teachings of the Prophet Joseph Smith.* Selected by Joseph Fielding Smith. Salt Lake City: Deseret Book, 1976.

Smith, Joseph F. *Gospel Doctrine.* Salt Lake City: Deseret Book, 1986.

———. "'I Know That My Redeemer Lives.'" *Improvement Era,* Mar. 1908, 379–87.

———. "Rest for the Peaceable Followers of Christ." *Improvement Era,* July 1904, 714–18.

Smith, Joseph Fielding. *Answers to Gospel Questions.* Compiled by Joseph Fielding Smith Jr. 5 vols. Salt Lake City: Deseret Book, 1957–66.

———. *Doctrines of Salvation.* 3 vols. Compiled by Bruce R. McConkie. Salt Lake City: Bookcraft, 1954–56.

———. *The Way to Perfection: Short Discourses on Gospel Themes.* Salt Lake City: Genealogical Society of Utah, 1931.

Sorenson, John L. *An Ancient American Setting for the Book of Mormon.* Salt Lake City: Deseret Book, 1985.

Sowell, Madison U. "On Measuring Flour and Forgiveness." In *Brigham Young University 1996–97 Speeches,* 47–56. Provo, Utah: Brigham Young University Press, 1997.

Strobel, Lee. *The Case for Christ: A Journalist's Personal Investigation of the Evidence for Jesus.* Grand Rapids, Mich.: Zondervan, 1998.

Talmage, James E. *Articles of Faith.* Salt Lake City: The Church of Jesus Christ of Latter-day Saints, 1966.

———. *Jesus the Christ.* Classics in Mormon Literature ed. Salt Lake City: Deseret Book, 1983.

"Things They're Saying." *New Era,* Feb. 1974, 18–19.

Uchtdorf, Dieter F. "Christlike Attributes—The Wind beneath Our Wings." *Ensign,* Nov. 2005, 100–103.

———. "Pride and the Priesthood." *Ensign,* Nov. 2010, 55–58.

———. "Two Principles for Any Economy." *Ensign,* Nov. 2009, 55–58.

Webster, Noah. *An American Dictionary of the English Language.* 1828. Reprint. San Francisco: Foundation for American Christian Education, 1980.

Webster's New World Dictionary. College edition. Edited by David B. Guralnik. New York: Macmillan, 1966.

Wernberg-Moller, Preben. *The Manual of Discipline.* Vol. 1 of *Studies on the Texts of the Desert of Judah.* Leiden, Netherlands: Brill, 1957.

Whitney, Orson F. *Life of Heber C. Kimball.* Salt Lake City: Bookcraft, 1945.

Widtsoe, John A. *Evidences and Reconciliations.* Arranged by G. Homer Durham. Salt Lake City: Bookcraft, 1960.

———. In Conference Report, Oct. 1940, 61–65.

Wirthlin, Joseph B. "Personal Integrity." *Ensign,* May 1990, 30–33.

———. "Seeds of Renewal." *Ensign,* May 1989, 7–10.

The Words of Joseph Smith. Compiled and edited by Andrew F. Ehat and Lyndon W. Cook. Provo, Utah: Grandin Book, 1991.

Young, Brigham. *Discourses of Brigham Young.* Compiled by John A. Widtsoe. Salt Lake City: Deseret Book, 1966.

INDEX

2:171–72; on becoming like
Jesus, 2:223; on Zion, 2:230;
on Americas as choice land,
2:260
Besora, 2:199
Beth-abara/Beth-avara, 1:45
Bethlehem, 1:399
"Beyond Jordan," 1:194
Bible, 1:61–63, 1:129, 1:247,
2:244–45
Bitter cup, 2:46–47, 2:133
Blessings: as part of mortality,
1:13; for children, 1:132;
asking and receiving, 2:175
Blood: atoning, 1:55–56;
redemption through, 1:60–
61; drinking, 1:294
Blood sacrifice, 2:212–13
Boasting, 2:33. *See also* Pride
Body: of God and Jesus Christ,
1:181–82; marking, 1:385–
86; controlling, 2:33–36,
2:151, 2:303–4; translated,
2:65–66, 2:224–26; joining
of spirit and, 2:111
Bondage: escaping, 1:333;
spiritual, 1:388
Book of Lehi, 1:8
Book of life, 1:395–96
Book of Mormon: importance
and value of, 1:1–4; title
page of, 1:5–7; translation
of, 1:6, 1:8; purposes of,
1:6–7, 2:241; witnesses
of, 1:7–9, 1:237, 2:270;
origins of, 1:8; holding to,
1:68; Bible and, 1:129,
2:244–45; Brigham Young
on Joseph Smith and, 1:206;

as prophets' voices from dust,
1:230–31; Isaiah prophesies
of, 1:236–38; exposes Satan's
tactics, 1:242–43; as ensign,
1:246; gathering of Israel
and, 1:249; and salvation
of Lamanites, 1:291–92;
possessors of, plates, 1:302–3;
meant for last days, 2:1; in
Jaredite record, 2:30; as
sign of covenant fulfillment,
2:227; as witness of Jesus
Christ, 2:239; blessings of,
2:245; receiving testimony of,
2:312
Book of Mormon lands, 1:431
Book of remembrance, 2:215
Bountiful Temple, 2:130
Bradford, William R., 1:309
Branch of Jesse, 1:205–7
Brass plates: overview of, 1:8;
obtaining, 1:24–27, 1:30–32;
importance and study of,
1:33–34; contents of, 1:87,
2:255; language of, 1:304
Brimstone, 1:316
Brinley, Douglas, 2:83
Broken heart, 2:127–28
Bronze, 1:33
Brooks, Phillips, 1:287
Brother of Jared, 1:8, 1:378–79,
2:255–57, 2:261–62, 2:264–
69
Brown, Hugh B., 2:161
Burning: refinement through,
1:98, 1:175, 1:183; of church
of devil, 1:108; and presence
of God, 1:182; symbolism
of, 1:278; of earth, 1:280;

judgment and, 1:281, 2:155, 2:215–16
Burton, Theodore M., 1:135, 1:324, 2:152
Bytheway, John, 1:160, 1:244

Cahoon, Reynolds, 2:256
Caldwell, C. Max, 2:300
Calendar systems, Nephite, 1:381, 2:113
Calling and election: of Lehi, 1:113; made sure, 2:26, 2:96, 2:162, 2:237, 2:265
Callings, magnifying, 1:260, 1:443
Callister, Tad R., 2:134
Cannon, George Q., 1:398, 2:42–43
Captivity, 1:218
Carnally minded, 1:156–57
Celestial kingdom, 1:249
Cezoram, 2:84
Change: through Jesus Christ, 2:5; societal, 2:84
Change of heart, 1:322, 1:389, 1:393. See also Spiritual rebirth
Charity, 1:235, 1:445, 2:23, 2:281, 2:299–303, 2:312
Chastening, 1:79, 1:367–68, 2:99–102, 2:107, 2:261–62
Chastity, 2:35–36
Cheer, 1:163–64. See also Happiness; Joy
Cheesman, Paul R., 1:272–73
Cherubim, 1:413
Chichen Itza, 1:235
Children: Book of Mormon's influence on, 1:3; wayward,

1:38–39; blessing, 1:132; as blessing, 1:173–74; parents' responsibilities to, 1:260, 1:320; innocence of, 1:313; resurrection and exaltation of, 1:357–58; father's interviews for, 2:65; naming, 2:85–86; becoming as, 2:137; putting off, 2:170; Jesus blesses Nephite, 2:185–86; baptism of, 2:306–10
Children of Christ, 1:322–24, 1:350–51, 1:352, 1:356
Children of God, 1:233–34
Chomsky, William, 1:296
Christ, 1:43. See also Jesus Christ
Christos, 1:43, 1:160
Christians, 2:67
Church of Jesus Christ of Latter-day Saints, The: fundamental principles of, 1:149; as ensign, 1:210; threats to, 1:242–43; discipline in, 1:372; addressing members of, 1:396; sharing, 1:442–43; growth of, 2:204; spreading of, 2:208–9, 2:246; name of, 2:222–23; retention in, 2:291–92. See also Gospel
Circumcision, 2:308
Clark, J. Reuben Jr., 2:260
Cleanliness, 2:199–200
Cleave, 1:281
Clothing, 1:383, 1:386, 2:67–68
Cloud of smoke, 1:175
Cockatrice, 1:207–8
Cognate accusative, 1:25
Coinage, Nephite, 1:407–8

Enoch, 2:230, 2:244, 2:282–86
Enos, 1:12, 1:286–92, 2:28–29
Ensign, 1:179, 1:210
Envy, 1:445
Episcopos, 2:222
Equity, 1:176
Eretz Horbah, 2:240
Errant leaders, 1:200
Essenes, 2:160
Ether (book), 2:254
Ether (prophet), 2:276
Ether, plates of, 1:8
Ethiopian court officer, 1:344–45
Evans, Richard L., 2:108
Ever HaYarden, 1:194
Everlasting Father, 1:197–98
Evil(s): war with, 1:63–64,
1:393–94; and moral
absolutes, 1:178; denounced
by Isaiah, 1:199–201;
discerning, 2:294–97. *See also*
Wicked and wickedness
Exaltation: doctrines of,
1:1; made sure, 1:113; of
Mormon, 2:237
Execution, of Nephite dissenters,
2:68, 2:72–73, 2:78
Exodus, 1:70, 1:77–78
Extremes, 1:321–22
Eye of faith, 1:391
Eyring, Henry B.: on wayward
children, 1:39; on prayer,
1:289; on war between good
and evil, 2:59; on Spirit of
God, 2:136

Faith: mercy and, 1:16; sacrifice
and, 1:17, 1:298; rewards

of, 1:22–23; of Nephi, 1:26;
on strait and narrow path,
1:39; results of true, 1:72;
through trials, 1:82–83,
2:24–26; through scripture
study, 1:253; as first gospel
principle, 1:317; eye of,
1:391; signs and, 2:3–4, 2:94;
precedes revelation, 2:9–11,
2:278; Alma's discourse on,
2:11–13; unto repentance,
2:19; importance of, 2:64;
fasting and prayer for, 2:82;
trials of, 2:219–20; in spirit
world, 2:246; miracles and,
2:250, 2:299; of brother of
Jared, 2:264–69; hope and,
2:276–77, 2:299; of ancient
prophets, 2:279; and spiritual
attainments, 2:281; of
Moroni, 2:289; praying for,
2:299; despair and, 2:313
Fall: and plan of salvation,
1:116, 1:118, 1:270–71,
1:413–14, 2:48–49, 2:50;
as transgression, 1:121–23;
effects of, 2:263–64; defined,
2:264
Fallen man, 2:100–102
False prophets, 2:176–77
Fame, 2:100
Family: influence of Book of
Mormon on, 1:3; Joseph
Fielding Smith on, 1:37;
Satan's attack on, 1:171–72
Family history, 2:218–19
Famine, 1:177, 2:99
Fasting, 2:65, 2:82, 2:168,
2:221–22

Jehoahaz, 1:10–11
Jehoiachin, 1:11
Jehoiakim, 1:11
Jehovah, 1:212, 1:355, 2:111–12
Jensen, Kurt, 2:186
Jeremiah, 1:34, 2:276
Jerusalem: Lehi and, 1:11, 1:16–18; destruction of, 1:14, 1:170–79; retrieving brass plates from, 1:24–27, 1:30–32; Ishmael leaves, 1:34–37; persecution of, 1:86; salvation of, 1:97; dedication of, 1:103–4; suffering of, 1:147; two prophets in, 1:147–49; as birthplace of Jesus, 1:399–400; defined, 2:284; building up of, 2:284–85
Jeshimon, 1:18
Jesse, branch of, 1:205–7
Jesus Christ. *See also* Atonement; Messiah; Second Coming; Teachings of Jesus to Nephites
Doctrine concerning
names and titles for, 1:43; scriptures lead to, 1:54; and covenant people, 1:64, 1:103, 1:141; relationship of, with earth, 1:78–79; setting, at naught, 1:84–85; honoring, 1:102, 1:324–25; millennial reign of, 1:110, 1:175; salvation through, 1:115–17, 1:155, 1:229, 2:17–19, 2:292; role of, in plan of salvation, 1:118–19, 1:123, 1:150; as Mediator,

1:123–24; as Rock of our salvation, 1:142–43, 2:87; worshipping, 1:229–30; spirit of prophecy and, 1:259; as Jews' stumbling block, 1:275; taking upon name of, 1:305, 1:322–25, 2:289; announced to King Benjamin, 1:311–16; law of Moses and, 1:336–37; as Father and Son, 1:354–56, 2:265; in our countenance, 1:390; coming unto, 1:393, 2:142–43, 2:282; becoming like, 1:402–3, 2:223; change through, 2:5; as Son of God, 2:13–15; healing through, 2:15–17; as Second Comforter, 2:97; knowing, 2:177–78; as example, 2:187–88; love of, 2:281; seeking, 2:282; merits of, 2:292; perfection in, 2:314
Life events of
rejection of, 1:160–61; baptism of, 1:250–51; temptation of, 1:312–13; crucifixion of, 1:351–53, 2:124–29; suffering and empathy of, 1:400–402; signs of, given, 2:104–5, 2:106, 2:109–13; visits Nephites, 2:129–35, 2:185–87, 2:193–94, 2:210–11; prayer of, 2:190–93
Prophecies and witnesses of
Book of Mormon as witness of, 1:1, 2:239; Lehi on,

Memory, 1:153–54, 1:267–69, 1:391
Mentally handicapped, 2:309
Mercy: faith and, 1:16; at day of judgment, 1:154; justice and, 2:49–50; in war, 2:65; for others, 2:145; application of, 2:298
"Meridian of time," 1:123
Merits of Christ, 2:292
Messengers, heavenly. *See* Angel(s)
Messiah: Lehi testifies of, 1:15; to come through Judah, 1:42; defined, 1:43, 1:160; rejection of, 1:139, 1:347; second coming of, 1:140; Isaiah prophesies of, 1:190–99; psalms of praise for, 1:211–12; Nephi prophesies of, 1:227; prophecies on, 1:337–43, 1:347–48; Abinadi prophesies of, 1:344–61; form of, 1:345–46. *See also* Jesus Christ
Messianic prophecy, 1:188, 1:221–22
Metal plates: Nephi commanded to make, 1:41–42, 1:83–84, 1:138; discovery of, 1:272–73. *See also* Brass plates; Gold plates
Micah, 2:194–95
Midbar, 1:18
The mighty God, 1:197
"Mighty ones," 1:214–15
Millennium: description of, 1:108–10; symbols of, 1:175; peace during, 1:207–9;

psalms for, 1:211–12; revelations during, 1:250; healing and salvation in, 2:217; translated beings and, 2:226; preparation for, 2:282–86; resurrection of children in, 2:310
Millet, Robert L.: on salvation, 1:97, 1:429–30; on visiting Babylon, 1:246; on learning gospel, 1:410–11; on scriptures among ancient Saints, 1:421–22; on famine, 2:99; on attributes of wicked, 2:110; on Lamanites' dark skin, 2:114; on "healing in his wings," 2:217; on Jaredite civil war, 2:287–88
Mind, firmness of, 1:269–70, 1:434
Minefield, 2:164–65
Miracles: in missionary work, 1:404–5; in conversion process, 1:426–27; faith and, 2:31, 2:250; criteria for performing, 2:124; and constancy of God, 2:249, 2:250–52, 2:297; prerequisites for, 2:298, 2:299. *See also* Sign-seeking
Miriam, 1:312
Mishpat/Mishpakh, 1:176
Missionary Training Center, president of, 1:73–75
Missionary work and missionaries: families prepared for, 1:35–36; attend rock concert, 1:41–42; teaching plan of salvation

Priestcraft, 1:234, 1:235, 1:282, 1:383–84, 2:91–92
Priesthood: Lehi and, 1:20; authority and power, 1:81, 1:362–63, 2:87; as putting on strength, 1:144; in Judah, 1:147; defined by Brigham Young, 2:242; Holy Ghost and, 2:290–91. *See also* Melchizedek Priesthood
Prince of Peace, 1:198–99
Priorities, 1:262–63, 1:321–22, 2:171–72
Problem resolution, 2:156
Procrastination, 2:21
Progress. *See* Spiritual growth
Promised land: Americas as, 1:124–27, 1:161–62, 1:291, 2:181, 2:258–61; for Israel, 2:196–97; for Jaredites, 2:256–57
Prophecy: spirit of, 1:93, 1:222, 1:259; among Jews, 1:221–22; logic and, 1:283
Prophetic tense, 1:359–60
Prophet(s): warn of destruction, 1:13–14; Lehi as, 1:14–15; knowledge of, 1:53, 1:155, 1:398–99; John's revelation on two, 1:147–49; consulting, 1:193; denial of, 1:240–41; defined, 1:330; repentance of, 1:362; threats to, 2:15; Nephi as, 2:94–97; following, 2:103–4, 2:108, 2:128–29; false, 2:176–77; as witnesses of God, 2:265–66; record keeping and, 2:267;

of Jaredites, 2:276; faith of ancient, 2:279
Prosperity, 2:100–101, 2:275–76
Provisions, 2:200–201
Provo, Utah, windstorm in, 1:21
Psalm of Nephi, 1:132–36
Psalms of praise, 1:211–12
Pure in heart, 2:145–47
Purification, 1:175. *See also* Refinement

Quarreling, among children, 1:320
Quetzalcoatl, 1:235, 2:16, 2:131

"Rabbanah," 1:426
Raca, 2:154
"Rahab," 1:144
Ram, 2:7
Rameumptom, 2:7
Ratzakh, 2:151
Ravak, 2:154
Reason, 1:283
Rebellion, 2:231, 2:272
Rebirth, spiritual, 1:322, 1:393. *See also* Change of heart
Record keeping: Lehi and, 1:10; Nephi and, 1:34; on metal plates, 1:272–73; importance of, 1:297, 2:26–29; Alma the Elder and, 1:360; for revelation, 1:372–73; Jesus corrects, 2:210; judgment and, 2:223–24; of prophets, 2:267
Redemption: through blood, 1:60–61; through Atonement, 1:115–17,

on suffering of righteous, 1:421; on neutrality, 1:434; on apostates, 2:2–3; on Atonement, 2:18; on outer darkness, 2:43–44; on resurrection, 2:44; on translated bodies, 2:65–66, 2:226; on heavenly beings, 2:88; on calling and election made sure, 2:96; on other Comforter, 2:97; on missionary work, 2:139; on meekness, 2:144; on fulfillment of law, 2:150; on loving enemies, 2:160; on forgiveness, 2:166; on spreading of gospel, 2:208–9, 2:246; on Malachi, 2:217; on Elijah and sealing power, 2:218; on knowledge of Church members, 2:219–20; on earth's exaltation, 2:264; on Jerusalem, 2:285; on unpardonable sin, 2:293–94; on baptism of children, 2:307–8; on deceased children in Millennium, 2:310
Smith, Joseph F.: on angels, 1:29; vision of, 1:49–50; on remembering mortality, 1:153–54; on threats to modern Church, 1:242–43; on sign seeking, 1:283–84; on conversion, 1:427; on resurrection, 2:44–45; on problem resolution, 2:156; on conscience, 2:296

Smith, Joseph Fielding: on families, 1:37; on binding of Satan, 1:110; on Fall, 1:121; on earth's resurrection, 1:143; on Church as ensign, 1:210; on sin and tolerance, 1:242; on Jesus Christ, 1:346, 2:111–12; on exaltation of children, 1:358; on Urim and Thummim, 1:379; on Melchizedek Priesthood, 1:414–15; on being taken home to God, 2:42; on resurrection, 2:45; on fire, 2:105; on blood sacrifice, 2:212–13; on Americas, 2:257; on prophets seeing God, 2:265–66; on New Jerusalem, 2:286; on mentally handicapped, 2:309
Smith, Joseph Sr., 1:128
Smith, Lucy Mack, 1:209
Smoke: cloud of, 1:175; meaning of Hebrew term, 1:182
Snakes, 1:207–8. *See also* Serpent(s)
Snow, Erastus, 1:35, 1:406
Snow, Warren S., 2:316
Soap, 2:212
Sober, 2:234
Society, deterioration of, 2:82–85
Solomon's temple, 1:137
Son of God, Jesus Christ as, 2:13–15, 2:131
Sons of Mosiah, 1:374–77, 1:423–24, 1:428
Soothsayers, 1:193

Tyler, Daniel, 1:434
Types, in scriptures, 2:32

Uchtdorf, Dieter F.: on pride,
2:8–9; on hope, 2:63; on
remaining in homelands,
2:117–18
Ugarit, 1:144
United States Constitution,
1:61, 1:373, 1:380, 2:260
United States of America:
prophecies on, 1:107,
2:201–2; as promised land,
1:111–12, 2:260; as Zion,
1:168; secret combinations
and, 2:274. *See also* Americas
Unity, 1:354–55, 2:90, 2:191–
92
Universe, Mormon's
understanding of, 2:102
Unworthiness, feelings of,
1:182–83
Uriah, 1:190
Urim and Thummim, 1:330,
1:378–79, 2:253, 2:267
Uru Shalem, 1:198
Uzziah, 1:180

Vain repetitions, 2:163–64
Vaya con Dios, 1:285
Vespasian, 1:226
Via Maris, 1:194
Vine, 1:68
Vineyard, Israel as Lord's,
1:175–79
Viper, 1:207–8
Virtue, 2:5
Vision, spiritual, 2:277–78

Voice: of Jesus Christ, 2:130; of
God, 2:131
Vows. *See* Oaths

War in heaven, 1:219–20, 2:59
Warnings, 1:13–14, 1:201–4,
1:224–25, 2:122
War(s): between good and evil,
1:63–64, 1:219; Zion and,
1:169; missionary work and
imagery of, 1:180; effects of,
1:386, 2:78; in Ammonihah,
1:423; justified, 1:433, 2:77,
2:238; accounts of, 2:51–52;
teachings on, 2:52–60;
LDS hymns on, 2:60–63;
mercy in, 2:65; for peace,
2:68; Nephites prepare for,
2:69–71; Nephite loyalty and,
2:72–73, 2:78; negotiations
and counter-negotiations in,
2:74; righteous deaths in,
2:75; stripling warriors' role
in, 2:75–77; siege warfare,
2:115; total war, 2:241; final
battle at Cumorah, 2:243–44;
among Jaredites, 2:287–88
Washington, George, 2:68
Water, 1:191–92, 1:212
Waters of life, 2:50
"Way of the sea," 1:194
Wayward children, 1:38–39
Weakness(es): following spiritual
experience, 1:14, 1:87, 1:426,
1:440; purpose of, 1:129–30,
2:279–81; of Nephi, 1:134;
giving in to, 1:135
Wealth: as spiritual challenge,
1:156; pride and, 1:158,

369

Jesus Christ, 1:229–30; true, 1:291; privacy in, 2:163, 2:168

Worthiness: for students of Isaiah, 1:93; and softness of heart, 1:412; for sacred things, 2:174–75; to take sacrament, 2:188. *See also* Unworthiness, feelings of

Wounds, of Jesus Christ, 2:134

"Wrest," 1:419

Yah, 1:212

Yarn, David H. Jr., 1:56

Yehovah, 1:212

Yesha-Yah, 1:88

Yeshua, 1:43, 1:87, 1:102, 1:131, 2:199, 2:338

Yeshua haMashiakh, 1:227

Yod, 2:150

Young, Brigham: on refinement, 1:98; on Book of Mormon and Joseph Smith, 1:206; on prayer, 1:257; on struggle for spiritual growth, 1:287; on trials, 1:397; on apostates, 2:4; on spirit world, 2:43; on gold plates, 2:81; on prosperity, 2:101; on judgment, 2:239; on priesthood, 2:242; on Bible and Book of Mormon, 2:244–45; on Creation and Fall, 2:264; on spiritual

gifts, 2:312; on Manti Utah Temple, 2:316

Young, Edward J., 1:180–81, 1:187–88

Youth: repentance and, 2:206–7; righteousness of, 2:234

Zacharias, 1:286–87

Zarahemla, 1:296–97, 1:330, 1:370–72, 1:373

Zebub, 1:189

Zebulun, 1:194, 1:195

Zechariah, 1:190

Zedekiah, 1:11, 2:93

Zeezrom, 1:408, 1:410, 1:420–21, 1:422, 2:5

Zeniff, 1:299, 1:331–32

Zenock, 1:85–86

Zenos, 1:85–86, 1:276–81

Zion: bringing forth, 1:63, 1:144; defined, 1:145; Americas as, 1:161–62, 2:257, 2:258–59; defined, 1:167–68; laboring for, 1:235; service and, 1:320–21; Isaiah's teachings on, 2:184–85; unity and, 2:191–92; and gathering of Israel, 2:197–98; establishment of, 2:201–2, 2:229–31; survival and prosperity of, 2:208–9; of Enoch, 2:282–86; as center place, 2:314

Zoram, 1:31–32, 1:423

Zoramites, 2:4–8, 2:23